Methodological Approaches to the Study of Career

Methodological Approaches to the Study of Career

Edited by
Richard A. Young
and
William A. Borgen

PRAEGER

New York
Westport, Connecticut
London

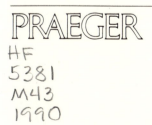

Library of Congress Cataloging-in-Publication Data

Methodological approaches to the study of career/edited by Richard A. Young
  and William A. Borgen.
      p. cm.
   Papers presented at a research workshop, held at the University of British
Columbia, Sept. 1988. Sponsored by the Social Sciences and Humanities
Research Council of Canada and the University of British Columbia.
   Includes bibliographies and indexes.
   ISBN 0-275-93299-0 (alk. paper)
   1. Career development—Study and teaching—Congresses. 2. Career
development—Research—Congresses. I. Young, Richard A. II. Borgen,
William A. III. University of British Columbia. IV. Social Sciences and
Humanities Research Council of Canada.
HF5381.M43   1990
158.7—dc20   89-33969

Library of Congress Catalog Card Number: 89-33969
ISBN: 0-275-93299-0

First published in 1990

Praeger Publishers, One Madison Avenue, New York, NY 10010
An imprint of Greenwood Publishing Group, Inc.

Printed in the United States of America

∞

The paper used in this book complies with the
Permanent Paper Standard issued by the National
Information Standards Organization (Z39.48-1984).

10 9 8 7 6 5 4 3 2 1

Contents

Table and Figures

Acknowledgments

This volume represents the compilation of papers presented to the research workshop "Methodological Diversity and the Study of Career," held at the University of British Columbia in September 1988. The workshop was sponsored by the Social Sciences and Humanities Research Council of Canada through its Strategic Grants Program "Education and Work in a Changing Society" (Grant No. 484-87-2009) and by the University of British Columbia. We are indebted to the Council and the University for their support of the workshop and the publication of this volume.

We are also indebted to the authors of these papers who initially responded favorably to our invitation to attend the workshop and to prepare papers for presentation and discussion. The workshop was intentionally small, but a number of others who attended contributed to the lively and important interchange that occurred. It is difficult to convey the openness that the participants, who represented quite different perspectives, engaged in during our discussions. This volume not only represents their individual work, which was substantial, but their willingness to see the project to completion by preparing their papers for this publication.

Terri Collett, Lisa Barnes, Gary Ladd, Kathleen VanAndel, Elly Davis, and Beth Helsley, graduate students at the University of British Columbia, assisted with various aspects of preparing this manuscript for publication. Their assistance is gratefully acknowledged. We are also grateful to Ilona St. Anne and Bay Gumboc who typed the manuscript, and to Patricia Good who prepared the camera-ready copy.

Introduction

The study of career exemplifies many issues about research in the social sciences today. Not only does it attract attention from a host of social science disciplines, as well as some beyond the social sciences, but career is the subject of interdisciplinary study. Career studies also engender many of the same methodological questions that have been the subject of debate and discussion in the social sciences in recent years (for example, Kuhn, 1970; Morgan, 1983; Popper, 1975; Reason & Rowan, 1981; Rosnow, 1981; Taylor, 1971).

This book attempts to address a range of methodologies that have been used to investigate career, with particular emphasis on alternative approaches. It is not our intention to resolve the tensions that exist among the various disciplines and methodologies that are represented here, nor do we propose to reinvent the methodological "wheel." Some of the approaches discussed in this volume have relatively long and respected lineages. Others, although more embryonic, are representative of definitive movements in the social sciences and need no introduction here. Rather, our intent is to examine in greater detail how each of them applies to the study of career.

The definition of career itself, which is one subject of Edwin L. Herr's chapter in this book, is not unrelated to research issues. We recognize the difficulty of defining it to everyone's satisfaction, but for purposes of orienting the reader, we will follow Super's (1976) description of career as:

> The course of events which constitutes a life; the sequence of occupations and other life roles which combine to express one's commitment to work in his or her total pattern of development, the series of remunerated and nonremunerated positions occupied by a person from adolescence through retirement of which occupation is only one. (p. 4)

For most people in Western society, career represents a practical construct both individually and socially. Thus, like many social sciences topics, it is studied for its own sake—to extend our understanding. However, its study is also enormously important in order to develop appropriate social and educational policy and to identify effective programs and interventions that aid individuals in their own development. This point is taken up by Hall (1987) who, in his review of the field of socialization and careers since the mid-1970s, concluded that career practice has outstripped career research and corresponding theory development. He recognized, however, that during the same period the study of career has come into maturity.

METHODOLOGICAL ISSUES

Sechrest (1986) described the term "methodology" as a "broad generic reference to the ways we go about planning and carrying out research" (p. 319). This description represents the way in which many researchers approach the issues of methodology and is apt to focus attention on specific procedures such as research design, sampling, and instrumentation used to carry out particular studies. Bryman (1984) defined the term "methodology" more particularly in an effort to shed light on the methodological debate. He proposed that methodology refers both to an epistemological position and to method and technique. The chapters in this volume address both these aspects of methodology.

The methodological controversy that has occurred in the social sciences over the past two decades has influenced, and, no doubt, in some small ways, has been influenced by the study of career. Career has largely been the subject of psychology (for example, Crites, 1969; Walsh & Osipow, 1983) and sociology (for example, Blau & Duncan, 1967; Deem & Salaman, 1985; Watson, 1980). However, its practical importance has led to the development of a number of subdisciplines and specializations such as counseling psychology, management sciences, organizational development, industrial and personnel psychology, and vocational guidance. Its relation to a variety of subdisciplines within education, such as career education, needs to be acknowledged as well.

Each of these areas is not discrete in its study of career, and the results of research efforts are seen in such disciplinary and interdisciplinary journals as the *Journal of Vocational Behavior*, the *Journal of Counseling Psychology*, *Human Relations*, *Career Development Quarterly*, and the *Journal of Occupational Behavior*. Much of the research reported in these and similar journals reflects the positivist, empirical tradition. Both in psychology and sociology, the quantitative approach has prevailed. These discipline-based research efforts have been able to inform social policy and professional practice in career counseling, organizational behavior, and other areas. However, Hall's (1987) observation that career practice has eclipsed career research may be indicative of problems with research perspectives and procedures in this field.

Critical examinations of the career literature have engendered several criticisms, not the least of which are problems with definitions and terminology, the inadequate integration of individual and contextual factors, and the real limitations of some of the reported research in terms of external validity (for example, Collin & Young, 1986; Sonnenfeld & Kotter, 1982). Although specific studies have been found wanting in particular ways, the more fundamental issue for the social sciences has been identified by Manicas and Secord (1983) as the failure of the positivist/ empirical tradition to deal meaningfully with the complexity of human action, and with human consciousness and agency. The core of these concerns was restated by Georgoudi and Rosnow (1985) when they suggested that "current thinking in philosophy of science recognizes that not all useful hypotheses (those that provide scientists with vantage points from which to concretize or objectify their observations) are subject to critical empirical scrutiny" (p. 5). As a result of these and other criticisms, a range of alternative approaches have been adopted in recent years.

Polkinghorne (1984) identified three alternative systems of inquiry that respond to the criticisms leveled at the "received view of science," particularly regarding the ability of researchers to respond meaningfully to personal and social concerns. Essentially, these systems of inquiry, namely systemic and structural designs, human action inquiry, and phenomenological and hermeneutical inquiry, address a different kind of knowing than the deductive reasoning characteristic of traditional science. Similar methodological alternatives were proposed by Collin and Young (1986) as a "way forward" for career theory.

Systemic Research

Systems theory addresses the interaction between the individual and the environment in a reciprocal and integrative way. Polkinghorne (1984) described systemic inquiry as focusing on "the interconnectedness within the unit of investigation rather than on the various parts. It uses a language and a logic of context instead of closed sets" (p.422). The systemic mode of inquiry also incorporated an open systems perspective that allows input from the environment from which new elements can be generated (compared to the closed system which loses energy and organization). Collin and Young (1986) found the systemic perspective particularly useful for the study of career in that "it conceptualizes the nature of the person's environment, its influence on the person, the person's response to it, and the internal and external adjustments which flow from this response" (p. 845).

Human Action Inquiry

Action theory and research represent a relatively new approach to the issue of the intentional behavior of humans (for example, Chapman, 1984; Cranach, Kalbermatten, Indermuhle, & Gugler, 1982). As Ladislav Valach points out later in this text, "action theory refers to an actor's consciously goal-directed, planned and intended behavior which is cognitively and socially steered and controlled" (p. 107). Constructs such as plans, goals expectancies, and personal agency, so important to the study of career, are subsumed in action theory. Although there is not a single action theory, human action, as conceived within a range of action theories, is not amenable to the causal explanations characteristic of the traditional approach. Rather, it looks to teleological explanations that can be understood retrospectively as well as contextually.

Phenomenological and Hermeneutical Inquiry

The subjective dimensions of career suggest that career behavior, including goal-directed actions, is meaningful to individuals, and that its meaningfulness is represented in how they describe it. Phenomenological approaches to research in the social sciences, which has increased in recent years (see for example, Bogdan & Taylor, 1975; Giorgi, 1970; Mackie, 1985; Scudder & Mickunas, 1985) emphasizes the meaningfulness and intelligibility of human experience, particularly to the person whose experience it is. Taylor's (1971) view is that the aim of hermeneutics is to bring to light an underlying coherence or sense of an object of study. From a methodological perspective, hermeneutics adds the notion of the framework from which the actions can be understood. Young and Collin (1988) have argued for the use of a hermeneutical methodology in career studies. Moreover, several career studies in a variety of disciplines that have used a hermeneutical approach explicitly or implicitly have been reported (for example, Borgen & Amundson, 1984; Ochberg, 1988; Willis, 1977).

Because of their appropriateness for the study of career issues, as well as representing fairly well the delineated approaches to inquiry, these alternative systems underlie many of the alternative methodologies proposed in this volume.

The important place that the hypothetico-deductive methodology has, and will continue to have, in the social sciences and in the study of career is also recognized in this book. Even in systemic-oriented inquiry, the use of this method has been supported. For example, Bednar, Burlingame and Masters (1988) uphold its use in research on systems of family treatment because it most readily meets the essential characteristic for the development of scientific knowledge, that is, "the demonstration of an acceptable level of correspondence between facts generated by careful observation and scientific propositions (formal assumptions and relations between events)" (p. 402).

The argument in favor of alternative methodologies does not negate the contribution that can be made to knowledge through the use of the hypothetico-deductive method. Rather, it leads to but one way of knowing. As Howard (1984) pointed out, there are likely "elements of truth in subjectivist and objectivist perspectives" (p. 437). In his view, the challenge is to integrate them for a full explanation of human action.

INTRODUCTION TO THE CHAPTERS THAT FOLLOW

The goal of this book, to examine methodological approaches to the study of career, is accomplished in three specific ways represented by the three parts into which the book is divided: broad research issues in the study of career (Part I), an overview of the study of career from the perspective of specific methodologies (Part II), and the use of a range of methodologies in specific research programs and studies (Part III).

Part I

The range of disciplines involved, the practical importance of career in the lives of individuals and families, the efforts of institutions and individuals to intervene in career development, and the continuously changing social and economic conditions all contribute substantively to issues that career researchers must address. In Chapter 1, Edwin L. Herr identifies a number of specific questions, involving terminology, assessment, samples, culture, and outcomes that represent the complexity of career research. These questions do not beget simple solutions. Their complexity, however, provides a framework for the remainder of this work.

Part II

Part II contains seven chapters, each of which addresses a generic research approach with relevance for research in the career area. Both epistemological issues and the specifics of methods and techniques are raised in these chapters. Arnold R. Spokane, in Chapter 2, reviews the enormously productive differential research tradition in vocational psychology. This tradition and the concomitant practice of career counseling has relied heavily on the empirical tradition in psychology, and has been found to be effective for interventions with individuals. Spokane also identifies the areas in which this tradition can be profitably supplemented.

The methodological debate in psychology has been sparked, in part, by the need to recognize the reciprocal and interactive nature of the environment in developmental studies (Bronfenbrenner, 1979; Lerner & Busch-Rossnagel, 1981). In Chapter 3, Fred W. Vondracek presents his developmental-contextual approach to career development research. His model goes beyond the differential tradition and conceptually recognizes the range and fluidity of the variables involved in career research. However, as Freeman (1984) pointed out, the introduction of a developmental-contextualist approach raises more questions than it can answer. Specifically, the empirical method does not capture all the dimensions of the context-person interaction.

The next three chapters deal with narrative approaches. They represent other methodologies based on alternative epistemologies that are required at this juncture. Charles Bujold, in Chapter 4, introduces us to the biographical-hermeneutical approach used in a variety of social sciences, and based on a phenomenological epistemology. In Chapter 5, Larry R. Cochran uses narrative as a paradigm for career research, and in doing so extends our methodological reach to literature, drama, and myth. Finally, in Chapter 6, Donald E. Polkinghorne frames narrative in career research from an action theory perspective, and thus addresses the epistemological question directly. In action theory, the human capacity to choose freely from among alternatives in the context of other life choices and events is recognized.

In Chapter 7, Ladislav Valach adds a European perspective to action theory. Specifically, he presents a model adapted from Cranach et al. (1982) for use in career research. In contrast to the previous chapter, Valach proposes more microanalytic means to study action.

Part II ends with a chapter by Donald Fisher in which he reviews the use of ethnography in career education studies. He focuses particularly on the relation between school and other educational institutions and career development. Identified in this chapter are important studies in the career field are that frequently are overlooked in the study of career. More importantly, he argues for fieldwork as a powerful and viable methodology for career research.

Part III

Part III is based on the assumption that "the proof of the pudding is in the eating." A range of alternative methodologies is used to address appropriate questions in the career field. In the six chapters in this part of the book, specific research studies which are either completed or underway are discussed. Each of these studies addresses an explicit topic in the career field. In Chapter 9, Richard A. Young and John D. Friesen introduce their research program on the intentional behavior of parents regarding the career development of their adolescent children. Several of the approaches discussed in earlier chapters, including the contextual and action theory approaches, are used to delineate their research framework.

Chapters 10 and 11 deal with the problem of unemployment. In Chapter 10, Thomas Keiselbach uses a qualitative methodology based on interview data to address the relation between unemployment and help-seeking behavior. This chapter demonstrates the important link that can be established between alternative research methodologies and practical problems, such as help-seeking among unemployed persons. William A. Borgen and Norman E. Amundson (Chapter 11) describe a series of qualitatively based interview studies that chart the individual's experience of unemployment and identify factors that help or hinder people during that time. Their work has important implications for the practice of career counseling with unemployed clients.

Audrey Collin (Chapter 12) also presents a qualitatively based study, in this case on mid-life career change. She uses methods that are referred to in Part I of this book as biographical-hermeneutical and narrative in an effort to account for the subjective experience of career change and the contexts in which it occurs.

Two issues specific to women's career development are discussed in Chapters 13 and 14. In Chapter 13, Jane Gaskell argues that the relationship among politics, women's careers, feminism, and methodology cannot be ignored, and demonstrates the evolution of her own methodological approach to account for these factors. In

Chapter 14, Bonita C. Long and Sharon E. Kahn return to the empirical tradition that initiated Part II by illustrating how the introduction of structural equation modeling can assist in the development of career theory, specifically in their research, in the relationship between stress and women in management positions.

REFERENCES

Bednar, R. L., Burlingame, G. M., & Masters, K. S. (1988). Systems of family treatment: Substance or semantics. *Annual Review of Psychology, 39,* 401-434.

Blau, P. M., & Duncan, O. D. (1967). *The American occupational structure.* New York: John Wiley.

Bogdan, R., & Taylor, S. J. (1975). *Introduction to qualitative research methods: A phenomenological approach to the social sciences.* New York: John Wiley.

Borgen, W. A., & Amundson, N. A. (1984). *The experience of unemployment.* Scarborough, ONT: Nelson Canada.

Bronfenbrenner, U. (1979). *The ecology of human development: Experiments by nature and design.* Cambridge, MA: Harvard University Press.

Bryman, A. (1984). The debate about quantitative and qualitative research: A question of method of epistemology. *British Journal of Sociology, 35,* 75-92.

Chapman, M. (Ed.). (1984). Intentional action as a paradigm for developmental psychology: A symposium. *Human Development, 27,* 113-144.

Collin, A., & Young, R. A. (1986). New directions for theories of career. *Human Relations, 19,* 837-853.

Cranach, M. von, Kalbermatten, U., Indermuhle, K., & Gugler, B. (1982). *Goal-directed action.* New York: Academic.

Crites, J. O. (1969). *Vocational psychology.* New York: McGraw-Hill.

Deem, R., & Salaman, G. (Eds.). (1985). *Work, culture and society.* Milton Keynes, England: Open University Press.

Freeman, M. (1984). History, narrative, and life-span developmental knowledge. *Human Development, 27,* 1-19.

Georgoudi, M., & Rosnow, R. L. (1985). Notes toward a contextualist understanding of social psychology. *Personality and Social Psychology Bulletin, 11,* 5-22.

Giorgi, A. (1970). *Psychology as a human science: A phenomenological approach.* New York: Harper & Row.

Hall, D. T. (1987). Careers and socialization. *Journal of Management, 13,* 301-321.

Howard, G. S. (1984). A modest proposal for the revision of strategies for counseling research. *Journal of Counseling Psychology, 31,* 430-441.

Kuhn, T. S. (1970). *The structure of scientific revolutions* (2nd ed.). Chicago: University of Chicago Press.

Lerner, R. M., & Busch-Rossnagel, N. A. (1981). Individuals as producers of their development: Conceptual and empirical issues. In R. M. Lerner & N. A. Bush-Rossnagel (Eds.), *Individuals as producers of their development: A life span perspective* (pp. 1-36). New York: Academic Press.

Mackie, F. (1985). *The status of everyday life: A sociological excavation of the prevailing framework of perception*. London: Routledge & Kegan Paul.

Manicas, P. T., & Secord, P. F. (1983). Implications for psychology of the new philosophy of science. *American Psychologist, 38*, 399-413.

Morgan, G. (Ed.). (1983). *Beyond method: Strategies for social research*. Beverly Hills, CA: Sage.

Ochberg, R. L. (1988). Life stories and the psychosocial construction of careers. *Journal of Personality, 56*, 173-204.

Polkinghorne, D. E. (1984). Further extensions for methodological diversity for counseling psychology. *Journal of Counseling Psychology, 31*, 416-429.

Popper, K. (1975). The rationality of scientific revolutions. In R. Harré (Ed.), *Problems in scientific revolutions* (pp. 72-101). Oxford: Clarendon.

Reason, P., & Rowan, J. (Eds.). (1981). *Human inquiry: A sourcebook of new paradigm research*. Chicester, England: John Wiley.

Rosnow, R. L. (1981). *Paradigms in transition: The methodology of social inquiry*. New York: Oxford University Press.

Scudder, J. R., & Mickunas, A. (1985). *Meaning, dialogue, and enculturation: Phenomenological philosophy of education*. Washington, DC: University Press of America.

Sechrest, L. (1986). Modes and methods of personality research. *Journal of Personality, 54*, 318-331.

Sonnenfeld, J., & Kotter, J. P. (1982). The maturation of career theory. *Human Relations, 35*, 19-46.

Super, D. E. (1976). *Career education and the meaning of work* (Monographs on Career Education). Washington, DC: U.S. Office of Education.

Taylor, C. (1971). Interpretation and the sciences of man. *Review of Metaphysics, 25*, 3-51.

Walsh, W. B., & Osipow, S. H. (Eds.) (1983). *Handbook of vocational psychology* (Vols. 1-2). Hillsdale, NJ: Erlbaum.

Watson, T. J. (1980). *Sociology, work and industry*. London: Routledge & Kegan Paul.

Willis, P. (1977). *Learning to labour: How working class kids get working class jobs*. Farnborough, England: Saxon House.

Young, R. A., & Collin, A. (1988). Career development and hermeneutical inquiry: Part I — The framework of hermeneutical approach. *Canadian Journal of Counselling, 22*, 153-161.

Part I

Issues

Issues in Career Research

Edwin L. Herr

Given the level of specific and substantive analysis of research methodologies in this book, an issues chapter becomes one derivative of that substance, more oblique and impressionistic, less quantifiable and, in some sense, an attempt to create a metalanguage of methodology and career. To those ends, I hope to address several topical areas under which are subsumed issues in career research. For the purpose of this chapter, I will address the following:

- The language of career,
- The assessment of career behavior,
- Samples in the study of career,
- Cultural diversity vis a vis career behavior, and
- Disciplinary and interdisciplinary research in career.

THE LANGUAGE OF CAREER

Perhaps the primary issue in the study of career is, what do we mean by career? Is it different from occupation or job? When we speak of career, are we concerned with the lifelong behavioral processes and the influences upon them that lead to individual work values, choice-making style, work salience, preferences and interests, continuity and discontinuity of a career pattern, work salience, role integration, self and career identity, pre- and postwork involvement, and related phenomena? On the other hand, are we principally concerned with the subset of individual career development, which might be defined in organizational terms as the stages that one undergoes in different work settings from induction to consolidation to retirement? Do we really mean that we are concerned with who enters particular occupations and why, the individual differences in interests and abilities found in particular groupings, and the overlap in these characteristics across occupational grouping, or are we really concerned with job satisfaction and work adjustment?

The answers to the above questions are neither right nor wrong, but they suggest that the study of career requires attention to the vocabulary of behavior, processes, mediating variables, barriers, motivations, and contexts subsumed by the term career. In broad terms, this question is, "What are the boundaries in which research can be legitimately conceived to express the study of career?" Until such definition of the field of study of career ensues, it becomes difficult to know what the outcomes of research should be, how they should be addressed, or how research studies can be compared as to purpose and meaning. The issues of the language of career also have implications for methodology and methodological diversity.

To put the importance of this matter into historical perspective, one can cite the observations of Super in several classic papers in 1969 (Super, 1969a, 1969b). At that time he contended that vocational psychology from the early 1900s until shortly after 1950 was a "psychology of occupations." Beginning in the mid-1950s there began to emerge a "psychology of careers." For Super, the premise of concern was that the psychology of occupations and the psychology of careers have different implications for research methodology. In his view, methodological models in a psychology of occupations typically focus on the occupations as subjects and persons in the occupations as the source of data about the occupation. This model takes predictor data at an early period in one's life or at least at preoccupational entry and employs regression methods to predict later success in one occupation or discriminant analysis techniques to determine the likelihood of being found in the future in each of several possible occupations. Super (1969b) contended that, while important for many purposes, such approaches tend to represent differential psychology, the study of individual differences, in a somewhat static sense. However, this is not the essence of the psychology of careers. The study of careers is by Super's perspective a developmental issue—a search for elements that underlie the etiology of career behavior, not just its classification.

Careers embody complex interactions between the affective, cognitive, and psychomotor characteristics of persons, potentially mediated by their values, family history, school climate, community reward system, and many other possible variables that unfold across time. Careers do not simply exist, they are forged in what persons do and what they avoid doing, in the decisions made or not made. Tyler (1978) has suggested in this regard, that "individuals create themselves. . . . It is development we must study, but the development of the shaper rather than the shaped" (pp. 223-224). Careers, then, are created as persons sort among and convert potentialities into actualities. Careers are not classifiable nor chosen in precise terms as occupations or jobs can be; they become identifiable entities as one's behavior unfolds in a complex decision tree across time. There is a *Dictionary of Occupational Titles*, but no *Dictionary of Career Titles*. In this sense, individual careers are better understood after the fact than before, in ipsative rather than normative terms, and in qualitative rather than quantitative terms. In such a premise, biographical and case study methodologies have a potential richness and explanatory power that many quantitative processes do not.

To return to the contrast in methodological diversity between the psychology of occupations and the psychology of careers as advanced by Super in 1969, in a career model the intent is not simply to predict placement in an occupation or prediction of likely success in several occupations that the individual might enter. Rather, a career model, as a developmental model, argues that the research intent is to predict the sequence of positions that a person will occupy in pursuing a career. Playing out such a model suggests that in order to understand career development, it is necessary to understand not only the sequence of positions one occupies across time, but the linkage between positions, the branching from one position to another, and the interrelationship of factors that cause persons to anticipate, plan for, and implement one position rather than another at any particular point in time.

Such a multiprobabilistic view of the challenge of the study of careers implies the study of complex interactions between an enormous array of data points, and argues for methodological approaches that are sensitive to time and context as well as the ebb and flow of direct and indirect effects of variables across time. In the latter challenge, there emerges the importance of such methodological possibilities, for example, as path analysis and causal modeling. Path analysis facilitates the examination of the cumulative indirect effects of one variable on another variable, and it permits the researcher to study not only the direct effect of x on y but when and under what conditions the direct effect of x stops being direct and becomes an indirect effect on y. The various paths of direct and indirect effect between exogenous and endogenous variables permit the examination of multiple hypotheses as combinations of variable effects occur across time. In addition, causal modeling (e.g., LISREL IV) techniques incorporate the functions of path analysis and increase the power to study alternative models of structural equations hypothesized to represent certain patterns of relationships between variables that occur over a period of time (Bentler, 1980). Causal modeling techniques also permit the researcher to examine the effect of several measured variables on one latent variable (unobserved) in order to increase the number of hypotheses that can be considered in relationship to how underlying structures affect career outcomes across time, with respect, perhaps, to the direct and indirect effects of latent variables on each other or the composition of latent variables themselves. Another methodological approach of relevance to the study of career behavior across time is P-technique factor analysis, which is a special case of single-subject research involving intense repeated measurement of an individual. This technique allows one to study in depth the consistency or variability of individual interests, values, preferences, or other characteristics to test whether such characteristics are stable or whether they are labile and dynamic (Nesselroade & Ford, 1985).

The language of career, then, needs to be differentiated from the language of occupations, leisure, or general personal development in such a way that outcomes relevant to the study of career can be as sharply defined as possible. Having stated that issue, however, leaves a complex residual of matters to be addressed within the language of career. One has to do with the reality that however one defines and bounds the study of career, there are at least two major classifications of research. Although somewhat redundant to what has already been stated, the point needs to be clearly focused. The first type of research deals with the structure of career behavior; for example, the behavioral elements that comprise career maturity. The second type of research deals with the longitudinal expression of career behavior; its developmental or transitional cycling, sequencing, and refinement, and the factors that shape or stifle career behavior; for example, the degree to which the behavioral elements comprising career maturity are different or differently important at different points in time.

Within a developmental classification of career one can overlay a further template of research concerns and issues. For example, which vocational behavioral traits are developmental and, for those, how does change occur in some time-ordered paradigm of influence? (Jepsen, 1984). In response to what they see as the personological and unidimensional character of much of the research on career development, Vondracek and Lerner (1982) have cited the need for the study of career to be more dynamic and interactional. By this perspective, they advance the importance of three concepts, particularly with regard to the study of adolescent development but with generalizability to all developmental conceptions of research in career. These concepts include developmental, contextual, and relational dynamics as they are manifested in career behavior. A developmental perspective is captured in the notion that "events prior to adolescence need to be considered as possible antecedents of vocational development; in turn, adolescent developments provide key antecedents of development in later life" (Vondracek & Lerner, 1982, p. 604). A contextual perspective would essentially attend to the nature of the social, political, economic, physical, and cultural environments through which adolescent career development is negotiated and shaped. Such a view is an important transactional perspective that suggests that cohorts differ in the contextual affects likely to be of prime importance in the unfolding of career behavior. A relational perspective would consider the goodness of fit between adolescent and contextual developments. The implementation of such perspectives requires methodological diversity suitable to addressing a historical or sequential design for the study of career by which one can appraise age-, cohort-, and time-related variance. It would require the study of the mutually adaptive interchanges between adolescents, or other age cohorts, and their context, as well as the possible effects on career behavior that would emanate from "interventions targeted to the individual, the family, the community, and its institutions, and finally social policy" (Vondracek & Lerner, 1982, p. 612).

The observation immediately above introduces a further set of issues to the language of career. That is, the study of career involves not only a concern about the structure and the longitudinal expression of career behavior but also the study of interventions effective in stimulating, remediating, promoting, redirecting, or otherwise affecting the trajectory of career development for individuals or groups. Within the intervention arena, there are also definitional questions that affect potential outcomes that reasonably might be expected to occur from particular interventions. For example, one sometimes reads of counselors "doing" career development. That perspective suggests that career development is an intervention rather than the object or target of intervention. Similarly, one reads of terms such as career guidance, career education, and career counseling being used interchangeably. Are they the same or different? Should each form of career intervention be expected to yield the same outcomes or different ones? Such lack of precision in the use of career intervention terminology obviously increases the confusion in dealing with outcome expectations and, therefore, issues of methodological diversity in the study of careers. One can extend the point to ask the question of what constitutes an appropriate intervention in career behavior and, perhaps much more relevantly, how it can be described in precise terms so that it can be replicated under conditions and with samples that are sufficiently similar to the original research condition that a researcher can make a reasonable comparison.

Thus, in the view advanced here, career development describes the structure and longitudinal nature of career behavior, as well as the psychological, cultural, economic, and political influences that intervention strategies might modify in order to facilitate more positive and purposeful career behavior than would likely occur randomly. Acknowledging the value-based questions of whether one should intervene in career behavior and to what ends, the question then becomes what interventions should be included and how might they be described. While we do not have the time here to explore the matter in depth, permit me to raise the issue. For example, does career guidance encompass career counseling? Do career guidance and career education have similar purposes but use different modalities, for example, the teaching/learning process? Under what intervention rubric should the following be classified: computer-assisted approaches, psychoeducational models, gaming, vocational card sorts, work-study, directed group work, decision-making skills training, anger management, stress reduction, assertiveness training?

Perhaps I make too much of the matter, but I do not believe that the use of terms like career guidance, career education, or career counseling represent differences that are simply semantic or benign; they connote different implications for practice that can be obscured in the intervention literature. Many processes of intervention can be subsumed under a blanket term such as career guidance, and, certainly, career counseling is not in itself a singular process. However, career counseling is certainly not the same thing as decision-making courses, shadowing a worker, guided imagery, a time management workshop, or computer-client interaction for assessment of interests or retrieval of occupational information. While these methods might be used in conjunction with career counseling, they are not interchangeable with that particular intervention.

A further definitional problem is related to the interaction between interventions and definitions of career. As suggested by Rounds and Tinsley (1984):

> Progressively more encompassing definitions of career appear to have resulted in wider and more heterogeneous categories of behavioral difficulties to which interventions are applied. The vocational problem of occupational choice, once the primary focus of intervention, has become only one of many behavioral problems that now form the focus of intervention. Furthermore, the expansion includes not only persons with work-related or choice-related problems, but also persons who are progressing reasonably well in their chosen occupations but want to enhance their adjustment or prevent future difficulties related to work,

family, leisure, or retirement. . . . As a result, the range of potential career interventions seems almost unlimited; literally hundreds of different practices have been introduced, each designed to effect some particular change in vocational behavior. . . . The issue of how these interventions effect the measured outcomes is rarely addressed, and how these techniques change specific types of vocational behavior has never been a focus of inquiry in the career intervention literature. (pp. 137-138)

In view of the definitional problems associated with interventions as described above, it is difficult to attribute any set of outcomes to career guidance, career education, career counseling, or, indeed, any other intervention in career behavior without specifically delimiting how the term is being used, what specifically was done by a counselor, under what conditions, with what type(s) of client, within what context, and for what explicit purpose.

Campbell, Connell, Boyle, and Bhaerman (1983) have made a similar point well. In their recommendations relative to career guidance practice, they state:

Career guidance practices that are too general or ambiguous should be avoided. Carefully planned and highly structured career guidance activities should include (1) clearly stated objectives in terms of client outcomes, (2) specific and meaningful client activities to achieve the objectives, and (3) a measure of assessing client achievement of the objectives. (p. 60)

I do not mean to be pedestrian here. Seasoned researchers are quite cognizant that these matters are absolutely basic to high-quality research. These are less questions of methodological diversity than of research design, but I note them here as important issues in the study of career, particularly when one considers the matter of intervention. The issues are vital to advancing a systematic eclecticism or differential treatment approach that scientifically matches career interventions, some taxonomy of presenting problems related to either structural aspects of career behavior or to developmental characteristics, and the achievement of planned outcomes.

Perhaps Fretz (1981) said it best in his general conclusion:

Little progress can be made in improving the effectiveness of career interventions until more specific and systematic evaluative attention is given to (a) the treatment of parameters in myriad contemporary interventions; (b) the relationship of participant attributes to the effects of treatments; and (c) the relationship of both treatment parameters and participants' attributes to the diversity of career-related behaviors, sentiments, and learning that presently serve as outcome measures for evaluating career interventions. (p.77)

In this view, Fretz would argue that there are likely to be Attribute-by-Treatment Interactions that flow from the notion that the outcomes of career intervention are a function of the interaction of client attributes and the treatments they receive. Part of the problem here is, of course, that there has been relatively little systematic comparative study of the effects of several career treatments on the same outcome or across client groups differing in their particular attributes. A related element of this problem may reside in the frequent finding that virtually any career intervention seems to have some beneficial effect (Campbell, Connell, Boyle, & Bhaerman, 1983; Spokane & Oliver, 1983) even when studies of the additive effect of treatments or component analysis studies tend to be less frequent than studies of single treatments in relation to single sets of outcomes. Findings that virtually any career intervention has some type of effect may have caused researchers to be casual about probes of the best or most effective treatments under certain sets of conditions and with specific client groups which, in the last analysis, are required as the major content of differential treatments or systematic eclecticism. However, regardless of such observations, it is important to recognize that studies of intervention have yielded additional and important new methodological diversity in meta-analysis, the study of effect size, and the standardized mean difference in performance between treated and untreated subjects, a method about which much more knowledge will be gained in the future as the technique is applied to a wide range of career interventions (Spokane & Oliver, 1983).

Let me make a final observation about the status of the study of career relative to methodological diversity. In essence, our knowledge of careers and interventions in them is still relatively primitive. We know more about some elements of careers (e.g., interests) than about others (e.g., self-efficacy), although we do not know enough about either. We know more about some forms of intervention (e.g., assertiveness training) than about other forms of intervention (e.g., computer-assisted career guidance), and we have relatively little comparative data about these interventions in relationship to the same sets of outcomes. Therefore, the study of career continues to require the widest combination of traditional and nontraditional methodology possible in order to capture the richness, the multiprobabilistic nature, and the attribute times setting times intervention interaction of the field.

The study of careers continues to need between-group and within-group designs, passive observation or descriptive studies and experimental designs, and tests of theory and quasi-experimental field-based research. It needs:

(1) Survey research: to discover relevant variables for more systematic study and to establish the parameters of known variables. (2) Technique research: to develop methods, whether test or no test, for making observations which are quantifiable. (3) Theoretical research: to test hypotheses that have been deduced from theories or that have been formulated to account for empirical laws. (4) Applied research: to determine what course of action should be taken. (Crites, 1983, p. 306)

Certainly in experimental and, indeed, in quasi-experimental designs we must advance methodological diversity with heightened sensitivity to statistical conclusion validity, internal validity, construct validity, and external validity if the study of careers is to be increasingly congruent with the canons of the philosophy of science (Campbell & Stanley, 1966; Cook & Campbell, 1979).

THE ASSESSMENT OF CAREER BEHAVIOR

A second issue of concern is the assessment of career behavior. This issue is less a matter of methodological diversity and more a matter of the range of assessment instruments available and the potential effects they have on the study of career. In general, it seems fair to suggest that the scaling of career constructs and the careful and systematic analysis of their psychometric properties is considerably less than the universe of constructs typically subsumed by the notion of career (Slaney, in press). Several problems tend to be associated with the current state of the art in identifying suitable measures of career constructs. One is that the study of careers is in many senses restricted to and defined by what existing assessment instruments measure (Herr, 1979). Thus, there is a problem of having available adequate outcome measures for career interventions (Oliver, 1979), for exacerbating the "criterion problem" (Gelso, 1979), or, indeed, of causing researchers to use primitive measures for which the psychometric properties are unknown or inadequate, leading to significant concern about whether the outcomes obtained are valid, generalizable, and adequate for purposes of aggregation. The other possibility is that researchers tend to select assessment measures that really do not measure effectively what the intervention has been designed to achieve, thereby yielding no significant effects. Some researchers choose assessment instruments because they exist, and not because their content is precisely congruent with the desired outcomes of the career interventions to be studied or evaluated.

The concerns about assessment problems in the study of career have already been discussed in terms of the limited number of instruments available, their overuse, and their contribution to an ongoing criterion problem. There are, in addition, some methodological concerns in the research on careers reported in the literature that can be seen in terms of additional problems for assessment. Some observers have argued that a major problem in career research is the assumption in many research studies that all clients within a given study who seek and/or receive counseling are more or less alike, or that outcome criteria used in a given study are equally appropriate for all clients in a similar way (Myers, 1971). These observers would argue that there is considerable variation in the etiology of a particular presenting problem in career or, indeed, in the way different people experience it (e.g., immaturity in situation, lack of occupational information, indecision-indecisiveness, etc.). Therefore, it is not likely that either the clients or the outcomes in a given study should be treated as though they were alike. Such a view has led L. Oliver (1979) among others to argue for individual criteria to be developed for each client. This perspective is consistent with theoretical statements that career development is developmental and that interventions should begin wherever a client is in that development. However, it certainly compounds assessment and methodological problems. It argues for ipsative rather than normative assessment; either an incredibly large inventory of assessment instruments with known psychometric properties that can be used for research, or a research philosophy that is less concerned with quantitative research and more with qualitative research based on structural interviews, thematic or trend analyses, biographical and case study material, and n-of-one design.

A major problem in the development of assessment instruments is related to the classification of career problems and the characteristics that should be assessed. "The issue of what to measure is contingent on the diagnosis and classification of vocational problems" (Rounds & Tinsley, 1984, p. 63). Observers (e.g., Osipow, 1982; Rounds & Tinsley, 1984) have contended that a major requisite for assessment is that reliable vocational-problem diagnostic systems need to be developed so that both communication and prediction can be enhanced. Such diagnostic systems should describe the content and etiology of vocational problems so that appropriately homogeneous samples can be drawn for purposes of intervention research. Then, the mechanisms assumed to underlie vocational behavior change in each problem area should be specified so that interventions can be designed and evaluated under conditions that allow for testing the theory and identifying the reasons for change. Such notions mean that the diagnostic assumptions by which vocational problem behaviors are classified must be clear and able to be made operational in measurement instruments. These diagnostic classifications need to be predictive of likely outcomes and the causes or the etiology of the behavior and, therefore, must be able to be used for purposes of differential treatment. Currently, the status of diagnostic classifications of vocational behavior is much less precise than that suggested above and, therefore, the content and comprehensiveness of assessment instruments tends to reflect such deficits and become a methodological issue in its own right.

One can also cite several other notions that relate to the state of assessment in career. For example, only some of the dimensions of current models of career behavior are measured, including the elements that make up the popular concept of career maturity (Super, 1984; Westbrook, Sanford, O'Neal, Horne, Fleenor, & Garren, 1985). In 1978, Super and Hall observed that the most highly developed instruments assess only 1 to 6 factors out of a total list of 18 in the Crites model of career maturity (Crites, 1974) or 19 in the Super model. In the terms of Cook and Campbell (1979), construct underrepresentation, or operations that are not as inclusive as the construct, is one of two possible sources of error or variance that can adversely affect construct validity (Crites, 1983, p. 325). If one extrapolates beyond career maturity per se, there is a gap between the availability of instrumentation that is not construct-underrepresented and the enormity of the constructs that tend to be descriptive of careers. In many cases, the alternative seems to be that elements of career which are not represented in instruments which have been constructed in accordance with accepted psychometric technology are assessed by Likert scales or other self-report devices which, in turn, make the comparison of results difficult or, indeed, yield to the assumption that the results obtained are likely to be confounded with variables not measured in the particular study. Nonsignificant results, for example, may be a function of the unreliability of the measure rather than an actual lack of treatment effect.

However, given the assumptions of intellective versus nonintellective measures of career behavior or what has been called measures of process of choice (e.g., attitudes toward choice, independence for the consequences of choice, etc.), the typical psychometric standards of high reliability or high validity may not apply (Crites, 1983). While it is important to be able to define the stability of the behavior in which one is interested, and, therefore, that there is sufficient test-retest reliability in the instrument assessing such behavior, it is also important that the scale or inventory not be so stable that there is no possibility of measuring systematic maturational variance (Karren, Crites, & Bobko, 1979). Although we will not pursue the discussion here, Crites (1983) has suggested that, in relation to our discussions of issues in methodological diversity, in dealing with measurement or assessment problems it is important to recognize that both principal components factor analysis and hierarchical forms of factor analysis are important to determine whether a behavior can be conceived in multidimensional or multifactor terms, on the one hand, and how these factors or dimensions are interrelated in structural terms, on the other. Thus, approaches to factor analysis that use principal components to isolate the factors or dimensions of behavior and those that seek the hierarchical structure of career orthogonal or oblique factors each have their own methodological purpose or role, but they are not the same. A further example of methodological diversity in measurement of some aspects of career is that emerging from the multitrait-multimethod matrix, originally formulated by Campbell and Fiske (1959), and its emphasis on both convergent and divergent validity as ways of assessing whether traits or behaviors under study are, in fact, correlated with other traits with which they should be correlated and not correlated with traits with which they should not be correlated. While such a method may not be appropriate for all traits in career studies, it does again suggest the importance of methodological diversity as a way of clarifying the relationships among traits and the importance they hold for research measurement.

A major concern in measurement has to do with the outcomes to be expected from career education, career counseling, or career guidance. Are each of these categories of intervention intended to affect the same behaviors, or are they to serve different purposes? Should there be a specified range of outcomes by age or by population for each such intervention, or for all? Crites (1981) has indicated that for career counseling there are three broad outcomes: making a career choice, acquisition of decisional skills, and enhanced general adjustments. However, as has been identified elsewhere (Herr, 1979; Osipow, 1982; Slaney & Russell, 1987) the outcomes expected to derive from career interventions are diverse and changing. Some are affective, others are cognitive, and still others are behavioral. Some deal with client progress in decision making, degree to which they experience indecision, knowledge of self-characteristics or occupational or educational options, attitudes toward or independence in choice, degrees of anxiety, quality of job-search skills, achievement, persistence, work adjustment, academic performance, or other behavior. Are any of these terms different? Are they too abstract to be helpful? What are the criterion variables inherent in such terms? What are the proxies or measurement indicators appropriate to each of these terms? Finally, what is the current availability of instruments relevant to each of these terms?

SAMPLES IN THE STUDY OF CAREER

A perennial issue in career research is the nature of the samples employed. Sometimes this issue is translated into questions of sample size as well. Since sample size is primarily a function of the power of the statistical tests used, it will not be elaborated here. Suffice it to say that many studies use either such small samples or such large samples in correlation studies that the optimal power for the correlation coefficient (approximately $df = 125$) where the "statistical significance and magnitude estimate appear to be balanced" (Crites, 1983, p. 321) is not met. Thus, small samples tend to produce such wide confidence intervals that r tends to approach .00 and large samples yield statistically significant r's so small that their practical meaning for theory or prediction is doubtful. In either case, the advancement of knowledge in the field when such statistical approaches and sample sizes are used is questionable at best.

Samples themselves vary in their relationship to research purposes. Frequently, college students tend to be the subjects of both theoretical and applied research in the study of career. Such samples obviously skew research findings into a somewhat restricted band of largely higher SES (socioeconomic status) and Caucasian subjects, thereby obscuring the knowledge base about those individuals who do not go to college, are poorer on average, or are members of minority groups. However, aside from the issue of the appropriateness of college students as prime subjects for the study of careers or career interventions, there is also the important question of the similarity of data from such a population. To wit, are college students the same regardless of where they go to college and regardless of when in a semester or in their college matriculation data are collected from them? Is there likely to be more extraneous anxiety in the life of college students at some institutions and at some points in the semester than at others? Is this likely to be extraneous "confound" that is not typically addressed, or are factors of transfer and adjustment to college, which are not reflected in grade point average per se, likely to be confounding variables that are unmeasured and unrecognized in the amount of variance they may explain in certain research findings? Are some groups of college students (for example, psychology students), so frequently tested that they are quite adept at hypothesis guessing and can alter outcomes of experiments through deliberate response sets?

Moving from college student samples to other types of samples raises similar issues. Is generalizing from samples in particular occupations in one setting to those in the same occupation but a different setting appropriate? Are there metaphors and environmental or geographic conditions at work that so change the work context or the psychosocial conditions that the researcher is really studying different types of samples? Does the likelihood that persons of even the same age and gender in the same workplace vary substantially in their career maturity or the mini- and maxi-decision cycles in which they are engaged alter substantially or wash out differences in such phenomena as job satisfaction, job success, productivity, and so forth?. The likely answer is yes, but what does this mean for methodological diversity? Among other possibilities it likely means that it is important to use multiple criteria to eliminate as many threats as possible to the internal or external validity of what one is studying. In addition, given the importance of contextual effects, the use of qualitative measures to assess climate and psychodynamics in environments and their comparability, in addition to quantitative measures, are important extensions of methodological diversity. Thus, case studies, the use of participant observers, and structured interviews become important methods of helping to understand the meaning of the results of tests and questionnaires.

Cultural Diversity vis-a-vis Career Behavior

Given the growing pluralism of populations in North America, a major issue of concern to methodological diversity is the lack of systematic study of the career behavior of minority groups or culturally different samples, whether classified racially, ethnically, or religiously (Tinsley & Heesacker, 1984). While some research has shown that existing career theories, originally validated on white males, are also applicable to women, minority groups, or lower-income persons, much research needs to be done on the career behavior of the culturally different (Kidd, 1982; Salomone & Slaney, 1978). Relatively little attention has been given to the rural poor compared to the urban poor. Virtually no attention has been given to the effects upon career behavior of being homosexual, the limitations this population faces, or career interventions that may be particularly useful.

Obviously, within culturally different populations there is extensive within group variance on many factors. Therefore, it is inappropriate to generalize findings from one cultural group at a certain age to another of a different age, setting, occupation, or other categorical difference. Replication and validation of findings must be undertaken across samples that diverge in characteristics from those on whom the original findings were obtained. Certainly within the notion of methodological diversity in the study of careers, the use of ethnographic methodology applied to cultural differences in career behavior or to cross-cultural interventions needs to be expanded (Wehrly & Watson-Grego, 1985). A qualitative rather than quantitative approach, ethnography studies naturalistic interaction and behavior, ways of living, expectations for behavior, specific cultural patterns, and rules for interpreting shared meaning among members of particular groups. The combining of the qualitative methodology of ethnography with traditional quantitative approaches is likely to bridge the understanding of career-related phenomena among culturally different groups in relation to such issues as career salience, the meaning of work, time management, information processing, and other cognitive or affective elements important in the study of career.

There is a growing literature that indicates that culturally different groups do not differ simply in their skin color or their socioeconomic status. They differ in their metaphors about work and its importance to the individual, what is defined as normal and abnormal behavior, whether one should seek individual achievement and recognition or subject oneself to group goals and collective effort, and how one should define and experience mental illness or mental health. Culturally different groups tend to experience different contingencies of reinforcement that result in cultural differences in perceptual selectivity, information-processing strategies, self-concepts, cognitive structures, habits, categorizations of experience, attitudes, beliefs, self-instructions about how to behave, norms, roles, and values (Draguns, 1980; Triandis, 1985). Cultures differ in terms of who people are (in-group, out-group, family, strangers) or what they do; in whether they are tight (very regulated) or loose; and in whether they are homogeneous or heterogeneous in traditions, religious background, child-rearing practices, and so on. Cultures differ in the attributes that are emphasized: for example, race, ideology, tribal membership, sex, religion, age, nationality, or past-present-future orientation.

In societies where immigration has been intense and of long duration, such as the United States and Canada, research findings indicate that traditions and cultural belief systems persist across generations as family rituals, ethnic churches, and other culturally reinforcing mechanisms (for example, barrios and ghettos) perpetuate the customs from the nations of origin (McGoldrick, Pearce, & Giordano, 1982). Other research indicates with considerable persuasion that national characteristics do differ. Peabody's (1985) research in the psychological characteristics of persons in a variety of European and Asian nations as well as in the United States indicates that national groups tend to have comparative differences based on (1) social relationships, (2) social rules, (3) control of hostility, (4) impulse control, and (5) authority and hierarchical relations. Modal relationships across these variables are likely to be different for one national group than for another. Garreau (1981) has extended the point to indicate that there are also regional differences in North America related to different perspectives on self-sufficiency, pride, teamwork, achievement, freedom, and duty.

In essence, cultures are similar to maps or templates that provide rules of behavior and perceptual cues to persons of a given culture that influences the things to which they are likely to attend and give meaning, their views of right and wrong behavior, and their self-perceptions and manners of expression. Each of these elements manifest themselves in some fashion in career behavior and, indeed, in the likelihood that some career interventions will be more appropriate or effective than will others. Clearly, our application of research, methodological diversity, and ethnography to the study of careers across culturally different populations and in the depth needed is both sparse and necessary. As such, it becomes a major issue in the study of career.

The Disciplinary Focus of Research in Careers

A final issue in career research and in the study of careers relates to psychological models of research versus interdisciplinary research in the study of careers. In the United States in particular, the study of careers has been principally a study of individual behavior and action, not that of the effect of environments, organizations, or social policy on individual behavior. Watts (1981) illustrates the point in his comparison of the evolution of career development theory in the United States and in Great Britain. He states:

> It is intriguing that theories of career development in the USA have been so heavily dominated by psychologists whereas in Britain the contributions of sociologists have been much more prominent. The dominant focus in the USA has been on the actions of individuals, while in Britain indigenous theoretical work has been more preoccupied with constraints of social structures . . . . The failure of the American socialstructural evidence to have much influence on career development theory seems to be due basically to cultural and historical factors. From the beginning of its independent existence, the USA has been formally committed to the proposition that all men are created equal.   . . . As a result, there is a belief that the individual controls his own destiny, that if he has appropriate abilities and, if these can be appropriately developed, his fate lies in his own hands. (p. 3)

Watts has implicitly suggested that one of the issues in the study of careers and methodological diversity concerns the potential disciplinary "windows" that should be applied to career behavior. Career behavior, depending on how it is defined in either structural or developmental terms, is of interest to many disciplines. While differential and developmental psychologists may have primary interest in the topic, as Watts indicated, so do sociologists as students of the social structure and its implications for the career mobility of subpopulations. Certainly, specialists in organizational behavior are concerned about the interaction between different organizational environments, individual career paths, and productivity; human resource specialists are concerned about the effects of treating workers in holistic terms, helping them to shed problems extraneous to the workplace that interfere with work identity and growing competence within the particular firm; and industrial psychologists are concerned about worker motivation and how human factors engineering can increase it. Similarly, specialists in personnel acquisition and retention are concerned about factors predicting success in different occupations or jobs, how to assess them, and how to maximize person-job fit; vocational educators and others are interested in planning preparation and training for the workplace that will build a competent and literate work force and reduce the likelihood of structural unemployment; psychiatrists have long had an interest in occupational mental health, stress, and substance abuse in the work place; and economists look at the characteristics and requirements of a nation's human capital, and implicitly at the career behavior of subgroups of persons relative to labor demands, costs of productivity, benefits of education, and related factors in terms of contributions to the Gross National Product and international competitiveness. Many other such examples could be cited in behalf of the interdisciplinary nature of the study of careers.

The point is, however, that knowledge about career behavior tends to be reported in disciplinary-based publications and contexts rather than in interdisciplinary formats. Thus, researchers on career behavior within disciplines tend to use perspectives and tools that are limited to the standard methodology of that field, and therefore do not understand or appreciate the methodological diversity inherent in interdisciplinary approaches to the study of career. Among other consequences of such a condition is a lack of researchers trained to view career behavior and its intervention through multidisciplinary lenses.

Awareness of the need to increase the multidisciplinary nature of the study of careers is periodically discussed in the professional literature. For example, Free and Tiedeman (1980) have argued that the study of economics has much to contribute to effective career guidance practice. They contend that both econometric and psychometric models need to be applied in the foundational study of individual behavior and career interventions. Obviously, econometric models represent expanded methodological diversity, so, too, does increased understanding and the study of the characteristics of labor markets. For example, Doeringer and Piore (1971) have described a dual labor market in the United States that has different ports of entry for workers depending on the industry involved, and different levels of security, benefits, training, and possibilities of internal mobility. In such a view, the primary and secondary labor markets require different job search strategies, skills, and personal characteristics. There are also informal labor markets outside the corporate or organizational structures that represent different forms of self-employment (Gershung & Dahl, 1979-1980). Such perspectives on organizational and social factors that emanate from sociology and economics and that affect the shape and flow of career offer potential expansion of methodological diversity in the study of career.

Voices arguing expanded interdisciplinary perspectives on the study of careers have come from within the ranks of psychologists in several of the annual reviews that occur, for example, in the *Journal of Vocational Behavior* or the *Annual Review of Psychology*. Illustrative of the point, Bartol observed in 1981 that

> As greater emphasis is placed on the work life of individuals after initial occupational choices are made, researchers on vocational behavior and career development will increasingly find it necessary to synthesize

research findings from the area of industrial/organizational psychology, organizational sociology, and organizational behavior and theory. This factor may suggest greater collaboration among researchers across these fields in the future. In any event, the broadening base of relevant research, while challenging, also is an exciting development with rich potential for increased knowledge of vocational behavior. (p. 151)

Fretz and Leong (1982) extend such observations with their findings in a major review of the literature on career development, which suggest that more researchers are attending to environmental and organizational variables as major factors. They observe that

> The affirmative results from this emphasis will have to be asserted repeatedly to encounter the impact of several generations of intrapsychically oriented career counselors and researchers. Understanding both the unique and interactive contributions of environmental and organizational, as well as organismic variables to the development and implementation of careers may well be a challenge we can meet in the 1980's. (p. 152)

Finally, it is possible to cite the review of vocational behavior published in 1987 in the *Journal of Vocational Behavior* (Slaney & Russell, 1987). The coauthors, a counseling psychologist and an industrial psychologist, collaborated in this annual review to combine the perspectives on vocational behavior from their respective fields. They believe these two perspectives to be those most centrally concerned with vocational behavior. They individually found large literatures in each of their areas but a lack of overlap between the literatures of the two specialties. While some of the research topics were the same—for example, sex discrimination, sexual harassment, dual careers, burnout, and retirement—most were not and neither literature tended to reference the other. Slaney and Russell argue the need for discussions about specific topics where collaboration would be most beneficial to both perspectives. They asked the question, for example,

> Would it be productive for I/O [industrial/organizational] psychologists to examine closely the research on career interventions in developing programs to aid the career development of employees? Conversely, would it make sense for counselors who deal with reentry women or retired persons to have a greater awareness of what provisions are made by employers for helping persons reenter the employment market, on the one hand, or depart successfully from paid employment, on the other? (p. 157)

It seems apparent that as such collaboration continues to ensue between I/O psychologists and counseling psychologists, the study of career will likely be enriched and more comprehensively understood, and methodological diversity will likely increase. Similar expectations would likely be achieved if increased interdisciplinary research were to occur between psychologists, economists, anthropologists, political scientists, sociologists and others. However, such goals themselves spawn issues of communication, training, common language and meaning systems, and mutual respect for the research tools used if interdisciplinary research and the sharing of findings in the study of careers is to grow.

CONCLUSION

Career research is proceeding in comprehensive ways across populations, time, and settings. However, there continue to be issues in career research that recur or emerge as theoretical perspectives, interventions, and settings related to the study of career change. While the issues in career research are wide-ranging, this paper has focused on those concerns that are reflected in the language of career, the nature of assessment, samples used in the study of career, and cultural diversity related to career behavior, as well as disciplinary and interdisciplinary research in the study of career.

REFERENCES

Bartol, K. M. (1981). Vocational behavior and career development, 1980: A review. *Journal of Vocational Behavior, 18*, 123-162.

Bentler, P. M. (1980). Multivariate analysis with latent variables: Causal modeling. *Annual Review of Psychology, 31*, 419-456.

Campbell, D. T., & Fiske, D. W. (1959). Convergent and discriminant validation by the multitrait-multimethod matrix. *Psychological Bulletin, 56*, 81-105.

Campbell, D .T., & Stanley, J. C. (1966). *Experimental and quasi-experimental designs for research.* Chicago: Rand-McNally.

Campbell, R. E., Connell, J. B., Boyle, K. K., & Bhaerman, R. D. (1983). *Enhancing career development: Recommendations for action.* Columbus, OH: National Center for Research in Vocational Education. Ohio State University. (ERIC Document Reproduction Service No. ED 227-303)

Cook, T. D., & Campbell, D. T. (1979). *Quasi-experimentation: Design and analysis issues for field settings.* Chicago: Rand-McNally.

Crites, J. O. (1974). Career development processes: A model for vocational maturity. In E. L. Herr (Ed.), *Vocational guidance and human development* (pp. 296-320). Boston: Houghton Mifflin.

Crites, J. O. (1983). Research methods in vocational psychology. In W. B. Walsh & S. H. Osipow (Eds.), *Handbook of vocational psychology: Vol. 1* (pp. 305-353). Hillsdale, NJ: Erlbaum.

Doeringer, P. B., & Piore, M. J. (1971). *Internal labor markets and manpower analysis*. Lexington, MA: Lexington Books.

Draguns, J. (1980). Psychological disorders of clinical severity. In H. C. Triandis & J. Draguns (Eds.), *Handbook of cross-cultural psychology: Vol. 6* (pp. 99-174). Boston: Allyn & Bacon.

Free, C. G., & Tiedeman, D. V. (1980). Counseling and comprehension of the economics of change. *Personnel & Guidance Journal, 58*, 358-367.

Fretz, B. R. (1981). Evaluating the effectiveness of career interventions. *Journal of Counseling Psychology, 28*, 77-90.

Fretz, B. R., & Leong, F. T. L. (1982). Vocational behavior and career development, 1981: A review. *Journal of Vocational Behavior, 21*, 123-162.

Garreau, J. (1981). *The nine nations of North America*. New York: Avon Books.

Gelso, C. J. (1979). Research in counseling: Methodological and professional issues. *Counseling Psychologist, 8*, 7-35.

Gershung, J. I., & Dahl, R. E. (1979-1980). Work outside employment: Some preliminary speculations. *New Universities Quarterly, 34*, 120-135.

Gottfredson, L. S., & Brown, V. C. (1981). Occupational differentiation among white men in the first decade after high school. *Journal of Vocational Behavior, 19*, 251-289.

Herr, E. L. (1979). The outcomes of career guidance: Some current and future perspectives. *Journal of Counseling Services, 3*, 6-14.

Jepsen, D. A. (1984). The developmental perspective on vocational behavior: A review of theory and research. In S. D. Brown & R. W. Lent (Eds.), *Handbook of counseling psychology* (pp. 178-215). New York: Wiley.

Karren, R. J., & Crites, J. O., & Bobko, P. (1979). *Path analysis of the Career Maturity Inventory to estimate maturational variance*. Unpublished manuscript, University of Maryland.

Kidd, J. M. (1982). *Self and occupational concepts in occupational preferences and entry into work. Unpublished doctoral dissertation,* National Institute for Careers Education and Counselling, Cambridge, England.

McGoldrick, M., Pearce, J. K., & Giordano, J. (1982). *Ethnicity and family therapy*. New York: Guilford.

Myers, R. A. (1971). Research on educational and vocational counseling. In A. E. Bergin & S. L. Garfield (Eds.), *Handbook of psychotherapy and behavior change: An empirical analysis* (pp. 863-891). New York: Wiley.

Nesselroade, J. R., & Ford, D. H. (1985). P-technique comes of age: Multivariate, replicated, single-subject designs for studying older adults. *Research on Aging, 7*, 46-80.

Oliver, L. W. (1979). Outcome measurement in career counseling research. *Journal of Counseling Psychology, 26*, 217-236.

Osipow, S. H. (1982). Research in career counseling: An analysis of issues and problems. *Counseling Psychologist, 10*, 27-34.

Peabody, D. (1985). *National characteristics*. Cambridge: Cambridge University Press.

Rounds, J. B., & Tinsley, H. E. (1984). Diagnosis and treatment of vocational problems. In S. D. Brown & R. W. Lent (Eds.), *Handbook of counseling psychology* (pp. 137-177). New York: Wiley.

Salomone, P. R., & Slaney, R. B. (1978). The applicability of Holland's theory to nonprofessional workers. *Journal of Vocational Behavior, 13*, 63.

Slaney, R. B. (in press). The assessment of career decision-making. In W. B. Walsh & S. H. Osipow (Eds.), *Advances in vocational psychology: Vol. II. Career decision making, development and maturity.* Hillside, NJ: Erlbaum.

Slaney, R. B., & Russell, J. E. A. (1987). Perspectives on vocational behavior, 1986: A review. *Journal of Vocational Behavior, 31*, 111-173.

Spokane, A. R., & Oliver, L. W. (1983). The outcomes of vocational interventions. In W. B. Walsh & S. H. Osipow (Eds.), *Handbook of vocational psychology: Vol. 2* (pp. 99-136). Hillsdale, NJ: Erlbaum.

Super, D. E. (1969a). The natural history of a study of lives and of vocations. *Perspectives on Education, 2*, 13-22.

Super, D. E. (1969b). Vocational development theory: Persons, positions, and processes. *Counseling Psychologist, 1*, 2-9.

Super, D. E. (1984). Career and life development. In D. Brown & L. Brooks (Eds.), *Career choice and development: Applying contemporary approaches to practice* (pp. 192-234). San Francisco, CA: Jossey-Bass.

Tinsley, H. E. A., & Heesacker, M. (1984). Vocational behavior and career development: A review. *Journal of Vocational Behavior, 25*, 139-190.

Triandis, H. C. (1985). Some major dimensions of cultural variations in client populations. In P. Pedersen (Ed.), *Handbook of cross-cultural counseling and therapy* (pp. 21-28). Westport, CT: Greenwood.

Tyler, L. (1978). *Individuality.* San Francisco: Jossey-Bass.

Vondracek, F. W., & Lerner, R. M. (1982). Vocational role development in adolescence. In B. Wolman (Ed.), *Handbook of developmental psychology* (pp. 602-614). Englewood Cliffs, NJ: Prentice-Hall.

Watts, A. G. (1981). Introduction. In A. G. Watts, D. E. Super & J. M. Kidd (Eds.), *Career development in Britain* (pp. 1-6). Cambridge, England: Hobson's.

Wehrly, B., & Watson-Grego, K. (1985). Ethnographic methodologies as applied to the study of cross-cultural counseling. In P. Pedersen (Ed.), *Handbook of cross-cultural counseling and therapy* (pp. 65-71). Westport, CT: Greenwood.

Westbrook, B. W., Sanford, E. E., O'Neal, P., Horne, D. F., Fleenor, J., & Garren, R. (1985). Predictive and construct validity of six experimental measures of career maturity. *Journal of Vocational Behavior, 27*, 338-355.

Part II

Methodological Approaches

2

Supplementing Differential Research in Vocational Psychology Using Nontraditional Methods

Arnold R. Spokane

Most research in vocational psychology can be described by reference to two fundamental methodological viewpoints that have clearly stated assumptions and a large evidential and historical base underpinning their tenets. The status of these two viewpoints is sufficient to consider them Kuhnian paradigms (Borgen, 1986). These paradigms are (a) differential Vocational Psychology, and (b) developmental Vocational Psychology. Both of these paradigms are necessary if we are to fully understand career behavior. A more elaborate classification system is possible, of course, but this twin classification captures past contributions, present impasses, and future possibilities very succinctly. This chapter will focus on issues related to the differential tradition.[1]

The differential paradigm in Vocational Psychology includes two major underlying thrusts that parallel Cronbach's (1957) paper on the two disciplines in scientific psychology. The first thrust, often called "actuarial" in the literature, contains studies that involve the construction and validation of various interest, ability, style, and, occasionally, personality measures related to choosing and adjusting to work for normal individuals. These test development efforts account for the largest share of effort expended by traditional differential Vocational Psychologists. The acturial emphasis also includes studies that employ ANOVA, ANCOVA, MANCOVA, factor analysis, multidimensional scaling analysis, or other multivariate techniques in an effort to test a theory, where control over the independent variable rather than construction of a new instrument is the principal focus of the study. A special issue of the *Journal of Counseling Psychology* edited by Wampold (1987) provides an excellent overview of these approaches.

The second, but less common, research undertaking in the differential tradition, is what Cronbach (1957) called "experimental." In Vocational Psychology, these experimental studies test the effects of a variety of career interventions and treatments ranging from a single 20-minute session of reinforcement for exploratory behavior to semester-long evaluations of the effectiveness of curricular/class interventions. Inventory interpretations logically fall within the experimental thrust of the differential tradition.

The differential tradition assumes the existence of a stable trait that is more or less normally distributed, and which, once identified, can be related to other constructs of interest via a nomological net or series of systematic interrelationships with other observable phenomena. Stable traits can also be the target of an experimental manipulation. The principal contribution of this differential tradition to psychological research is the concept of reliability of measurement, or the notion that it is possible to characterize, in a dependable and precise manner, the nature of an individual or group of individuals on a variable of interest. According to the differential viewpoint, aggregate behaviors or tendencies are presumed to represent stable dispositions, and changes over time are regarded as error variance to be minimized in the test construction process. McCrae and Costa (1986) remind us that it has taken 20 years for differential psychologists to recover from Walter Mischel's (1968, 1984) damning attacks on the cross-situational consistency of behavior. Reviewers such as Seymour Epstein (1979) have reestablished, with some considerable effort, that enduring traits do exist that maintain themselves over time, and that these traits can be accurately and reliably measured using scales or self-reports. Epstein concludes that single episodes of behavior are unreliable in the way that single items are unreliable in psychological tests. Repeated instances of behavior averaged over multiple measurements, however, are quite reliable, and can be related to other psychological traits.

EXPERIMENTAL STUDIES IN DIFFERENTIAL VOCATIONAL PSYCHOLOGY

My research encompasses both the acturial and the experimental research areas of the differential tradition. My goal here is to summarize briefly the contributions of each area and to provide an example illustrating how nontraditional methodology offers an advance where traditional methodology does not. I will start with the experimental emphasis. Early in my career I conducted a few studies of the effects of brief career interventions on the function of post-counseling, but it was not until 1979 when John Holland, Tom Magoon, and I undertook to review career psychology for the *Annual Review of Psychology* that I realized just how much, and also how little, had been done in experimental studies Holland, Magoon & Spokane, 1981). In the course of our efforts, we reviewed hundreds of studies that varied vastly in sophistication. In our first narrative, or literary, review we concluded that there were four essential ingredients necessary for a successful career intervention. These were:

a. the acquisition of a cognitive framework for understanding self, the world of work, and the relational aspects of both—which could be supplied directly—for example, Holland's theory (1985)—or implied from the materials used in the intervention;

b. information about self and the world of work—generally supplied by systematic exploratory activity, inventories, and so forth;.

c. cognitive rehearsal of career aspirations, dreams, and so on; and

    d. social support or reinforcement—from a counselor, workshop member, family member, or other such figures.

We drew these conclusions from close examination of the content of the treatments employed, rather than from any specific data supplied in the experimental methods used in these studies.

My second attempt at a review grew out of frustration with the speculative nature of literary reviews, and the conclusion that hard data were needed to verify the treatment effects we saw in the career intervention studies. Laurel Oliver and I reanalyzed 58 studies of career interventions containing more than 7,300 subjects and published from 1948 to 1980 (Spokane & Oliver, 1983). We calculated Glassian effect sizes for each study by subtracting the mean of the control group from the mean of the treatment group and dividing by the standard deviation of the control group. In this way, we obtained a standardized mean difference between treatment and control subjects across studies and measures.

We drew three conclusions from our work:

    a. the status of the average client receiving any type of vocational intervention exceeded that of 80 percent of untreated controls;
    b. the outcome status of the average client receiving group/class interventions exceeded that of 87 percent of untreated controls; and
    c. the outcome status of the average client receiving individual interventions exceeded that of 81 percent of untreated controls.

We also made suggestions to authors, reviewers, and editors for improving the quality of career intervention outcome studies, many of which have been incorporated in subsequent research.

We were taken to task by Rounds and Tinsley (1984) for not separating out group and class interventions and for not looking at the characteristics of studies that contributed to greater effect size. Because we wanted to examine relationships among study variables and respond to Rounds and Tinsley, we recoded all of our studies on 14 different study characteristics, including counselor experience level, reactivity of measures employed, type of client, and age of client. We also updated our study base with two additional years of studies. A third effort was published in the *Journal of Counseling Psychology* (Oliver & Spokane, 1988). Here we weighted our effect sizes for sample sizes, removed outliers, broke treatments into five different classification levels, and corrected several problems in our original analysis.

Clearly, the class interventions were more effective than all the others, but they were also the most intensive, requiring more sessions and time. When we regressed all study characteristics against effect size, the only significant predictor of magnitude of outcome was number of sessions/hours, which we called treatment intensity ($F = 12.01$, $df = 9.81$, $p < .01$). To correct for the possible confounding of number of sessions with treatment, we calculated a dose-response ratio or the effect per hour for each treatment, an effect per client ratio, and a cost effectiveness figure.

Individual counseling, although twice as costly per client as a workshop/class, was more than four times as effective per hour of intervention. Thus, individual treatments were the most costly but the most effective, whereas the workshop/class interventions were the least expensive but also less effective per hour of treatment (Oliver & Spokane, 1988).

WHAT TRADITIONAL DATA COULD NOT TELL US ABOUT CAREER INTERVENTION

We confirmed the beneficial nature of career interventions in these reviews but there was little we could say about how and why those effects occur—about what was driving the positive outcomes we found. We know a little about a lot of clients from this traditional approach, and we would benefit from knowing a lot about one or two clients. This latter, nontraditional approach is called N-of-one or case study research, a good example of which follows.

In a recent doctoral dissertation, Kirschner (1988) conducted seven sessions of career counseling with a 43-year-old woman who was dissatisfied with her career as a speech therapist. The client was screened for overt pathology and found to be free of serious disorders. Prior to counseling, the client completed the *My Vocational Situation* (Holland, Daiger, & Power, 1981), the Career Exploration Survey (Stumpf, Collarelli, & Hartman, 1983), a goal attainment scaling procedure, and the Strong-Campbell Interest Inventory (SCII). Process measures were administered after each session, and a special debriefing procedure developed by Clara Hill (Hill, Helms, Spiegel, & Tichenor, 1988; Hill, & O'Grady, 1985) was utilized to determine the therapist's intentions and the client's reactions to each session. Each session was tape-recorded and "unitized" for later analysis. The client was contacted 18 months following counseling to study the longer-term outcomes of the intervention. Although it would be impossible to detail this more that 300-page effort, the careful scrutiny given to each session provides wonderful new data for model building in career intervention.

In addition to the session data, the client and counselor also indicated which materials were most helpful. Four change mechanisms (information about interests, methods of organizing information, counselor support and feedback, and discussions of self-concept and career obstacles) were identified that closely resembled our early thinking (Holland, Magoon, & Spokane, 1981). This nontraditional method, then, provided data that hundreds of studies employing more traditional experimental methods could not. Without the traditional backdrop of outcome studies we would have placed less weight on this N-of-one study. Since it emerged from the findings of preceding traditional studies, it could confirm and extend our understanding of career intervention. I can now foresee a wave of process-oriented career studies triggered by this novel methodology that will lead to a quantum advance in our understanding of the change process in career intervention. A blend of methodologies, especially if the findings agree, will enhance the depth and reliability of our understanding of the career intervention process.

ACTUARIAL STUDIES IN
DIFFERENTIAL VOCATIONAL PSYCHOLOGY

The second major research thrust in the differential tradition presumes the development and validation of dozens of vocational inventories as background, and tests the degree to which individuals make career choices consistent with the predictions of those inventories. More than 100 studies of person-environment congruence have been published since the introduction of Holland's first scale in the early 1960s. I reviewed a number of those studies in a monograph in 1985, and then guest-edited a special issue of the *Journal of Vocational Behavior* on Person-Environment Fit (Spokane, 1987).

In studying Holland's (1985) work and the work of students of the theory, my own studies included, I have repeatedly been struck by the observation that only a small portion of Holland's theory has ever been subjected to empirical study. As stated in the 1973 version of the theory, Holland offered the following three major theoretical propositions:

a. Congruent individuals will be reinforced, satisfied, and less likely to change environments than will incongruent individuals.
b. Incongruent individuals will be influenced by the dominant environment to change in the direction of congruence.
c. When placed in an incongruent environment, persons with consistent and differentiated personality patterns will be more likely to operate to make changes in the environment than will inconsistent and undifferentiated individuals; that is, they will clarify the influence of the environment.

I know of only a few studies that test either of the last two propositions of the theory, but there are hundreds that evaluate the first. The lion's share of the theory, and certainly the most complex portion, remain for study. What is conveyed to counselors and students of Holland's theory is a distorted caricature of Holland's position which no longer addresses the pertinent questions clients and counselors face in making difficult career decisions. In spite of the complexity of the original theory, the stasis notion has come to represent the Holland theory, and research testing the theory has overconcentrated on static fit analyses, with decreasing returns. I am bothered less by the lack of method diversity than by a lack of creative questioning that I see in these studies.

The weight of evidence from traditional Holland differential studies of person-environment fit and career behavior suggests that about half of the time individuals select an occupation congruent with their personality type. When there is a correspondence between expressed and measured interests, that predictive power jumps to 70 percent (Borgen & Seling, 1978). Secondly, congruence is correlated with job satisfaction in the range of about .20 to .55. The congruence-satisfaction relationship varies in strength depending on which correspondence indices are used and whether specialty within occupation is considered (Assouline & Meir, 1987).

Assouline and Meir's (1987) meta-analysis of congruence studies shows that when tested, even an oversimplified version of Holland's theory yields expected relationships between satisfaction and congruence. Under some circumstances, the correlation between congruence and well-being measures is over .50.

The prospects are better for an advance in our understanding of person-environment fit when a more complex approach to the theory is tested. For example, overall correlations between congruence and satisfaction increase, the more accurately the job environment is defined, and when moderators of the congruence-satisfaction relationship are considered. For example, when one considers the importance of group membership to the individual (Meir, Kelnan, & Segal, 1986), or differences between intrinsic and extrinsic job satisfaction (Smart, Elton, & McLaughlin, 1986), research findings are more in line with theoretical expectations. In another recent study, Grotevant, Cooper, and Kramer (1986) found an important link between congruence and actual behavior, showing that the more broadly adolescents explored career options, the more likely they were to make a congruent career choice.

It is hard to imagine how any reasonable person could adhere to a strictly static interpretation of person-environment fit, though one or two very capable individuals still do. Borgen (1986), for example, likens the choice of a career to the selection of an entrée in a restaurant. No change is implied; one simply selects an item. Although I do not believe that fit is entirely static, I am unsure whether some hybrid model of developmental fit, on the one hand, or an interactionist position in which we describe relatively stable individuals who influence the environments they inhabit more than the environments influence them, on the other hand, is the reasonable next step at this time. I remain convinced that there is much less change and development in most careers than is generally accepted. Vondracek, Lerner, and Schulenberg (1986) and Gottfredson (1981) provide different views of what a reframe of the differential paradigm might be. Gottfredson adheres to a more static fit model in which sex role and prestige level, once acquired, are added to field of interest and are fitted to the ability requirements of jobs. In contrast, Vondracek and colleagues (1986) offer a continuous, interactive or ecological description of the career development process. The two models are still in their formative stages. Vondracek and colleagues will have to become a good deal more specific about the content of the choices that develop across the lifespan. Gottfredson will have to describe specifically how ability dictates career selection.

The problems we face in person-environment fit are not unlike those faced in physics. Tiedeman (1980) tried to tell us that when he invoked Heisenberg's uncertainty principle. The uncertainty principle dictates that, even though the description of a single molecule at a particular moment in time is possible, as is an analysis of the direction of movement of that molecule over time, the random movement of molecules makes it impossible to describe both where the molecule is (equivalent to differential Vocational Psychology) and where it is headed (developmental Vocational Psychology) with sufficient certainty to predict its ultimate position. The more precisely we focus on one of these two processes, the more uncertain becomes the other. Vocational Psychology is approaching the same Heisenbergian wall that Newtonian physics faced in the early part of this century. Differential methods now confirm where an individual is, and developmental methods provide answers to where the individual might be going, but unified vocational theories may be out of reach for now. The best that contemporary physics can do is provide ranges or probabilities for estimating movement, a model that seems reasonable to me for career psychology and that Mischel now endorses for personality theory (Mischel, 1984). A unified theory in Vocational Psychology may take the same 100 year struggle that it has in physics.

I was very taken with a recent article by Sandelands, Bockner, and Glynn (1988) which studied the conditions under which individuals persist in a course of action, a problem that seems very central to career choice and that will become more so if we would concede that probability ranges are a more reasonable route to take than exact predictions (Spokane, 1985). For the most part, I believe that, except for social class, psychological traits (interest, ability, personality) will account for most of behavior, especially if we are willing to accept probability ranges for a series of behaviors over time. People are more consistent than they are variable across situations, especially when we refer to career situations, which are not as powerful as experimentally created lab conditions. There is a certain linearity to career behavior. The elementary-school child who gave up on math because it was too hard will become the adolescent who, without exploration, took the first available job at McDonalds, and the unemployed adult who finds retraining too much of a hardship.

Nontraditional methods can also inform traditional methods in this second differential thrust. In my own research, I am turning to an investigative reporting framework (Levine, 1980), for studying career decision making, in which we conduct a tape-recorded structured interview accompanied by traditional inventories, the results of which we will subject to multidimensional scaling analysis to determine the underlying dimensions in common career decision situations. In this way, we hope to capture the emotional, behavioral, and attitudinal requirements for successful coping in common career decision situations and then to examine personal characteristics as moderators of the behaviors people exhibit when faced with these situations. We should capture the essence of some of the mental accounting that Kahneman and Tversky (1984) describe, and ascertain the degree to which the subject is able to entertain disconfirming information as an indicator of the quality of the career decision made (Janis & Mann, 1977). Once we describe these career situations and constructive responses to them, we can begin to develop diagnostic measures to determine what constructive cognitions, behaviors, and emotional sets are lacking in an individual, and can build treatments to increase them directly.

PITFALLS NONTRADITIONAL METHODS CAN AVOID

A major failing of differential research in Vocational Psychology is the reporting of small-N studies whose results cannot be cumulated across samples or time

(Oliver & Spokane, 1983, 1988). Replications of influential studies in our field are almost never conducted. It is unusual when more than one or two studies are conducted by even the better research teams in Vocational Psychology. Adding a nontraditional method to a replication would greatly increase our understanding of the often subtle changes that occur in individuals across time. Reviews of a focused area of the field by a researcher who has been involved in a prolonged research effort are also infrequent. There have been a few notable exceptions, of course, and those are the instances where we have made the strongest gains (Myers, 1986). Most studies, however, are conducted as doctoral dissertations or isolated efforts, and many of those isolated efforts are reported without the basic data necessary for applying cumulative techniques such as meta-analysis. It is rare to see studies published in the Vocational Psychology literature that employ the large representative data bases gathered by the federal government, that is, the National Longitudinal Studies of Laborforce Participation (NLS), National Assessment Educational Progress data (NAEP), or Census data. We are not, then, doing as well as we might in producing cumulative and generalizable evidence in areas of importance to Vocational Psychology. Our sociological friends explain more variance and cumulate more effectively than we do. Any nontraditional effort should be launched with a long-term commitment to a series of studies and reviews, with an end goal in mind, and with sampling that will permit generalization beyond middle-class white college students.

A second pitfall that is particularly annoying to me is the repeated use of variables and measures that are of very little practical significance to clients or counselors. We should study what people actually do in their day-to-day lives, not what they respond to on an inventory, or indicate they wish they could do, or might do in the future. Pervin (1983) dubbed this outcome the "stream of behavior," a concept drawn from William James but Vocational Psychology has yet to embrace it. The behavior stream can be measured as rigorously as a psychometrically sound instrument (see Epstein, 1979), but we should not equate the two. What is needed are measures of what people do in the face of difficult environmental barriers, not what they promise to do, prefer to do, or hope to do. There is still confusion about whether expressed choice or measured interests are better reflections of eventual choice. We do know that agreement in these two domains results in higher predictability, but we do not know what disagreement between expressed and measured interests really means, and I have yet to read a convincing explanation of conflicts between the two. If nontraditional methods make exclusive use of self-report, which they often do, will we have an accurate picture of a person's life? If we stick with actual behaviors, we can then determine whether as Holland (1985) and Epstein (1979) contend, behavioral repertoires emerge from trait complexes, or whether they are situationally determined as Mischel (1968) believes. The only measures of actual behavior that I have seen are the vocational information-seeking measure developed by Krumboltz and Thoresen (1964); Azrin's (1980) work in which he calculates the number of welfare dollars collected by participants in his job club, and the treatment he uses, which essentially increases the volume of job search activity on a daily basis; and recent measures by Stumpf et al. (1983) on career salience. When students complete a course on personal career development, it is folly indeed to measure their post-course career maturity and then to assume that a measure of maturity will lead to a higher quality or more comfortable series of decisions thereafter. We need more relevant and verifiable career measures.

A third failing of traditional differential research, which nontraditional efforts might avoid, is the separation of career and personal concerns. Increasingly, it is apparent that the psychological and mental health consequences (and antecedents) of difficult career decisions are as important a topic for career psychology as the content of the decision itself. In his remarkably clear analysis of interest measurement, Borgen (1986) argues that interests are indeed related to normal personality, when neuroticism and psychopathology are removed first. Neuroticism by itself was unrelated to any personality type. Thus, maladjustment seems to affect all interest types equally. What Borgen did not say was that congruence (more appropriately incongruence) is repeatedly related to pathology and maladjustment. I would wager that people who make poor career decisions are affected in negative ways by having done so, and that people with antecedent maladjustment will make poor decisions and, having made these bad decisions, will suffer from a host of difficulties, including work inhibition, occupational stress, accidents, and counter- and nonproductivity. The more difficult the decision, the more likely a negative outcome. In a forthcoming special issue of the *Journal of Career Development,* Herr (in press) addresses this issue head-on.

In one setting, I recently interviewed young fast-track managers who were selected for their value to the company. Four of the six saw an uncertain or unhappy future for themselves in their personal lives, largely because they were too busy working, or in the case of the women, because they were afraid that most eligible men were not interested in a capable woman. What surprised me most, however, was the deep unhappiness these young managers expressed and the fact that three of the six indicated that they had felt some suicidal inclinations within the past six months. I was not about to give them a career maturity inventory. Career and personal problems can be intertwined during a difficult transition even when they are independent before and after the decision (Spokane, in press-a).

Lastly, I think it is especially important to use more than one method to investigate most topics. If the different methods produce largely the same results, then we can be more certain of our conclusions. If not, then we are obliged to find out why not. One excellent study used a combination of differential (discriminant analysis), developmental (Markov chaining) and case study methods, to examine career patterns in a longitudinal data base (Gribbons & Lohnes, 1982). The result was four clear patterns (degeneration, constant maturity, constant immaturity, and emerging maturity) that are full of rich clinical detail and supported by traditional quantitative data.

SUMMARY

In sum, the two traditions in vocational psychology, differential and developmental, have provided useful frames for understanding vocational behavior. The two major paradigms in the differential tradition, outcome studies and correlational studies, can be enhanced by employing nontraditional methods to enrich and confirm conventional findings. A unified theory of vocational behavior that attempts a convergence between the developmental and differential traditions is intuitively attractive but practically premature. Career measures that describe actual behavior rather than test attitudes are badly needed as a preparatory step to a future unified theory.

NOTE

As a matter of course, I would include under the *differential* rubric any studies evaluating interventions that were based on inventories or tests whose purpose was to distinguish one group of respondents from another, just as I would include under the *developmental* rubric any studies evaluating the effects of a career intervention that was based on developmental assumptions. This distinction is not always clear, but a third research class for interventions does not seem preferable to the inconvenience of this ambiguity.

REFERENCES

Assouline, M., & Meir, E. I. (1987). Meta-analysis of the relationship between congruence and well-being measures. *Journal of Vocational Behavior, 31*, 319-332.

Azrin, N. (1980). *Job club counselor's manual: A behavioral approach to vocational counseling.* Baltimore, MD: University Park Press.

Borgen, F. H. (1986). New approaches to the assessment of interests. In W. B. Walsh & S. H. Osipow (Eds.), Advances in vocational psychology, Vol 1: The assessment of interests (pp. 83-125). Hillsdale, NJ: Erlbaum.

Borgen, F. H., & Seling, M. J. (1978). Expressed and inventoried interests revisited: Perspicacity in the person. *Journal of Counseling Psychology, 25*, 536-543.

Cronbach. L. J. (1957). The two disciplines of scientific psychology. *American Psychologist, 12*, 671-684.

Epstein, S. (1979). The stability of behavior: I. On predicting most of the people much of the time. *Journal of Personality and Social Psychology, 37*, 1097-1126.

Gottfredson, L. S. (1981). Circumscription and compromise: A developmental theory of occupational aspirations [Monograph]. *Journal of Counseling Psychology, 28*, 545-579.

Gribbons, W., & Lohnes, P. R. (1982). *Careers in theory and experience: A twenty-year longitudinal study.* Albany, NY: State University of New York Press.

Grotevant, H. D., Cooper, C. R., & Kramer, K. (1986). Exploration as a predictor of congruence in adolescents' career choices. *Journal of Vocational Behavior, 29,* 201-215.

Herr, E. L. (in press). Career development and mental health. *Journal of Career Development.*

Hill, C. E., Helms, J. E., Speigel, S. B., & Tichenor, V. (1988). Development of a system for categorizing client reactions to therapist intentions. *Journal of Counseling Psychology, 35,* 27-36.

Hill, C. E., & O'Grady, K. E. (1985). A list of therapist intentions illustrated in a case study with therapists of varying theoretical orientations. *Journal of Counseling Psychology, 32,* 3-22.

Holland, J. L. (1985). *Making vocational choices: A theory of careers* (2nd ed.). Englewood Cliffs, NJ: Prentice Hall. (Original work published 1973)

Holland, J.L., Daiger, D., & Power, P.G. *My Vocational Situation.* Palo Alto, CA: Consulting Psychologists Press.

Holland, J. L., Magoon, T. M., & Spokane, A. R. (1981). Counseling Psychology: Career interventions, research and theory. *Annual Review of Psychology, 32,* 279-305.

Janis, I., & Mann, L. (1977). *Decision-making: A psychological analysis of conflict, choice, and commitment.* New York: Free Press.

Kahneman, D., & Tversky, A. (1984). Choices, values and frames. *American Psychologist, 39,* 341-350.

Kirschner, T. J. (1988). *A case study of the process and outcome of career counseling.* Unpublished doctoral dissertation, University of Maryland, College Park.

Krumboltz, J. D., & Thoresen, C. E. (1974). The effect of behavior counseling in group and individual settings on information seeking behavior. *Journal of Counseling Psychology, 11,* 324-333.

Levine, M. (1980). Investigative reporting as a research method: An analysis of Bernstein & Woodward's *All the President's Men. American Psychologist, 35,* 626-638.

McCrae, R. R., & Costa, P. T., Jr. (1986). Clinical assessment can benefit from recent advances in personality psychology. *American Psychologist, 41,* 1001-1003.

Meir, E. I., Kelnan, G., & Segal, Z. (1986). Group importance as a mediator between personality-environment congruence and satisfaction. *Journal of Vocational Behavior, 28,* 60-69.

Mischel, W. (1968). *Personality and assessment.* New York: Wiley.

Mischel, W. (1984). Convergences and challenges in the search for consistency. *American Psychologist, 39,* 351-364.

Myers, R. M. (1986). Research on educational and vocational counseling. In A. E. Bergin and S. L. Garfield (Eds.), *Handbook of psychotherapy and behavior change* (3rd ed., pp. 715-738). New York: Wiley.

Oliver, L. W., & Spokane, A. R. (1983). Research integration: Approaches, problems, and recommendations for research reporting. *Journal of Counseling Psychology, 30*, 252-257.

Oliver, L. W., & Spokane, A. R. (1988). Career intervention outcome: What contributes to client gain. *Journal of Counselling Psychology, 35*, 447-463.

Pervin, L. A. (1983) The stasis and flow of behavior: Toward a theory of goals. In R. Dienstbier (Ed.), *Nebraska symposium on motivation*. Lincoln, NB: University of Nebraska Press.

Rounds, J. B., & Tinsley, H. E. A. (1984). Diagnosis and treatment of vocational problems. In S. D. Brown & R. W. Lent (Eds.), *Handbook of counseling psychology* (pp. 137-177). New York: Wiley.

Sandelands, L. E., Bockner, J., & Glynn, M. A. (1988). If at first you don't succeed, try, try again: Effects of persistence-performance contingencies, ego involvement and self-esteem on task persistence. *Journal of Applied Psychology, 73*, 208-216.

Smart, J. C., Elton, C. F., & McLaughlin, G. W. (1986). Person-environment congruence and job satisfaction. *Journal of Vocational Behavior, 29*, 216-225.

Spokane, A. R. (1985). A review of research on person-environment congruence in Holland's theory of careers [Monograph]. *Journal of Vocational Behavior, 26*, 306-343.

Spokane, A. R. (1987). Conceptual and methodological issues in person-environment fit. *Journal of Vocational Behavior, 31*, 217-221.

Spokane, A.R. (in press-a). Are there psychological and mental health consequences of difficult career decisions? *Journal of Career Development*.

Spokane, A. R. (in press-b). *Career intervention*. Englewood Cliffs, NJ: Prentice-Hall.

Spokane, A. R. (in press-c). Self-guided interest inventories as career interventions. In E. Watkins & V. Campbell (Eds.), *Testing in counseling practice*. Hillsdale, NJ: Erlbaum.

Spokane, A. R., & Oliver, L. W. (1983). The outcomes of vocational intervention. In W. B. Walsh & S. H. Osipow (Eds.), *Handbook of Vocational Psychology: Vol. 1*, (pp. 99-136). Hillsdale, NJ: Erlbaum.

Stumpf, S. A., Colarelli, S. M., & Hartman, K. (1983). Development of the Career Exploration Survey (CES). *Journal of Vocational Behavior, 22*, 191-226.

Tiedeman, D. (1980). Personal communication.

Vondracek, F. W., Lerner R. M., & Schulenberg, J. E. (1986). *Career development: A life-span developmental approach*. Hillsdale, NJ: Erlbaum .

Wampold, B. E. (Ed.). (1987) Special issue: Quantitative foundations of Counseling Psychology research. *Journal of Counseling Psychology, 34*, 363-489.

3

A Developmental-Contextual Approach to Career Development Research

Fred W. Vondracek

During the past five or six years, some of my colleagues and students at Pennsylvania State University and I have attempted to formulate what we have called a developmental-contextual approach to career development. A fairly extensive exposition of this approach was accomplished in the 1986 book *Career Development: A Life-Span Developmental Approach.* This book was coauthored by me, my colleague Richard Lerner, and my former student John Schulenberg.

The formulation of a developmental-contextual approach to career development seemed to be an almost natural consequence of my own career development experiences as well as the important influences of several of my colleagues at Penn State University. Regarding my own career development experiences, it should suffice to note that I was destined to become a tile setter and stone mason according to a decision made by my father when I was only 10 years old. My formal schooling was terminated after I finished the eighth grade, and subsequently I became an apprentice tile setter. Three years later I obtained my journeyman's license and continued to practice my trade for another two years. Unconvinced that my father's decision about my occupational future had been correct, I left not only the occupation he had chosen for me but also the country so that I could pursue educational and career opportunities that were more to my liking. Less than eight years later, I obtained my Ph.D. in clinical psychology from the Pennsylvania State University and, after being sidetracked, among other things, to the U.S. Veterans Administration and to a tour of duty as department head at Penn State, I finally returned to a concern with career development: both my own and that of others. Changing the direction of my career so often convinced me that a developmental approach to career development was necessary; having worked not only in vastly different work environments but also in different countries persuaded me of the crucial importance of the context in career development.

In the meantime I had the great fortune of being associated with a number of outstanding individuals at Penn State who helped in shaping my thinking about career development. Individuals like Paul Baltes and John Nesselroade helped me to gain an understanding and appreciation of life-span developmental psychology. Richard Lerner has been instrumental in helping me and my former student John Schulenberg to describe the implications of the life-span developmental view for the field of career development (Vondracek, Lerner, & Schulenberg, 1983, 1986). His "goodness-of-fit" model of person-context relations has served as the basis for much of our thinking about a developmental-contextual approach to career development. Finally, John Nesselroade has made many important contributions to the methodology of studying "development in context," and it is to his methodological expertise and innovation that I remain indebted.

Two themes are clearly apparent in my thinking about careers: development and context. A third theme is implied by these two, and that is the theme of change. Individuals develop and contexts change. To study career development thus means to study a moving target (the developing individual) within a changing and complex context. Certainly, it would be simpler to study an individual at a specific point in time, and limited to a specific context. This would be analogous, however, to showing a silent series of black-and-white still pictures as opposed to showing a wide-screen movie in technicolor and with stereo sound.

What I would like to accomplish in this chapter is to (1) describe what I mean by a developmental-contextual approach to career development, (2) discuss some of the methodological implications of employing a developmental-contextual approach, and (3) give some examples from the research conducted by me and by my colleagues that demonstrates how our way of thinking about careers can be translated into actual research.

THE DEVELOPMENTAL-CONTEXTUAL APPROACH
TO CAREER DEVELOPMENT

As mentioned previously, the developmental-contextual approach to career development described here is heavily indebted to the thinking of Richard Lerner regarding developmental contextualism in general (e.g., Lerner, 1978, 1986, in press). Most importantly, in explaining the nature of the relationship between individual and context, Lerner uses the term "probabilistic epigenesis," which was introduced by Gottlieb (1970), to emphasize that the influence of the changing context on the developing person is to make the trajectory of development less certain with respect to the applicability of norms to the individual. In emphasizing the probabilistic nature of person-context interaction, Lerner deliberately departs from what Gottlieb (1983) has labeled "predetermined epigenesis," a characteristic feature of theories in which biology was seen as the prime mover of development (e.g., Erikson, 1959; Freud, 1949). Scarr (1982) has amplified the probabilistic epigenetic notion by stating that

> development is a probabilistic result of indeterminant combina-
> tions of genes and environments. Development is genetically
> guided but variable and probabilistic because influential events
> in the life of every person can be neither predicted nor explained
> by general laws. Development, in this view, is guide primarily by

the genetic program through its multilevel transactions with environments that range from cellular to social. (pp. 852-853).

An important additional consideration pointed out by Lerner is that the organism in developmental-contextualism

> is itself a qualitatively distinct level within the multiple, dynamically interacting levels forming the context of life. As such, the organism has a distinct influence on that multilevel context that is influencing the organism. As a consequence the organism is, in short, not a passive host, but an active contributor to its own development. (in press)

Developmental contextualism thus incorporates the notion that the context does not just produce alterations in the individual's development, but that the context itself is influenced and constrained by the characteristics of the individual. As a consequence, development can be conceptualized in terms of reciprocal organism-context relations or dynamic interactional relations (Lerner, 1978, 1984, 1985). Such development is not dispersive (or chaotic)—in spite of its probabilistic nature—because the individual (organism) has organization and internal coherence, and these features constrain the capability of the developmental context to affect the system (Gollin, 1981).

Although the organism has organization, structure, or internal coherence, each organism is individually distinct as a consequence of its genotype and experiential history. Similarly, the context enveloping the organism is unique and changing. It is impossible to predict what particular features of the context will exist at a particular time in a given individual's life course.

> As a consequence, we may only speak probabilistically of the effects a given person may have on his or her context, of the feedback the person is likely to receive from the context, and of the nature of the person's development that will therefore ensue (Vondracek, Lerner, & Schulenberg, 1986, p. 78)

Many theorists and researchers have attempted to describe the conceptual complexity of this framework, both from the perspective of life-span developmental psychology and career development. For example, Super's (1980) concept of the life space and individual development within it represents a prominent example from the career development literature. Another complex person-context model is presented by Schein (1971) who speaks of the structure of the individual and the structure of the organization, suggesting that a career is fashioned as the developing individual moves through the organization. A very recent example of concern with person-context relations in career development is the recent special issue of the *Journal of Vocational Behavior* edited by Spokane (1987). In life-span development a number of authors have made major contributions to the area of complex person-context relationships (e.g., Baltes, Baltes, & Reinert, 1970; Belsky, 1984; Bronfenbrenner, 1979; Nesselroade & Baltes, 1974; Schneirla, 1957; Tobach & Schneirla, 1968).

A GRAPHIC REPRESENTATION OF THE MODEL

Figure 3.1, which is reproduced from our career development book (Vondracek, Lerner, & Schulenberg, 1986, p. 79) is an attempt to graphically represent the basic features of the developmental-contextual model applied to career development. What is implied by the model is that both individuals and the world they inhabit are composed of multiple dimensions, which are thought to be interdependent, and developing and/or changing over time. Keeping this in mind, it must be understood that the figure, complex as it may seem, represents a gross oversimplification. It should thus be emphasized that the figure is meant to be only descriptive of the relations that various theorists and researchers have noted as being involved in person-context relations. The bidirectional arrows in the figure are meant to be suggestive of some of these relations as identified in the human development and career development literature.

There are a number of limitations inherent in this type of graphic. First and foremost is the consideration that the components of the macro context, such as "economic conditions," "job opportunities," or "organizational/institutional context" have been chosen rather arbitrarily and represent only a small sample of the relevant macro context. To a lesser extent, arbitrary choices had to be made in the depiction of other components of the developmental-contextual (dynamic interactional) model of career development. It should also be stressed that the model is not presented with the idea that it could be tested as a whole. Instead, this type of representation of person-context relations should be viewed as a useful guide to theory development and a guide to the selection of specific individual and ecological variables in one's research.

What is clearly illustrated by graphics of this type is that there are three essential components in theory-guided research on person-context relations. First, one must have an understanding of the nature of the person-attributes of the person(s) one is interested in studying. Second, one must have an understanding of the features of the person's context one wishes to explore and a rationale for why those features of the context are pertinent to the person-attributes one is examining. Third, one needs a conceptualization of the relation between the individual attributes and the contextual features chosen for study.

Figure 3.1. Graphic representation of a developmental-contextual model of career development.

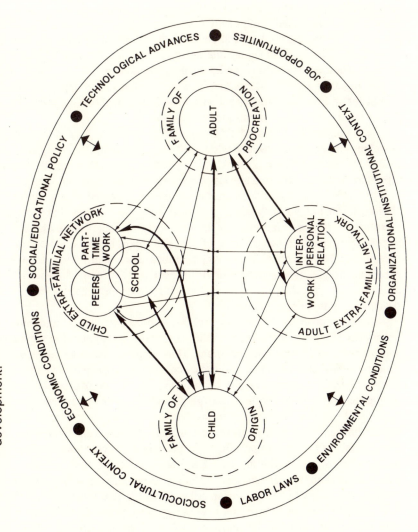

SOME METHODOLOGICAL IMPLICATIONS OF A
DEVELOPMENTAL-CONTEXTUAL APPROACH

The developmental-contextual perspective suggests that career development be conceptualized as part of developmental processes encompassing the entire life span: as involving relationships within the person (e.g., between biological and psychological processes), between persons, and between persons and their contexts, ranging from the immediate interpersonal context to the societal and cultural contexts. There are a number of methodological implications of this view, which are offered together with the observation that methodological strategies and choices should derive from one's theory or conceptual model; methodological preferences should not dictate the questions one investigates.

The complexity of the model, however, places great burdens on the researcher in making choices about research design and data collection. Obviously, the overall goal is to examine whole persons who possess an incredibly varied behavioral repertoire and who exist in a myriad of contexts over their lifetimes. Nesselroade (1988) has recently examined some of the issues involved in making difficult choices in order to design "doable" empirical work. He observed that in practice it is possible to only acquire a subset of the potentially available information that quite imperfectly represents the universe of data that might be classified according to person, variable, and occasion. These limitations are exemplified by, for example, extensive samples of persons measured only once, by small convenient samples that are measured repeatedly, or by studies in which large test batteries with variable psychometric properties are used.

The consequences of making such difficult choices result in limitations (i.e., on generalizability) that Nesselroade (1988) observes are not neutral in regard to the substantive conclusions one can draw. Thus, explicit decisions must be made concerning persons, variables, and occasions in order to develop an experimental design. Nesselroade presents a version of Cattell's (1966a) data box, which is adapted and presented as Figure 3.2, to graphically show how sampling by persons, by variables, and by occasions limits the data in such a way as to produce selection effects that can create distortions in the conclusions reached concerning the nature and generality of relationships reflected in the data. Most vocational psychologists have preferred to live with the selection effects that come from focusing on the person dimension (via the individual differences approach) or with those that come from selecting the variable dimension in the universe of data represented by the data box. Thus, the concepts of representative sampling (of persons) and variables (from content domains) are familiar to most psychologists (see Nesselroade & Ford, 1987, for a recent discussion). It is by no means unusual, however, to have some aspects of the data box poorly represented in a given study, and to thus have conclusions that reflect the consequent selection effects (Nesselroade, 1988).

Figure 3.2. Adaptation of Cattell's data box.

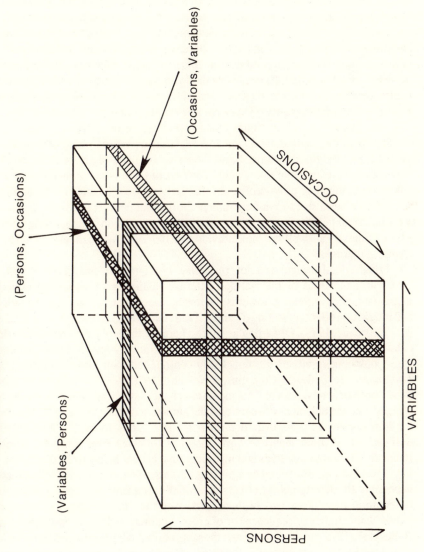

It is the occasion dimension, however, that is most important for developmentalists, and hence for the developmental-contextual approach. It is particularly important from the developmental viewpoint because questions having to do with change over time or with the assessment of stability require multiple occasions of measurement. Since one of the basic premises of the developmental-contextual approach to career development is that careers change as people develop and as their circumstances change, one can readily appreciate the importance of the occasions dimension for examining questions from this perspective. There is another reason, however, and that is that the occasions mode does not just represent time but that it also represents different contexts and situations. Thus, at each occasion of measurement a different occasion *or context* may be sampled.

When two or more occasions of measurement are effected one can ordinarily speak of having a longitudinal design. Indeed, I shall now turn to a discussion of two longitudinal designs that have been shown to be particularly relevant to the developmental-contextual framework. The first of these is the sequential design, either longitudinal or cross-sectional (e.g., Baltes, 1968; Schaie, 1965), and the second involves a short-term longitudinal design that permits the examination of intra-individual change patterns that are related to occasion (either time or situation/context), as well as interindividual differences in such intraindividual change patterns.

Longitudinal designs are not, of course, without problems, most of which center around issues of internal and external validity, such as testing effects, instrumentation, regression towards the mean, selection, experimental mortality, and interaction effects of testing (Campbell & Stanley, 1963; see also Baltes, Reese, & Nesselroade, 1977). Of particular interest here are the problems associated with cohort effects. Specifically, when only one birth cohort is involved in a longitudinal study, ontogenetic effects are hopelessly confounded with historical effects on development (e.g., Baltes, Cornelius, & Nesselroade, 1979). For example, because of technological advances and sociocultural changes, the timing and sequence of "stages" and the outcomes of vocational developmental processes may be different for those born in the 1940s than for those born in the 1960s. In short, in longitudinal designs, unless more than one birth cohort is followed over time, the unique interaction of individual lives and historical time cannot be uncovered.

The advent of sequential designs (e.g., Baltes, 1968; Schaie, 1965) has made it possible to identify cohort effects. Essentially, sequential designs involve the observation of at least two birth cohorts over time in a succession either of longitudinal studies or sequences or of cross-sectional studies or sequences (e.g., Baltes et al., 1979). In the former case, the same individuals are measured repeatedly at different ages (thus involving the problems associated with repeated measurement), and in the later case, independent observations with respect to age and cohort are gathered (thus circumventing problems associated with repeated measurement, but creating problems associated with the inference of intra-individual change). These two forms of sequential strategies can be exploited in various ways, combined or repeatedly, to describe and explain cohort effects on development. It should be noted, however, that disagreement exists over methods of estimation and the utility of such designs in *explaining* cohort effects (see Baltes, 1968; Schaie, 1965; Schaie & Baltes, 1975).

A second analytic procedure that is meaningful in addressing questions posed by the developmental-contextual approach is that of P-technique factor analysis (Cattell, 1963). When coupled with a research design involving intense, repeated measurement of an individual, it allows one to address empirically the contention that vocational phenomena, such as vocational interests or work values, may not be as stable as they are assumed to be. To demonstrate the utility of this approach, we must remind ourselves that most vocational measurement, especially in applied settings, presumes that we are dealing with relatively stable, trait-like constructs. Thus, when we suggest to a student that he or she should pursue a career in business because his or her vocational interests (measured on one occasion) and work values (also measured on one occasion) point in that direction, we implicitly reject the notion that these dimensions could vary significantly and systematically on a day-to-day basis, and we assume that these dimensions are stable. However, the proper empirical support for this assumption may not be present.

If we believe that it is possible that a person's vocational interests and/or work values may change from day to day, and that these changes may be systematic, we need to do at least two things. One of these is to administer a measure of vocational interests and work values repeatedly, at least for about a hundred occasions, in order to obtain a sufficient number of observation points to statistically test for the presence or absence of systematic change. This requirement is analogous to what is needed in more conventional approaches, such as R-technique factor analysis, wherein one wants to see how items covary within a single occasional measurement across a large number of subjects: This is because people in our analogue to measurement occasions also constitute observation points. The point is that in all types of factor analytic procedures, one needs to have sufficient observations of that "entity" one wishes to generalize across—people in R-technique factor analysis, and occasions in P-technique factor analysis. Since we want to test the possibility that our vocational variables may be labile and may therefore show variation from day to day or from context to context, we need a sufficient number of days or contexts in our "sample" to perform this test.

The second thing that needs to be done to test the possibility of lability in our vocational variables is to analyze the data derived from our intensive measurement design. Without going into the technical details of P-technique factor analysis, it should suffice to note that the procedure permits one to determine if change occurs from day to day or context to context, and whether that change is systematic. If day-to-day or context-to-context change or variation does not occur, no correlations among variables across occasions will be found; in such a case, the result of the P-technique factor analysis would lead to the rejection of the idea of lability within a person over time or contexts. If, however, significant patterns of covariation are found, this would indicate systematic change within a person over time or contexts. It would indicate that the person did change from day to day or context to context but that the change was not random. Indeed, the change could be grouped into a factor or factors—statistical constructs that describe, in this case, a given person's state-like day-to-day or context-to-context fluctuations in vocational interests and work values.

One particular point of importance regarding the P-technique is that its use is obviously not limited to studying intra-individual variability over time. Instead of varying occasions according to time (such as day by day), one could vary occasions according to contexts; that is, if a sufficient number of different contexts (possibly several work-related contexts) could be obtained, one could ascertain intra-individual variability across various contexts. It is clear, therefore, that P-technique represents a data analytic procedure that is sensitive not only to the requirements of a developmental perspective but also to contextual variation.

Finally, it should be pointed out that one additional highly desirable, but not essential, component could be added to our intensive measurement P-technique study. This would consist of replicating our entire procedure with several individuals. This would reveal not only possible similarities among people in within-person change but also interindividual differences as well. Thus, by focusing on changes within individuals and also on the extent of similarities across change patterns, the P-technique is a powerful strategy with which to ascertain intra-individual change in vocational phenomena as well as to address differences and similarities across individuals with respect to such changes. In the next section, some findings from a P-technique study of work values will be presented to illustrate some of the above points.

PUTTING INTO PRACTICE WHAT WE PREACH: TWO EXAMPLES

A Longitudinal Sequential Study of Adolescent Career Development

In 1985, two of my former students, James Pendorf, now with the U.S. Veterans Administration, and John Schulenberg, now at Purdue University, and I started a longitudinal study of adolescent career development. One of my current graduate students, Michelle Hostetler, is continuing their work. We set out to investigate vocational development from a developmental-contextual perspective by focusing, in particular, on the issue of separating ontogenetic from generational or historical sources of change. The appropriateness of using such strategies with an adolescent sample has been underscored by the authors of two major longitudinal studies of youth (Jessor & Jessor, 1977; Nesselroade & Baltes, 1974). Referring to the Nesselroade and Baltes study, which used multivariate sequential strategies, the Jessors state that "such designs, especially when applied to those stages in the life trajectory when rapid change is characteristic, appear to have big promise of revealing both the contour and the process of growth and development" (1977, p. 8). Dusek and Flaherty (1981) also argue for the desirability of longitudinal approaches to the study of adolescence. They conclude that it is more informative to be able to test for cohort and time-of-measurement effects than to totally ignore them, even if one does not find them to be significant in a given comparison. Nesselroade and Baltes (1974) underscore the appropriateness of using longitudinal sequential designs by pointing out that during the adolescent period, grouping of individuals into one-year birth cohorts and conducting annual measurements are discriminations that are not, contrary to some expectations, too fine to make in sorting out ontogenetic, historical, and cultural influences on developmental change. Moreover, they point out that age- or stage-invariant sequence models of development are rightfully challenged by alternatives that stress the importance of recognizing contextual influences peculiar to the historical/cultural moment. Finally, they point out that longitudinal studies are necessary if one is to measure intra-individual change, but that simple longitudinal designs, which do not provide controls for threats to internal validity or permit between-cohort comparisons, are of limited value.

Design. The design of the present longitudinal sequential study (subsequently referred to as the Adolescent Career Development Study) involves varying age, sex, and cohort membership in a coordinated series of short-term longitudinal sequences, each requiring five times of measurement. The times of measurement occur annually; thus, the longitudinal sequences will extend over four years. The basic design of the study is presented in Table 3.1 The figure shows that four birth cohorts (1969, 1970, 1971, and 1972) are to be measured repeatedly, using the battery described below at five times, in 1986, 1987, 1988, 1989, and 1990. The subjects were seventh- through tenth-graders, who ranged in age from 13 to 16 years at the first time of measurement. By the fifth occasion of measurement (1990), ages will range from 17 to 20.

Table 3.1. The Core Longitudinal Sample

		Age							
Cohort	N	13	14	15	16	17	18	19	20
1972	250	1986	1987	1988	1989	1990			
	250								
1971	250		1986	1987	1988	1989	1990		
	250								
1970	250			1986	1987	1988	1989	(1990)	
	250								
1969	250				1986	1987	1988	(1989)	(1990)
	250								

Note: Years in parentheses represent potential follow-up samples.

As has been pointed out previously, there are two major limitations of this type of design that need to be guarded against. The first of these is selective dropout or attrition of the longitudinal sample, which can render the data from the core sample a biased representation of the population of observations to which generalization is intended; the second is the problem of retest effects which can result in the longitudinal subjects, showing apparent increases or decreases in level over time that are unrelated to normative ontogenetic change. Without going into much detail, I shall note that we have taken steps to limit attrition, in collaboration with the responsible school authorities, and thus far have succeeded in limiting attrition (among those subjects who produced usable data protocols at the first time of measurement) to less than 20 percent. With regard to the confound of retest effects, we have selected a control group at random from the total sample, they received the test battery for the first time at the second occasion of measurement. Continued selection of such control groups will eventually permit a comparison of data sets between those subjects who have been exposed repeatedly to the test battery and a randomly selected subset of those subjects who have not had repeated exposure to the test battery. Such comparisons will then permit the application of data analytic techniques to examine the effects of repeated testing and to make corrections according to the outcomes (Labouvie, Bartsch, Nesselroade, & Baltes, 1974).

Subjects. The subjects for the Adolescent Career Development Study are students in a single junior/senior high school in western Pennsylvania. The school in question is located in a generally rural area. While this limits the generalizability of the findings, using a single school is virtually a matter of necessity in conducting such a large-scale longitudinal study. The degree of cooperation and assistance required is possible only in a setting where wholehearted support is forthcoming not only from the top levels of administration but also from teachers and students. Needless to say, such circumstances are most difficult to find.

Subjects consist of the entire population of the school, consisting of more than 900 students, approximately half of whom are male. Students are fairly evenly distributed across grades 7 through 12. (It should be noted that for practical reasons all students are asked to participate in each data collection occasion. For purposes of the present study, however, only those subjects were considered who fit into the sequential longitudinal cohort design outlined in Table 3.1)

Measurement Battery. Selection of measurement devices for use in a multi-variate study such as the present one is a critical planning feature. As Campbell and Stanley (1963) have pointed out, one of the primary aspects of external validity or generalizability concerns the domain of measurement variables. Would the same conclusions be reached had other measures been used? These concerns force a conscientious examination of domain representativeness and other psychometric properties such as reliability prior to settling on a specific set of measuring instruments. These and additional criteria were attended to in selecting the measures used in the present study.

Three major content domains are involved in the present study. They are related directly to the area of vocational development, and they consist of the domains of vocational interests, work values, and career indecision.

The specific measures used were:

1. *The Career Decision Scale (CDS)* (Osipow, Carney, Winer, Yanico, & Koschier, 1976). This scale has been used extensively to ascertain the extent and specific nature of career indecision. It consists of 19 items, but only 16 of those, namely, items 3 through 18, are used as the CDS Indecision score. The items are scored on a Likert scale with a score of 1 corresponding to "not at all like me," and a score of 4 corresponding to "exactly like me." Satisfactory reliability and validity have been documented. For reviews, see Allis (1984), Harmon (1985), Herman (1985), and Slaney (1985, 1988).
2. *Work Aspect Preference Scale (WAPS)* (Pryor, 1981). Work values are being measured with Pryor's Work Aspect Preference Scale. It measures 13 distinct work values and consists of 52 items that are scored on a 5-point scale that ranges from 1, corresponding to "totally unimportant," to 5, corresponding to "extremely important." Validity and reliability have been reported to be acceptable (e.g., see Pryor, 1983).
3. *California Occupational Preference System (COPS)* (Knapp, Grant, & Demos, 1966; Knapp & Knapp, 1976). The COPS is a vocational interest measure that consists of 168 items that describe a wide range of occupationally relevant activities. It is based on Roe's (1956) classification of occupations. There are 14 interest scales, each of which consists of 12 items. Respondents rate each item on a 4-point scale ranging from 1, "dislike very much," to 4, "like very much." Scale construction is based on factor analysis (Knapp, 1967).

Current status. As of summer 1988 three occasions of data collection (1986, 1987, 1988) have been completed. Since we are operating without outside funding, however, only limited progress has been made in data analysis. However, what has been accomplished in collecting and managing three occasions of data is not inconsiderable. Moreover, with the collaboration of former and present students, progress has been made in examining data collected with one of the instruments, namely, the CDS. This was due in part to the fortunate circumstance of having a visiting professor from Japan, Kazuaki Shimizu, spend the 1986-1987 academic year working with me on the analyses of data collected at Occasions 1 and 2.

Two studies (Schulenberg, Shimizu, Vondracek, & Hostetler, 1988; Shimizu, Vondracek, Schulenberg, & Hostetler, 1988) have resulted from those collaborative efforts. In the first of these studies (Shimizu et al., 1988) the factor structure of the CDS was examined by comparing the findings of seven previous factor analytic studies with the results of a factor analytic study conducted on our longitudinal sample. Inconsistent findings regarding the factor structure of the CDS from previous studies could generally be accounted for by communality estimation. It was also found that all previous studies relied on orthogonal rotational procedures, and that when their solutions were recalculated using oblique rotational procedures, the overall factor solutions were less complex and greater similarity in factors across studies was found. Finally, the study suggested that a "simple" model of the CDS factor structure could be derived in which each CDS item loaded saliently on only one factor.

The second study (Schulenberg et al., 1988) utilized confirmatory factor analytic strategies to test for factorial invariance across groups of adolescents (junior-high versus high-school by gender). A four factor model derived from Shimizu et al. (1988) was tested via LISREL on the resulting four subgroups. It was found that a model depicting equivalent factor loadings and factor variances and covariances across all four groups provided the most acceptable fit to the data, indicating that factorial invariance was obtained across the four groups.

A third manuscript has just been completed (Vondracek, Schulenberg, Hostetler, & Shimizu, in press), which capitalizes on the findings of the above two studies through the development of factor scales to measure dimensions of career indecision. Findings indicate that different kinds of career indecision can be reliably identified and measured. Moreover, males and females appear to follow different patterns of change in career indecision over time.

I want to be clear at this time that the findings reported above do not yet take full advantage of the richness of the data collected or the above-discussed advantages of the longitudinal sequential design. Time and money will take care of those shortcomings. In the meantime, it should be noted that the work done in examining the structure of career indecision and refining the identification and measurement of career indecision subtypes could have been successfully concluded only with the type of longitudinal data that my students and I are collecting. Moreover, I would like to emphasize that the data currently available will offer significant insight into how work values, vocational interests, and career indecision change over time, and how changes in one may be related to changes in the other. Finally, a comparison of response patterns or factor structures across cohorts may offer important information regarding the differential impact of historical change (or the macrocontext) and ontogenetic change on the variables under investigation.

Patterns of Short-term Changes in Individuals' Work Values: P-Technique Factor Analyses of Intraindividual Variability

This study was conducted by John E. Schulenberg as his Master's thesis under the joint supervision of John Nesselroade and myself (Schulenberg, Vondracek, & Nesselroade, 1988). This study represents an important departure from traditional conceptual and empirical work on the stability of work values by focusing on changes within individuals. Moreover, the study uses multiple single case designs for data collection and analysis. Nesselroade (1988) has recently discussed such an idiographic focus as complementary to the pursuit of nomethetic relationships. Thus, by first identifying idiographic patterns and then ascertaining the extent of interindividual similarities and differences in intra-individual patterns, it may be possible to provide a more powerful and adequate identification of the laws governing behavior.

Design. The present study utilized a multivariate, replicated, single-subject design (Nesselroade & Ford, 1985), the data from which are analyzed by P-technique factor analysis (Cattell, 1963, 1966b). In contrast to the more familiar R-technique factor analysis, P-technique combines the sampling of variables and occasions for one subject, rather than the sampling of variables and subjects on one occasion. Factors derived from P-technique describe the structure of intra-individual variation or change over the times of measurement, while the more traditional R-technique yields factors that describe interindividual differences at the time of measurement. Thus, P-technique emphasizes the examination of systematic, occasion-to-occasion covariation among variables for the single case. Generalizability across persons can be studied by comparing the factors that result from several P-technique analyses to examine the extent of interindividual similarities in short-term intra-individual change (Hertzog & Nesselroade, 1987).

Subjects. The present study involved seven single case replications. Consequently, seven subjects were recruited. They were college students in their junior or senior year of study. A relatively homogeneous group of subjects was recruited to facilitate efforts to determine the possible degree of similarity of intra-individual variability patterns.

Measure. Super's (1970) *Work Values Inventory (WVI)* was used to measure work values. The WVI is a self-administered, 45-item inventory composed of 15 scales (with 3 items per scale), with each scale designed to tap a different work value. The response format is a 5-point Likert scale with choices ranging from "unimportant" to "very important." Test-retest reliabilities and internal consistency estimates for the WVI scales have been found to be acceptable (Hendrix & Super, 1968; Zaccaria, Jacobs, Creaser, & Klehr, 1972).

Procedures. Each of the subjects completed the WVI each day for approximately 100 consecutive days. They were instructed to respond to the WVI according to their *present* feelings (i.e., those on each given occasion) without attempting to introduce consistency or inconsistency into their responding across occasions. In an effort to reduce occasion-specific sampling error, participants were encouraged to vary the times during the day which they responded.

Results and discussion. Results of the study indicated that the WVI can be characterized as reflecting, at least in part, state dimensions. Specifically, the P-technique factor analyses resulted in meaningful factor solutions for six of the seven subjects, calling into question the assumption within the vocational literature that work values behave exclusively as trait-like phenomena.

Regarding the extent of similarities across subjects in the state dimensions of work values scores, the outcome was mixed. Similarities were found for some factors, but others were largely idiosyncratic. The patterns of factor intercorrelations were generally peculiar to each individual. Schulenberg, Vondracek, and Nesselroade (1988) explain, however, that in R-technique factor analysis, factor intercorrelations vary from group to group as a function of selection effects (Meredith, 1964; Thurstone, 1957), and group differences in factor correlations will be observed even when the factor loading patterns are invariant. The parallel of R-technique person selection is occasion selection in P-technique data. Thus, differences in factor intercorrelations among P-technique solutions can reflect important differences in the samples of occasions on which participants responded, without necessarily indicating structural differences in the nature of state dimensions. Unfortunately, models for defining and representative sampling from populations of occasions are primitive, despite the salience of occasion sampling for the study of development and other change processes. (1988, page 390)

The discovery of state-like variability in work values does not to deny the possible existence of a trait-like component of work values. As a matter of fact, for five of the seven subjects, one or more WVI scales manifested low or no variability across occasions. Moreover, those scales that did demonstrate systematic variability may also contain components of stability. Distinguishing between trait and state components is necessary, however, for a complete understanding of the properties of work values. Cattell (1952) noted that "some psychologists have been prone thoughtlessly to assume that day-to-day variations in measurements on an individual are largely experimental errors of measurement" (p. 104). The findings of the present study indicate that day-to-day intra-individual variability in work values measurements is not simply error variance. They do not offer evidence, however, of simplicity in the work values domain. Nonetheless, the findings lend empirical support to those who have urged that vocational development be conceptualized as a dynamic process characterized by multivariate and multidirectional change (e.g., Super, 1980; Vondracek, Lerner, & Schulenberg, 1986).

CONCLUSION

In the preceding pages I have attempted to describe a conceptual framework, some of the methodological implications of that framework, and some ways in which my colleagues and I have tried to translate these considerations into actual research. As with any task of this scope, many omissions were made and much needs to be done. We are painfully aware of the fact that the scope and complexity of the developmental contextual framework make it difficult to implement in its entirety. We are also painfully aware of the fact that without substantial financial resources, the translation of the framework into research is a very slow process.

We are encouraged that just as a fine house can be built brick by brick, the further development and implementation of our work can proceed piece by piece.

At the same time, we realize that we cannot do all that needs to be done. We are hopeful that our work will inspire others to pursue a developmental contextual perspective in their vocational or career research, and that our efforts to bring about a merger of ideas from developmental and vocational psychology will bear better and bigger fruit in the future.

REFERENCES

Allis, M. R. (1984). Test reviews: Career decision scale. *Measurement and Evaluation in Counseling and Development, 17*, 98-100.

Baltes, P. B. (1968). Longitudinal and cross-sectional sequences in the study of age and generation effects. *Human Development, 11*, 145-171.

Baltes, P. B., Baltes, M. M., & Reinert, G. (1970). The relationship between the time of measurement and age in cognitive development of children: An application of cross-sectional sequences. *Human Development, 13*, 258-268.

Baltes, P. B., Cornelius, S. W., & Nesselroade, J. R. (1979). Cohort effects in developmental psychology. In J. R. Nesselroade & P. B. Baltes (Eds.), *Longitudinal research in the study of behavior and development* (pp. 61-88). New York: Academic.

Baltes, P. B., Reese, H. W., & Nesselroade, J. R. (1977). *Life-span developmental psychology: Introduction to research methods.* Monterey, CA: Brooks/Cole.

Belsky, J. (1984). The determinants of parenting: A process model. *Child Development, 55*, 83-96.

Bronfenbrenner, U. (1979). *The ecology of human development.* Cambridge, MA: Harvard University Press.

Campbell, D. T., & Stanley, J. C. (1963). *Experimental and quasi-experimental designs for research.* Chicago, IL: Rand McNally.

Cattell, R. B. (1952). *Factor analysis.* New York: Harper.

Cattell, R. B. (1963). The structuring of change in P-technique and incremental R-technique. In C. W. Harris (Ed.), *Problems in measuring change* (pp. 167-198). Madison, WI: University of Wisconsin Press.

Cattell, R. B. (1966a). The data box: Its ordering of total resources in terms of possible relational systems. In R. B. Cattell (Ed.), *Handbook of multivariate experimental psychology* (pp. 67-128). Chicago, IL: Rand McNally.

Cattell, R. B. (1966b). Patterns of change: Measurement in relation to state dimension, trait change, lability, and process concepts. In R. B. Cattell (Ed.), *Handbook of multivariate experimental psychology* (pp. 355-402). Chicago, IL: Rand McNally.

Dusek, J. B., & Flaherty, J. F. (1981). The development of the self-concept during the adolescent years. *Society for Research in Child Development Monograph, 46*(4, No. 191).

Erikson, E. H. (1959). Identity and the life-cycle. *Psychological Issues, 1*, 18-164.

Freud, S. (1949). *Outline of psychoanalysis.* New York: Norton.

Gollin, E. S. (1981). Development and plasticity. In E. S. Gollin (Ed.), *Developmental plasticity: Behavioral and biological aspects of variations in development* (pp. 231-251). New York: Academic.

Gottlieb, G. (1970). Conceptions of prenatal behavior. In L. R. Aronson, E. Lobach, D. S. Lehman, & J. S. Rosenblatt (Eds.), *Development and evolution of behavior: Essays in memory of T.C. Schneirla* (pp. 111-137). San Francisco: Freeman.

Gottlieb, G. (1983). The psychobiological approach to developmental issues. In M. M. Haith & J. J. Campos (Eds.), *Handbook of child psychology: Vol. 2. Infancy and biological bases* (4th ed.) (pp. 1-26). New York: Wiley.

Harmon, L. W. (1985). Review of S. H. Osipow, C. G. Carney, J. L. Winer, B. Yanico, & M. Koschier, "Career Decision Scale." In J. V. Mitchell, Jr., (Ed.), *Ninth mental measurements yearbook: Vol. 1* (p. 270). Lincoln, NE: University of Nebraska Press.

Hendrix, V. L., & Super, D. E. (1968). Factor dimensions and reliability of the Work Values Inventory. *Vocational Guidance Quarterly, 16,* 269-274.

Herman, D. O. (1985). Review of S. H. Osipow, C. G. Carney, J. L. Winer, B. Yanico, & M. Koschier, "Career Decision Scale." In J. V. Mitchell, Jr., (Ed.), *Ninth mental measurements yearbook: Vol. 1* (pp. 270-271). Lincoln, NE: University of Nebraska Press.

Hertzog, C., & Nesselroade, J. R. (1987). Beyond autoregressive models: Some implications of the trait state distinction for the structural modeling of developmental change. *Child Development, 58,* 93-109.

Jessor, R., & Jessor, S. L. (1977). *Problem behavior and psychosocial development: A longitudinal study of youth.* New York: Academic.

Knapp, R. R. (1967, November). *Classification of occupational interests into groups and levels.* Paper presented at the Society of Multivariate Experimental Psychology meeting, Berkeley, CA.

Knapp, R. R., Grant, B., & Demos, G. D. (1966). *The California Occupational Preference System.* San Diego: EDITS.

Knapp, R. R. & Knapp, L. (1976). *California Occupational Preference System technical manual.* San Diego: EDITS.

Labouvie, E. W., Bartsch, T. W., Nesselroade, J. R., & Baltes, P. B. (1974). On the internal and external validity of simple longitudinal designs. *Child Development, 45,* 282-290.

Lerner, R. M. (1978). Nature, nurture, and dynamic interactionism. *Human Development, 21,* 1-20.

Lerner, R. M. (1982). Children and adolescents as producers of their own development. *Developmental Review, 2,* 342-370.

Lerner, R. M. (1984). *On the nature of human plasticity.* New York: Cambridge University Press.

Lerner, R. M. (1985). Adolescent maturational change and psychosocial development: A dynamic interactional perspective. *Journal of Youth and Adolescence, 14,* 355-372.

Lerner, R. M. (1986). *Concepts and theories of human development* (2nd ed.). New York: Random House.

Lerner, R. M. (in press). Developmental contextualism and the life-span view of person-context interaction. In M. Bornstein & J. S. Bruner (Eds.), *Interaction in human development*. Hillsdale, NJ: Erlbaum.

Meredith, W. (1964). Notes on factorial invariance. *Psychometrika, 29,* 177-185.

Nesselroade, J. R. (1988). Sampling and generalizability: Adult development and aging research issues examined with the general methodological framework of selection. In K. W. Schaie, R. T. Campbell, W. Meredith, & S. C. Rawlings (Eds.), *Methodological issues in aging research* (pp. 13-42). New York: Springer.

Nesselroade, J. R., & Baltes, P. B. (1974). Adolescent personality development and historical change: 1970-1972. *Monographs of the Society for Research in Child Development, 39*(1, Serial No. 154).

Nesselroade, J. R., & Ford, D. H. (1985). P-technique comes of age: Multivariate, replicated, single subject designs for studying older adults. *Research on Aging, 7,* 46-80.

Nesselroade, J. R., & Ford, D. H. (1987). Methodological considerations in modeling living systems. In M. E. Ford & D. H. Ford (Eds.), *Humans as self constructing living systems: Putting the framework to work* (pp. 47-79). Hillsdale, NJ: Erlbaum.

Osipow, S. H., Carney, C. G., Winer, J. L., Yanico, B. J., & Koschier, M. (1976). *Career Decision Scale* (3rd ed., rev.). Odessa, FL: Psychological Assessment Resources, Inc.

Pryor, R. G. (1981). *Manual for the Work Aspect Preference Scale.* Sydney, New South Wales: NSW Department of Industrial Relations.

Pryor, R. G. (1983). *Manual for the Work Aspect Preference Scale: 1983 version.* Sydney, New South Wales: NSW Department of Industrial Relations.

Roe, A. (1956). *The psychology of occupations.* New York: Wiley.

Scarr, S. (1982). Development is internally guided, not determined. *Contemporary Psychology, 27,* 852-853.

Schaie, K. W. (1965). A general model for the study of developmental problems. *Psychological Bulletin, 64,* 92-107.

Schaie, K. W., & Baltes, P. B. (1975). On sequential strategies in developmental research: Description or explanation? *Human Development, 18,* 384-390.

Schein, E. H. (1971). The individual, the organization, and the career: A conceptual scheme. *Journal of Applied Behavioral Science, 7,* 401-426.

Schneirla, T. C. (1957). The concept of development in comparative psychology. In D. B. Harris (Ed.), *The concept of development* (pp. 78-108). Minneapolis: University of Minnesota Press.

Schulenberg, J. E., Shimizu, D., Vondracek, F. W., & Hostetler, M. (1988). The factor structure of career indecision in junior and senior high school students. *Journal of Vocational Behavior, 33,* 63-81.

Schulenberg, J. E., Vondracek, F. W., & Nesselroade, J. R. (1988). Patterns of short-term changes in individuals' work values: P-technique factor analyses of intraindividual variability. *Multivariate Behavioral Research, 23,* 377-395.

Shimizu, K., Vondracek, F. W., Schulenberg, J. E., & Hostetler, M. (1988). The factor structure of the career decision scale: Similarities across selected studies. *Journal of Vocational Behavior, 32,* 213-225.

Slaney, R. B. (1985). Review of S. H. Osipow, C. B. Carney, J. L. Winer, B. Yanico, & M. Koschier, "Career Decision Scale." In D. J. Keyser & R. C. Sweetland (Eds.), *Test critiques: Vol. II* (pp. 138-143). Kansas City, MO: Test Corporation of America.

Slaney, R. B. (1988). The assessment of career decision making. In W. B. Walsh & S. H. Osipow (Eds.), *Career decision making* (pp. 33-76). Hillsdale, NJ: Erlbaum.

Spokane, A. R. (Ed.). (1987). Conceptual and methodological issues in person-environment fit research. *Journal of Vocational Behavior, 31,* 217-221.

Super, D. E. (1970). *Manual of the Work Values Inventory.* Boston: Houghton-Mifflin.

Super, D. E. (1980). A life-span, life-space approach to career development. *Journal of Vocational Behavior, 16,* 282-298.

Thurstone, L. L. (1957). *Multiple factor analysis.* Chicago: University of Chicago Press.

Tobach, E., & Schneirla, T. C. (1968). The biopsychology of social behavior of animals. In R. E. Cooke & S. Levin (Eds.), *Biologic basis of pediatric practice* (pp. 68-82). New York: McGraw-Hill.

Vondracek, F. W., Lerner, R. M., & Schulenberg, J. E. (1983). The concept of development in vocational theory and intervention. *Journal of Vocational Behavior, 23,* 179-202.

Vondracek, F. W., Lerner, R. M., & Schulenberg, J. E. (1986). *Career development: A life-span developmental approach.* Hillsdale, NJ: Erlbaum.

Vondracek, F. W., Schulenberg, J. E., Hostetler, M., & Shimizu, K. (in press). Dimensions of career indecision. *Journal of Counseling Psychology.*

Zaccaria, L., Jacobs, M., Creaser, J., & Klehr, H. (1972). Work values of college bound students. *Psychological Reports, 31,* 567-569.

4

Biographical-Hermeneutical Approaches to the Study of Career Development

Charles Bujold

In every investigation, and particularly in those that focus on human beings, the level of understanding that we can reach is never equivalent to the level of complexity of the phenomena under study. A life history, including the history of a career, entails a certain amount of mystery, and it will no doubt always remain much more fascinating as such than all the theories, schemes, paradigms, or models that would claim to help us discover its thread or to identify satisfactorily the mechanisms underlying the development of a particular individual.

Furthermore, ambitions in this direction would not only be naive, but could almost be labeled as disrespectful. Just as it would be odd to try to confine in a numerical formula the poetics of springtime, so would it be utopian to assert that the final equation of a human existence is possible. This is what Tiedeman meant when he said that in fact, some 4.8 billion theories of career development exist, thus suggesting, of course, that every individual life, at one point or another, escapes the general explanations that science could propose, that there exists a specific explanation for every vocational behavior, and that the role of counselors should consist essentially in facilitating the discovery of this explanation for each individual (Olson & Roberts, 1985).

The foregoing puts us in contact with the paradox faced by researchers who, while pursuing their quest for Truth, nonetheless know better than anyone that this Truth will remain forever out of their reach. However, a paradox or two, more or less, does not matter, as we can see in both our personal and our professional lives.

MY INTEREST IN THE TOPIC

When tackling the topic of biographical-hermeneutical research in career development, I am not referring to a research project in which I am involved at an operational level. However, the mass of autobiographical data with which I have been in contact with for quite some time has nourished my interest for this approach, and has brought me to consider its application in future studies. For nearly two decades I have been teaching an undergraduate course in theories of career development. Year after year, the students registered in this course are provided with the same opportunity that I had when I received my basic training in career development theory: I ask these students to write a paper in which they describe their own career development, attempt a critical interpretation of their development in reference to some of the models and theories that have been studied, and finally draw the perspectives that seem most plausible to them with regard to their future career process.

The considerable investment, in terms of time and effort, to which the students consent in carrying out this assignment gives strong evidence of the value of this exercise with regard to conceptual integration, but also as an opportunity for growth and integration on a personal level. Many express their "gratitude" for this opportunity to reflect seriously about their vocational and personal trajectories. The relationships between vocational, personal, and social development are sometimes manifested by the very difficulties encountered in the realization of this task by students who have not yet achieved a satisfactory integration of the various aspects of their development. The delays that students ask for in these cases have nothing to do, it seems to me, with procrastination, but rather reveal their desire to find their position in a somewhat arduous developmental process.

Many of the texts that are handed over in this course are revealing, and some of them are particularly touching. Through these pages lives unfold, marked by calculated moves and adventurous bounds, by painful questionings and insightful moments, by victories and retreats, by fierce resistances and courageous acceptances, by blockages and sudden accesses to higher levels of integration. A student who was delaying the moment of writing because he feared he could not find all the answers he was seeking reconciles himself with the fact that the constant presence of questions will stimulate his progress. However, these papers also provide opportunities to realize how human beings create themselves through their decisions, to see the interpenetration of self and world that Levinson (1978) talks about, to examine the interactions of the various roles that the person is assuming, and to witness the integrations of the polarities and paradoxes that are observed throughout human existence.

BIOGRAPHICAL-HERMENEUTICAL APPROACHES AND INTERACTIONAL CONCEPTIONS OF CAREERS

Some theorists in the field of career development have shown an interest in biographical data (e.g., Ginzberg, Ginsburg, Axelrad & Herma, 1951; Roe, 1951a, 1951b, 1953; Tiedeman & O'Hara, 1963). White (1975) published studies on subjects who had been followed up over a long period of time. Levinson and his colleagues (1978) interviewed 40 men and described their "life structure." Nevertheless, it seems that autobiography as a research method in the specific domain of career research has not been used to a significant extent, at least not in North America. The fact that research efforts have concentrated on relatively young subjects, not very advanced in their career development, may explain in part the greater popularity of other approaches. No doubt, the qualitative character of this method, in comparison with the prestige of the quantitative approaches in science, also has something to do with this state of affairs.

Not only are we currently in an era in which interactional conceptions of career development and career guidance interventions are proposed (e.g., Gendre, 1985; Lecomte, 1984; Vondracek, Lerner, & Schulenberg, 1983, 1986), but we are also in a period when traditional methods and even the very nature of science are being questioned while qualitative approaches are regaining the favor of social scientists (Le Gall, 1987; Soulet, 1987). In such a period of activity, it is important to carefully reexamine the research methods currently in use. Young (1984) has proposed some landmarks for studying career development in an ecological perspective, and is among those who have considered research approaches likely to be better adapted to this conception. It is worth recalling some of his ideas.

Drawing from many sources, Young (1984) presents the ecological approach under four headings: (1) it proposes a perspective, in the sense that while attempting to take into account a great number of variables, it seeks, through this multiplicity, what is "unique" rather than what is "similar"; (2) it focuses on the dynamic interaction between the developing person and the environment. This notion of dynamic interaction invites us to see the individual as an active agent of his or her own development, and as someone who understands his or her environment and acts on it, contrary to some conceptions that tend to see the person as a being whose development is determined by external influences; (3) it constitutes an aspect of systems theory, because the individual is seen here as an open system in inter-action with his or her environment; (4) finally, the ecological perspective invites us to consider the way an organism lives in its environment instead of the environment itself.

This approach, of course, has implications at several levels, and specifically at the research level. Ecological research, for Young, is of the biographical-hermeneu-tical type, and aims at bringing to light the articulation underlying the story the person tells about his or her development and his or her plans for the future. Originally the science of the interpretation of texts, hermeneutics becomes, in the context of career development research, the method by which one attempts to draw out the meaning of human behavior. The method gives us access to the continuous flow of actions that always happen in a given context, and consequently, to the phenomena that are at the heart of individuals' lives. It also involves the develop-ment of conceptual schemes to understand these phenomena, and in this sense, in Young's opinion, it should not replace but should rather precede the use of traditional empirical methods.

It is not without interest to add that for him, the ecological perspective invites us to consider the problems of research and practice simultaneously, since the major interest, in this perspective, is centered on the interaction between the organism and its environment—interaction that models both the organism and the environment. Biographies are seen, in this context, as a link between research and practice, the role of the counselor being, according to R. J. Roberts (in Young, 1984), to help people construct their own reality and to find the meaning of their life in the environment of which they are a part and to which they contribute.

What precedes invites us to examine more extensively the notions of biographical and hermeneutical approaches, to consider, among other things, the close relationship that can be observed between research and practice, at least in some of the biographical methods, and to look at the perspectives that these approaches offer for the study of careers.

Some Notions, Principles, and Illustrations

A first glance at the literature in this area reveals that a number of investigators in various fields or disciplines have studied the lives of individuals and groups with a variety of means. Sociologists, psychologists, anthropologists, educators, and historians, to name but a few, are among these scientists. No less variety is found in the terms they use to identify their methods; for example, autobiography, biography, life story, life history, psychobiography, and narrative. This suggests once more that the study of career is likely to be enriched by borrowing from many fields of study. At the same time, however, it points to the fact that drawing sharp distinctions between methodologies is not an easy task. While not devoting much space to a comparative analysis of terms, it might be worthwhile, before going further, to bring to light some theoretical distinctions, even though they are not always clearly taken into account in the scientific literature.

Grell (1986) refers to the *autobiography* as the description of a person's life by that same person, whereas he defines *biography* as the description of a person's life by another person. These are familiar notions. However, Grell also suggests another distinction, namely between *life stories (récits de vie)* and *life histories (histoires de vie)*. The former are biographical stories that are limited to the material provided by the narrator. In life histories, on the other hand, elements from other sources are collected in addition to what the narrator reveals about him- or herself.

Psychobiographies are not so much defined by their sources as by the method by which the material is processed, which brings McAdams (1988) to speak of the psychobiography as "the systematic use of psychological (especially personality) theory to transform a life into a coherent and illuminating story" (p. 2). The same author notices an upsurge of interest among scholars from many disciplines for the concept of the *narrative,* which applies to the lives of people and their social environments, and which has hermeneutical connotation in the sense that human lives may be conceived as texts that the researcher must interpret, as we shall see later.

Life Histories

A special issue of the French journal *Education Permanente* (72-73, March 1984) constitutes a rather rich documentation on life histories as a research method and as a tool in adult education, but as we will see, the concepts discussed in this publication clearly have relevance for career research as well.

The double function of the life history is affirmed by Jobert (1984b) who sees it as work upon oneself and as a *production* that can become an object of study for a researcher. With regard to the first of these aspects, he speaks about it as "an exploratory venture into one's life itinerary, an involved and often painful effort to call to mind and to translate into words . . . the facts of one's life (or of some of its aspects)" (p. 7, my translation). There is a clear similarity between this and what I have described earlier. From a research point of view, Jobert cites Franco Ferrarotti, who speaks about biographies as "an organized but cryptic knowledge that one must learn to decipher" (p. 11, my translation), which illustrates well the close relationship between biographical and hermeneutical approaches.

A sociologist, Ferrarotti is in fact considered a leader with respect to the epistemological, theoretical, and methodological aspects of the biographical approach, which is still a marginal one, as Jobert (1984a) noted during an interview with him. It is important to mention that for Ferrarotti, the biographical method implies an interaction between experimenter and subject, an interaction that transforms both partners. However, this approach also involves a time of critical reflection. It is at this stage that the scientist will attempt to bring out the significant themes, to identify the strategic moments, and to examine the decision-making process carefully.

This time of reflection and research, in Ferrarotti's view, involves four parts that are not necessarily in temporal succession. For the sake of presentation, they will nevertheless be considered here in a sequential order. The first one is referred to as *contextualization*, which occurs when the researcher studies the relationships between the subject's life experiences and his or her primary membership group, his or her community, and also the social, cultural, economic, and political structures in which he or she has lived.

Temporalization, the second moment in the research process, is the moment in which an attempt is made to establish the difference between real time and time as it has been experienced by the subject. Ferrarotti (in Jobert, 1984a) explains that

> the subject's time is not homogeneous. There are moments of particular intensity, moments of truth which represent aoristic contractions of the chronological time. . . . Here, the time duration is qualitative and existentially expressed. It [time] is not to be measured but to be appreciated for its quality. . . . Temporalization is essential for understanding the relative interest of the narrators' experiences. One must resist the temptation of "framing" the biography. (p. 29)

The third step is that of *interaction*. This statement may seem surprising at first since the question of interaction was raised at the stage of data collection. However, Ferrarotti insists that, without losing sight of the fact they must remain detached, researchers must admit that they are collaborating with the research undertaking. Their involvement is even seen as an epistemological condition of this process in which they may be changed or transformed.

Finally, there is *saturation*. Here, Ferrarotti refers to the relationships that can be examined, through several biographies, between identical critical moments. These moments may throw into relief particular situations like the first work experiences, for example. It is at the saturation stage, in fact, that the predominant cultural themes are revealed, as are the core behaviors and structures around which the data of an individual's life can be reorganized and better understood.

If we are interested in studying an individual biography instead of comparing several protocols, this notion of saturation evokes the study of the relationships between various elements or aspects of this particular life. It also evokes the attempt to understand without garbling the facts and without imposing a preestablished conceptual scheme.

Ferrarotti's conception of the biographical approach is attractive, but it is also illuminating, I believe, to listen to some of the comments he made at the conclusion of the interview with Jobert (1984a):

> Up to now, we have pretended that we could understand before listening, even though, at the same time, we could discourse on the importance of the investigators' humility with respect to their objects of study. . . . Researchers, as technicians of the intellect, have persuaded themselves that they could think for others. They had nothing to learn from the actors, they simply had to confirm the hypotheses that they had put forward. In order to understand, one must listen. The epistemology as well as the methodology of the biographical approach could be understood as an effort to develop the technique of listening: listening to what is said, and listening to the silences. Psychoanalysis has something to offer here. Listening takes time and patience, but we often lack both of these elements because of the conditions under which research grants are awarded. We are always in a hurry and we do not have the time to let important things emerge, things which often are not said explicitly and thus cannot be grasped by the busy researcher. (p. 31, my translation)

It would probably be overly optimistic to hope that the subsidizing institutions could be easily convinced that Ferrarotti's vision is well founded, but in the meantime, it is encouraging to note, once again, the interest manifested by many researchers in the biographical approach. For instance, de Gaulejac (1984), who looks into the problem of the life history approach from a sociopsychological point of view, discusses, amongst other things, the convergences and limits of the psychoanalytic approach in relation to life histories, and shows how every pulsion is socialized, in the sense that if, as Whilhelm Reich suggested, a sadistic pulsion underlies the vocational choices made by the butcher and the surgeon, it is, on the other hand, the socioeconomic context that helps to understand why one of them will sublimate this pulsion behind a meat stall and the other in the operating room.

Dominicé (1984), who is interested in educational biographies as a means for understanding the process of adult education, insists, like Ferrarotti, on the fact that in this approach, the subjects are both objects and partners in the research enterprise. Josso (1984), on her part, expresses the opinion that the educational biography, used as a tool in the field of adult education, provides the subject, the researcher, and the educator with food for thought in relation to the process of identity formation, a process in which one can observe identification (or refusals to identify) with some models, along with acceptances or refusals of the ways of thought proposed by the environment. In connection with this, she suggests that group biographies would be useful as elements of information concerning the elaboration of professional identify in its collective and individual dimensions. She suggests, at the same time, that this approach could perhaps give the narrators an opportunity to reappropriate their own life history.

Life Stories

D. Berthaux (1977, cited in Le Gall, 1987, p. 35) sees the life story as something more than a technique for collecting data: For him, it is a new sociological approach. While discussing the use of life stories in ethnosociological research, Berthaux (1986) makes a distinction between their exploratory, analytic, and synthetic or expressive functions. The exploratory function consists essentially of interviewing people in order, first, to collect facts on as many aspects as possible of the problem being studied and then, in subsequent interviews, to focus on some points that seem of particular significance. At the analysis stage, the researcher attempts to develop a preliminary theory to make sense of the observed phenomena, and checks the material collected by trying to find contradictory data. To this end, he or she tries to interview subjects who do not fit the preliminary model in order to refine or modify it. In Berthaux's view, the result of this stage is the construction of a coherent theory that can account for the processes under study without using a "representative sample" as in traditional approaches. Finally, the synthetic or expressive function—perhaps the most demanding one—consists of rephrasing the stories while retaining the essence of their content. If the researcher does not have the opportunity to go through the expressive stage while being once again in interaction with the interviewees, he or she can rewrite the stories in such a way as to bring to light the theory that has emerged while, again, providing a true synthesis of the content that has been collected.

Once more, it is in a sociological perspective that Le Gall (1987) writes about life stories. He agrees with Berthaux on the point that they constitute, per se, a particular sociological approach, in the sense that investigators using this approach are involved in a dialectical relationship in which they are constantly in the process of modifying both their perception of the object of study and the way they proceed to get the biographical material. Consequently, Le Gall does not consider that a strict and straightforward methodology should be defined with regard to this approach, although he suggests that it could be conceptualized as consisting of four phases: (a) the elaboration of a priori hypotheses, (b) the collection of the life stories, (c) their transcription, and finally, (d) the phase of analysis—interpretation involving the use of concepts and notions that seem appropriate to the subject matter.

Psychobiography and Life Narratives

There is strong evidence, as we have seen, that biographical approaches figure among the methodologies that are familiar to many contemporary sociologists. However, they also draw the attention of some psychologists, and in particular some personologists. Witness a recent special issue of the *Journal of Personality* (56(1), 1988) under the theme "Psychobiography and Life Narratives," a theme that McAdams (1988) introduces by saying that "today, personality psychologists seem less ashamed than they did 20 years ago to admit that the subject of their study is human lives" (p. 1).

McAdams (1988) distinguished between psychobiographies and life narratives, although the authors of the contributed papers did not always seem to take into account the distinctions he made. Nonetheless, this special issue of the *Journal of Personality* deserves a careful reading, for it provides us with a wealth of theoretical and research material (which could not be adequately summarized here) on current approaches to psychobiography and new uses of life narratives in social research. For example, Stewart, Franz, and Layton (1988) applied Erik Erikson's constructs of identity, intimacy, and generativity to the diary, correspondence, and retrospective autobiographical writings of Vera Brittain, a British feminist and pacifist, in order to understand her personality development, namely by comparing her experiences as described at the time they happened with her description of them at a later period. Stewart and his colleagues conclude that Brittain's experience, in psychological terms, is consistent with Erikson's theory of development in adolescence, although their analysis suggests that the crises of intimacy and generativity should be considered as factors influencing identity.

With regard to the topic under consideration, another interesting contribution, from a specifically methodological point of view comes from Alexander (1988), who proposes two major strategies for analyzing psychobiographical data. He calls his strategies letting the data reveal itself, and asking the data a question. With the first strategy, he attempts to extract the raw data according to their salience by using a set of rules or markers that he calls "principal identifiers of salience." They are identified as follows: primacy, frequency, uniqueness, negation, emphasis, omission, error, isolation, and incompletion. The second strategy—asking the data a question—can be used as a complementary means of getting more information about a person. Alexander points to the fact that the method he has elaborated

does not presuppose a particular theoretical stance on the psychological nature of human beings. Data that emerge from the
approaches suggested may be put together conceptually with any
kind of theory attractive to the investigator. It remains incum-
bent, however, on the investigator to make the connections clear.
(p.289)

Ochberg (1988) and Wiersma (1988) provide examples of the use of life narratives
in the study of careers, and the latter makes specific references to hermeneutics in
her analysis of career changes in a group of women.

The literature on hermeneutics is vast, varied, and complex (I would even say
hermetic!). This complexity is reflected by the fact that hermeneutics, which was
originally the science of the interpretation of texts, has been taking on added—and
not always convergent—meanings through the writings, for instance, of philosophers and social scientists, with the result that the specific impact of hermeneutics
on research on human phenomena is not particularly easy to identify. In addition,
whatever the field of application being considered, this literature still seems to be
the theater of many controversies, as can be seen in the recent reactions, including
some stinging ones, that were observed to Packer's (1985) article on hermeneutic
inquiry in the study of human conduct (Barratt & Sloan, 1988; Day, 1988;
Russell, 1988).

It is not, of course, the purpose of this chapter to discuss the foundations and
applications of this branch of knowledge called hermeneutics. Such an attempt
would be largely unrealistic, and, moreover, out of my field of competence.
However, a brief synthesis of some notions is in order, for it may help us to better
understand the contributions hermeneutics have made to investigations of the type
described by Ochberg and Wiersma.

Ricoeur (1969), one of the important figures in this field, suggests that if
exegesis raises a problem of interpretation, it is because the reading of a text takes
place within a particular community, in the context of a tradition or of a line of
thought. It is in this sense, for instance, that one can speak of the spiritual or
historical meaning of a text. Ricoeur also points to the fact that hermeneutics raises
the general problem of understanding, in the sense that no major understanding can
emerge without borrowing the ways of understanding that were popular in a certain
period, for example: myths, allegories, and so on. Further, he states that the task of
interpretation consists of deciphering the hidden meaning in the apparent meaning
provided by the symbols. Thus, for him, "the circumscription of the double meaning
expressions constitutes the proper domain of hermeneutics" (1969, p. 16).

In a more recent publication, Ricoeur (1986) assigns to hermeneutics the task
of finding in the text, first, "the internal dynamics underlying the structure of the
work, and then, the power of the work to project itself out of itself and to generate
a world which would really be the 'thing' of the text" (p. 32, my translation).

In his book about William Butlar Yeats' autobiography and hermeneutics,
O'Hara (1981) writes that for Ricoeur and for Yeats,

the task of interpreting the texts of one's life involves [this] idea of creative retrieval or "repetition" in which we look carefully at the habitual ways one has of understanding oneself as composing what Yeats calls "the tradition of myself," a tradition that must be continually put into question, so as to allow the metaphoric text of one's life to give a self to the ego. (p. 41)

Users of a hermeneutical approach consider people as subjects rather than objects, and instead of aiming at manipulation and control as in traditional scientific methods, they aim at mutual understanding (Outwaite, 1986). Later on, Outwaite makes his statement more explicit by saying that when we understand someone's feelings, we understand the context in which these feelings occur and "make sense"; it is this sort of understanding that he calls hermeneutic. It is worth pointing out that Outwaite distinguishes between understanding (or *verstehen*) and interpretation, although he does not suggest that a rigid distinction be made between these terms. He considers that interpretations are made from a particular theoretical perspective, whereas understanding "suggests a more all round approach" or attempts to overcome or neutralize the limitations of interpretation (p. 18).

The above paragraphs are illustrative, I hope, both of the intricacies and subtleties of hermeneutics, and at the same time of the potential that it entails for career research. This potential manifests itself in Ochberg's (1988) and Wiersma's (1988) studies.

Ochberg concentrated his investigation on the careers of two middle-aged businessmen. His basic hypothesis was that even if characters and situations are important parts of a life story, they are not the whole story in the sense that people's behavior in new situations and their memories of their life events are conditioned by the plot or scenario of their lives. In Ochberg's words, "Individuals have characteristic ways of navigating their lives" (1988, p. 174). He also had two other interpretive assumptions: (a) the formal structure of a life narrative is the joint product of the individual and the culture where he or she lives; and (b) the meaning of a narrative is a kind of psychodynamic symbol that can (and should) be decoded, since the individual may want to disavow or falsify the meaning of prior experiences. The detailed and elegant analysis conducted by Ochberg brought to light the way in which his male subjects' career strivings were related to the frustrations they had experienced as children, and how the pursuit of recognition, stimulated by their culture, was achieved at the cost of more personal satisfactions.

A symbol-decoding procedure is also apparent in Wiersma's (1988) critical account of the narrative that she collected in a group of women effecting career changes (from homemaker to the world of work). She identified in these accounts certain "prefabricated press releases," designating the "misleading, irrelevant and stereotyped character of the initial self-report statements" provided by her subjects, which concealed the relationships between the career changes that had occurred and some painful personal events that these women had experienced (p. 205). However, she also concentrated, in her analysis, on demonstrating that the "press releases" were not wrong answers but were to some extent true when reinterpreted in other contexts of meaning, particularly the social/cultural contexts, since the women attempted to distort experiences that were perceived as a violation of cultural requirements.

CONCLUSION

The brief examination presented above of some major notions and principles concerning the biographical-hermeneutical approaches and their applications to the study of career development supports Young's (1984) assumption about the pertinence of these strategies in our research endeavors. The elaboration and experimentation of such strategies by workers in various disciplines suggests at the same time that productive attempts to expand and deepen our understanding of career development should be helped by multidisciplinary approaches to the problem. It is a well known fact that researchers in the human sciences field often fail to take into account, and even to take an interest in, developments in disciplines other than their own. However, if Ginzberg and his colleagues (Ginzberg et al., 1951) from other specialties have contributed to paving the way for more satisfactory theorizing in the area of career development, joint efforts are surely still appropriate.

Young (1984) suggested that hermeneutical methods should precede the use of more traditional empirical approaches in career research. This suggestion seems to be sound. As Ferrarotti (in Jobert, 1984a) rightly reminds us, understanding takes time. Moreover, attempts to quantify before carefully listening to subjects and closely examining the phenomena under study are likely to prevent access to what is really going on in the life of individuals who are in constant interaction with both their past history and their present living conditions. In this connection, it is worth recalling Outwaite's (1986) statement to the effect that in hermeneutics, people are viewed as subjects, not as objects, and that mutual understanding between the investigator and the subject, rather than the latter's manipulation and control by the former, is the goal of the research enterprise.

It should be apparent at this point that biographical-hermeneutical approaches in career research do not only take time and patience, but that they may present the researcher with a particular challenge. Creativity and versatility are required in every research undertaking, of course. However, it is important to realize that looking at human lives from a biographical-hermeneutical perspective puts the focus, at least in many cases, more on the processes than on the outcomes, and thus, the target of the study is much more dynamic than it is—or rather, than it appears to be—if traditional methods are put to use. However, if this challenge is met successfully, fascinating research lies ahead, with the result that significant advances should be expected in career research and subsequent developments should occur in career theories.

REFERENCES

Alexander, I. E. (1988). Personality, psychological assessment, and psychobiography. *Journal of Personality, 56,* 265-294.

Barratt, B. B., & Sloan, T. S. (1988). Critical notes on Packer's "Hermeneutic inquiry." *American Psychologist, 43,* 131-133.

Berthaux, D. (1986). Fonctions diverses des récits de vie dans le processus de recherche. In D. Desmarais, & P. Grell, (Eds.), *Les récits de vie: Théorie, méthode et trajectoires types* (pp. 21-34). Montréal: Editions Saint-Martin.

Day, W. (1988). Hermeneutics and behaviorism. *American Psychologist, 43,* 129.

De Gaulejac, V. (1984). Approche socio-psychologique des histoires de vie. *Education Permanente, 72-73,* 33-45.

Dominicé, P. (1984). La biographie éducative: Un itinéraire de recherche. *Education Permanente, 72-73,* 75-86.

Gendre, F. (1985). Vers une orientation professionnelle individualisée: La méthode synthèse. *Revue de Psychologie Apliquee, 35,* 19-33.

Ginzberg, E., Ginsburg, S. W., Axelrad, S., & Herma, J. C. (1951). *Occupational choice.* New York: Columbia University Press.

Grell, P. (1986). Les récits de vie: Une méthodologie pour dépasser les réalités partielles. In D. Desmarais, & P. Grell, (Eds.), *Les récits de vie: Théorie, méthode et trajectoires types* (pp. 150-176). Montréal: Editions Saint-Martin.

Jobert, G. (1984a). Entretien avec . . . Franco Ferrarotti. *Education Permanente, 72-73,* 25-31.

Jobert, G. (1984b). Les histoires de vie: Entre la recherche et la formation. *Education Permanente, 72-73,* 5-14.

Josso, C. (1984). Des demandes aux processus de formation: Les apports de l'approche biographique. *Education Permanente, 72-73,* 87-96.

Lecomte, C. (1984). L'orientation, une question de transactions personne-environnement. In D. Pelletier & R. Bujold (Eds.), *Pour une approche éducative en orientation* (pp. 428-447). Chicoutimi: Gaëtan Morin.

Le Gall, D. (1987). Les récits de vie: Approcher le social par le pratique. In J. P. Deslauriers (Ed.), *Les méthodes de la recherche qualitative* (pp. 35-48). Sillery, Québec: Presses de l'Université du Québec.

Levinson, D. J., Darrow, C. N., Klein, E. B., Levinson, M. H., & McKee, B. (1978). *The seasons of a man's life.* New York: Knopf.

McAdams, D. P. (1988). Biography, narrative, and lives: An introduction. *Journal of Personality, 56,* 1-18.

Ochberg, R. L. (1988). Life stories and the psychosocial construction of careers. *Journal of Personality, 56,* 173-204.

O'Hara, D. T. (1981). *Tragic knowledge—Yeats's autobiography and hermeneutics.* New York: Columbia University Press.

Olson, S. K., & Roberts, V. F. (1985). David V. Tiedeman: Statistician, scholar and sage. *Journal of Counseling and Development, 63,* 597-604.

Outwaite, W. (1986). *Understanding social life: The method called verstehen* (2nd ed.). Lewes, East Sussex, England: Beacon.

Packer, M. J. (1985). Hermeneutic inquiry in the study of human conduct. *American Psychologist, 40,* 1081-1093.

Ricoeur, P. (1969). *Le conflit des interprétations—Essais d' hermeutique.* Paris: Editions du Seuil.

Ricoeur, P. (1986). *Du texte à l' action—Essais d' hermeutique II.* Paris: Editions du Seuil.

Roe, A. (1951a). A psychological study of eminent biologists. *Psychological Monographs, 65(14,* Whole No. 331).

Roe, A. (1951b). A psychological study of physical scientists. *Genetic Psychology Monographs, 43,* 121-239.

Roe, A. (1953). A psychological study of eminent psychologists and anthropologists and a comparison with biological and physical scientists. *Psychological Monographs, 67(2,* Whole No. 352).

Russell, R. L. (1988). A critical interpretation of Packer's "Hermeneutic inquiry in the study of human conduct." *American Psychologist, 43,* 130-131.

Soulet, M. A. (1987). La recherche qualitative ou la fin des certitudes. In J. P. Deslauriers (Ed.), *Les méthodes de la recherche qualitative* (pp.9-22). Sillery, Québec: Presses de l'Université du Québec.

Stewart, A. J., Franz, C., & Layton, L. (1988). The changing self: Using personal documents to study lives. *Journal of Personality, 56,* 41-74.

Tiedeman, D. V., & O'Hara, R. P. (1963). *Career development: Choice and adjustment.* New York: College Entrance Examination Board.

Vondracek, F. W., Lerner, R. M., & Schulenberg, J. E. (1983). The concept of development in vocational theory and intervention. *Journal of Vocational Behavior, 23,* 179-202.

Vondracek, F. W., Lerner, R. M., & Schulenberg, J. E. (1986). *Career development: A life-span developmental approach.* Hillsdale, NJ: Erlbaum.

White, R. W. (1975). *Lives in progress* (3rd ed.). New York: Holt, Rinehart and Winston.

Wiersma, J. (1988). The press release: Symbolic communication in life history interviewing. *Journal of Personality, 56,* 205-238.

Young, R. A. (1984). Toward an ecology of career development. *Canadian Counsellor, 18,* 152-159.

5

Narrative as a Paradigm for Career Research

Larry R. Cochran

A career is the course of a person's life, particularly in some pursuit or integrated set of pursuits as in a lifework. It is what would be included if one were to write the story of his or her life. "A career is one's life" (Norris, Hatch, Engelkes, & Winborn, 1979, p. 7), or, as Tiedeman and Miller-Tiedeman (1985) phrased it, "Life is career unfolding and, conjointly, career is life empowered" (p. 223). Research on career development is not of the same order as research on intellectual or physical development. The topic of career is not so much concerned with parts as with how parts are related and brought to a point in living. Without a synthesis that seems very like the composition of a novel (see Gardner, 1985, for instance), the very subject of study becomes invisible. The relevance of narrative to career research is direct. Narrative (story or drama) is a synthetic form, a coherent pattern through time that is capable of representing a career. To describe a person's career is to tell a story.

NARRATIVE AND HUMAN REALITY

Traditionally, science has been dominated by a materialistic viewpoint that stresses locations of objects in space (Whitehead, 1967). Regarding an object, we know nothing beyond what we sense, and what we can sense are such properties as figure, size, and motion. Quality has disappeared in favor of a quantification of attributes. Time entered this spatial view uneasily (as impersonal time or time of the clock), for one cannot see, touch, taste, smell or hear time. Unlike space and its objects, time corresponds to no sense organ; it has no definite location.

In contrast to the spatial emphasis of physical science, narrative emphasizes time as lived. Lived time relates to human consciousness, not to the senses. That is, we are conscious of time; we do not sense it. A story can be viewed as a temporal organization of consciousness in relation to a stream of doings and undergoings. From a positivistic perspective of what is really real, story is inherently fictional, a dressing on "the hurrying of material, endlessly, meaninglessly" (Whitehead, 1967, p. 54). While there is currently a different view emerging (e.g., Augros & Stanciu, 1986), and Bateson (1979) has argued for the applicability of story to the living world, it is difficult to grasp clearly how story could adequately represent physical reality, much less the mechanistic materialism of positivistic science. More than one proponent of narrative has, oddly enough, mistaken the reality to which story applies and, ended up denying that reality can be represented adequately in story (Mink, 1978; Ricoeur, 1984; White, 1981). While narrative might fare poorly in representing the reality of physical science, neither does the realm of hurrying material represent human reality as lived.

Briefly, a story has a beginning, a middle, and an end. The beginning is typically characterized as an upset, conflict, or tension, resulting in a gap between the way things are and the way they ought to be. There are two story lines. The first involves the direction of the hero or main character. The person seeks closure to what was aroused in the beginning. Optimally, beginning and end form an opposition as in the relationship of incomplete to complete. For example, the hero begins poor and ends wealthy. The second story line involves what actually happens, and the tension of a story revolves around the discrepancy between the hero's line of intention and the actual line of action (Weston, 1970). Thus, the actual end may deviate from a desired end. For example, the hero may become resigned to poverty or realize that his or her real wealth lies elsewhere, say in friends. The end forms an opposition to the beginning, but one cannot predict the exact opposition that will bring closure.

Opposition between beginning and end forms a dimension that establishes the relevance and significance of elements. For example, other people become aligned, opposed, and configured in relation to the thrust of the story. They facilitate or hinder movement; they support or thwart. Events may bring hope or despair, but irrelevant events are simply edited out as not part of the story. Since the end is unknown (and only anticipated), relevance and significance may change. For example, a person who was a steady friend all along to the ambitious hero may have been ignored or taken for granted, but may achieve great significance if the hero ends with the realization that his or her wealth lies in friendships. However, if the hero becomes financially wealthy, the friend may remain at the periphery of the story. From the line of intent, relevance and significance can be plausibly determined. From the actual line of action, relevance and significance are peculiarly open until the end.

The resurgence of interest in story form is based not on its power to illumine reality, but rather on its power to illumine human reality in particular (Brissett & Edgley, 1974; Bruner, 1986; Burke, 1957, 1965, 1969; Carr, 1986; Cochran, 1985, 1986; Crites, 1971; Danto, 1985; Hardy, 1968; Harré & Secord, 1973; MacIntyre, 1984; McCall & Simmons, 1978; Polkinghorne, 1988; Prado, 1986; Sarbin, 1986; Spence, 1982; Turner, 1974). Once destined for special audiences, the works of literary scholars (such as Barthes, 1977; Brooks, 1984; Frye, 1957; and Kermode, 1967) have significance far beyond their original intent, bearing directly on problems in other fields. The unique potency of narrative is not a recent discovery, however. Emile Zola, for instance, believed that narrative would eventually become a scientific approach for the study of persons and society (Walcut, 1948). In the sixteenth century, Erasmus used drama as a basis for appraising society. Our very word *theory* stems from an ancient Greek term for spectator, which is related to theater. The power of story was embodied in the role of the bard and the dramatist (Arendt, 1978). In the resurrection of narrative, one partakes of a very rich and ancient tradition.

Among the many ways that story mirrors human reality, four seem particularly salient. First, we live in story. In human experience, there is always before and after, memory and anticipation, without which the present is unintelligible (Carr, 1986; Crites, 1971). One can not even sharpen a pencil without awareness of what has been done and what is to be done informing the moving moment. Narrative emerges from and reflects human reality because the temporal organization of before, present, and after is already an incipient narrative.

Second, we represent life in story. In Hardy's (1968) often-quoted sentence, "We dream in narrative, daydream in narrative, remember, anticipate, hope, despair, believe, doubt, plan, revise, criticize, construct, gossip, learn, hate, and love by narrative" (p. 5). Whether termed a primary act of mind, a pattern that connects (Bateson, 1979), a cognitive schema (Mandler, 1984), a mode of cognitive functioning (Bruner, 1986), or a narratory principle (Sarbin, 1986), there is basic agreement that we represent (meaning fundamentally to re-present) ordinary existence in story. In telling jokes, giving anecdotes, describing an event, writing a life history, or planning the future, we tell stories. To prove that this is what we do is simply a matter of watching and listening. The evidence is so overwhelming that were someone to presumably test the proposition, we would think that he or she had misunderstood or missed the point. It might be argued, however, that just because we represent life through story in ordinary life, does not mean that we should do so as scientists. While other forms of representation might be legitimately and fruitfully used, this line of argument misses the point. If we represent life in story, then telling stories to ourselves and others is part of life as lived. Part of a career, for instance, is telling stories of the career we have had so far, have now, and want in the future. To represent a career, then, would partially involve representing the stories people construct about themselves and their life projects.

Third, we explain through story. While there are a variety of ways to support this claim, Danto's (1985) account is the most straightforward. For instance, X aspires to be an electrician at one time and changes his mind in favor of plumbing at a later time. Explanation is not concerned with one time or the other, but with the change over time represented by two contrasting states. Together, these two states, separated over time, constitute the explanandum. In between, something happens to account for, make intelligible, or explain the change. What happens in between to explain how X moved from electrician to plumber constitutes the explanans. An explanation takes the form of a story because it already has the story's form, with a beginning, middle, and end. Changes might be encompassed within changes such that increasingly complex middles are required, but the form remains the same. As Danto stressed, "A story is an account . . . of how the change from beginning to end took place" (1985, p. 234).

Last, we understand or comprehend through story. According to Mink (1970), comprehension is a grasping together into a coherent totality diverse and discrepant fragments. To comprehend, we seek larger patterns and syntheses in which parts fall into place. Narrative form is synthetic, a putting together or configuring of people, places, and events. As Bateson (1979) stated, "Any A is relevant to any B if both A and B are parts or components of the same story" (p. 13). Relevance, however, requires a judgment guided by the opposition between beginning and end. We comprehend through story because story is the natural form we use to put things together, to make them understandable.

Like the prior three claims, the claim that we understand through story opens a vast topic, and it is worthwhile indicating its richness to counter my effort at brevity and simplicity. A story integrates forms of explanation in cultivating understanding. For example, we have inherited four forms of explanation from Aristotle. Final explanation asks, for what purpose was something made? Material explanation asks of what is something made? Efficient explanation asks who or what made it? Formal explanation asks through what vision or design was something made? The four types of explanation were originally extracted from a story of a human crafting a product, and can be regarded as guides for telling a complete story, a story that resolves puzzlement. Whether Aristotle's four types are adequate or complete is irrelevant. For example, we could augment his types through Burke's (1969) pentad of explanatory resources, or through other works. What is significant is that explanations are drawn from and integrated within story. Although psychology has tried to operate with a narrow version of efficient causality (activators, controlling stimuli), the inadequacy of this mechanistic focus seems to be generally recognized, but the problem of fragmented types of explanation has not been faced. That is, if we use different types of explanation, we must find some way to make these types cohere into an integrated account. Narrative appears to be the only structure that seems capable of such an integration, and it does so with such ease and naturalness that understanding can be virtually equated with a complete story. For example, consider a mystery in which the detective is trying to solve a murder (consult Brooks, 1984). Gradually, the detective pieces together motive, opportunity, means, and the like; we do not feel that we understand the mystery until the gaps are filled in. For instance, in the classic locked-door mystery (i.e., a body is found in a room with doors and windows locked from the inside), stress falls on the means, on how on earth the murderer committed the crime. However, no one would be satisfied just with knowledge of the means. We want a complete story. As one who searches to construct a complete story that relieves puzzlement, the detective is a model for human science.

BARDIC VISION

Story also cultivates a kind of understanding that goes beyond explanation to something more akin to wisdom or illumination. This kind of understanding is concerned with the meaning of the story, and it was once the role of the bard to bring that meaning to fruition (Arendt, 1978). Writing 500 years before Christ, Pindar

(1976) exemplified the role of the bard in Homer's restoration of the reputation of Ajax, who had been undeservedly defamed. "Yet Homer has glorified him among men, and straightened the whole story of his valor in the rhapsode's magic words to charm all men thereafter" (p. 143).

The bard does not merely report, but straightens the story, sets things right, or as Pindar put it, "The muse is increased also by true interpretation" (p. 73). The story is not falsified, but straightened or corrected from the disorder of circumstances, transient opinions, impositions, and disruptions. The effect of straightening the story is to grasp the meaning of what has happened clearly. In the Odyssey of Homer (1946), Odysseus became a guest of the Phaecians during his wanderings after the Trojan war. Twice during his stay, a bard sang story-songs of Odysseus's war experiences, and twice his host had to halt the tales because Odysseus wept and groaned and sighed so miserably. "Only when he hears the story does he become fully aware of its meaning" (Arendt, 1978, p. 132).

The power of story to reveal meaning rests in part on a peculiar limitation of experience. In the festival of life, to use an ancient anecdote attributed to Pythagoras, one can take part in activities as a participant or stand back from participation as a spectator. The difference between these standpoints is profound, with the strengths of each complementing the weaknesses of the other.

A participant is someone who is immersed in the affairs of everyday life, who is trying to get something done (Britton, 1970; Harding, 1937). In striving toward an end, aspects of the participant's world are sized up as means or hindrances, taking on functional significance to the extent that they forward or thwart movement toward an end. As a participant, one decides, plans, and acts, living out a story.

However, the functional orientation of a participant carries with it serious limitations on perspective. The narrowness of this perspective, and the consequent muffling of meaning, can be characterized in four ways. First, in taking a part or a particular role in the ongoing story, a person is limited to the perspective of that role. For example, if we received a version of Shakespeare's Hamlet from the perspective of but one participant, it would be a very different play, lacking appreciation of the whole, and, in particular, lacking understanding of the perspective of others. Second, in a functional orientation, the functional aspects of things dominate to the detriment of an appreciation of things in themselves. The world collapses to the level of one's aim. Third, the temporal vista of a participant is apt to be short, restricted in urgent situations to immediately before and immediately after. How the moving moment is anchored in the past and bears on future plans and aspirations might be only dimly sensed, if at all. While we live in story, this does not mean that we live a coherent life story. We might instead live a scattered clutter of short stories that do not add up to a larger story. Last, while participating, a participant might know more or less clearly what is being strived for, but may not know how it will all turn out. The participant lacks the vantage point of the end, which marks the true meaning of the story. In the middle, one does not know really what will bear on the end, nor what end is really being fashioned by one's participation. The middle is open and uncertain.

A spectator is someone who is withdrawn from the affairs of the moment, not seeking to get anything done. Freed from the demands of action, the spectator might be engaged or involved, but will still be detached, able to take a broader perspective to evaluate events more richly. Spectators are able to savor, recount, and embroider, "to assess the event in light of all the interests, desires, sentiment and ideals that they can relate it to" (Harding, 1937, p. 250). The emotions experienced as a participant might be completely different from the emotions experienced in going back over an event as a spectator. According to Britton (1970), the spectator is more concerned with a total worldview. While a participant uses an established representation of the world to get things done, a spectator works directly on the way he or she is representing life and can alter that representation. This concern for the total can be seen in the way novelties are incorporated, expectations are clarified, and the livability of life is portrayed, each requiring more comprehensive adjustments that go beyond a single event. The spectator searches more broadly and deeply for the event's meaning.

> Without spectators the world would be imperfect; the participant, absorbed as he is in particular things and pressed by urgent business, cannot see how all the particular things in the world and every particular deed in the realm of human affairs fit together and produce a harmony, which itself is not given to sense perception, and this invisible in the visible would remain forever unknown if there were no spectator to look out for it, admire it, straighten out the stories and put them into words. . . . The meaning of what actually happens and appears while it is happening is revealed when it has disappeared; remembrance, by which you make present to your mind what actually is absent and past, reveals the meaning in the form of a story. (Arendt, 1978, pp. 132-133).

As participants, we act largely in the dark, in need of the spectator to reveal the fuller meaning of events. However, we also cycle from one role to the other as a natural part of living. We act and reflect. It is just that we are not necessarily very good at it, particularly in an age that values pragmatic doing and devalues story telling. If the cycle were strengthened and developed, it is entirely possible that each person could become his or her own bard, pausing to charge the past, present, and future with more meaning. More realistically, perhaps, we still stand in need of a bard who can listen and help to straighten our own stories, endowing lives with the wisdom of bardic vision.

In the ancient Greek view, the bard was always blind, symbolically meaning that he or she was undistracted by the immediate and visible. Through hindsight and foresight, through searching the invisible, the bard was able to discern the hidden harmonies and possibilities, able to take the long view that impregnates the present with meaning. The price of this vision is withdrawal from affairs. "The Muse . . . had mingled good and evil in her gifts, robbing him of his eyes but lending sweetness to his song" (Homer, 1946, p. 123).

For many psychologists, the Greek contribution is apt to seem like flowery drivel, yet it is my position that something very like bardic vision is needed in career research. To grasp the point experientially, consider walking in on a good movie near the end. Without a grasp of what came before and what is at stake, the scene is apt to seem flat and overdone. However, if one had seen the movie from the beginning, the same scene might be deeply moving, highly meaningful, and entirely appropriate. Bardic vision rests on narrative organization, putting what is invisible and past or invisible and future together with the present. It is this that yields meaning in the form of a story, and it is this depth of perspective that is most needed in a field whose research methods often resemble walking in on a good movie near the end.

NARRATIVE AND CHRONICLE

A chronicle is a purely sequential description of an event or period of time. As Danto (1985) noted, an ideal chronicle would still be just a chronicle, differing only in amount of detail. A chronicle is preparation for a story, but lacks the plot that would make details cohere into a unifying temporal organization. In Forster's (1927) famous statement, if the king died and then the queen died, it is merely an arrangement of events in a time sequence. However, if the king died and the queen then died of grief, it is a kernel statement of plot. The two deaths become plausibly connected, forming a whole.

Most research in counseling psychology and psychology generally is chronicle in search of plot. For example, a standard pretest-posttest control group design has a beginning (pretest and orientation), a middle (treatment), and an end (posttest and debriefing). In the way in which such an experiment is usually conducted, it cannot rise above a chronicle. There are no grounds for development into a full story. Consider the beginning. What is the real beginning of an experiment? Perhaps a college sophomore reads a notice on a bulletin board. One person sees an opportunity to make a little money. Another cannot resist a chance to smirk at the superficial claptrap of psychologists. Another wants to figure out what is being tested to sabotage or support the hypotheses. A person relates the idea of a psychological experiment to whatever he or she can in order to define the coming experience. However, what is reported would only be how subjects were recruited and what instructions and tests were given, as if one were dealing with objects or organisms. Similarly, the middle of the chronicle amounts to a description of treatment conditions as experienced by the experimenter, not as interpreted and given meaning by those who live through the treatment. Finally, the post-test provides a one-sided and usually narrow view of the end. Without knowledge of individuals as persons who think, feel, and do; who have aims, beliefs, and values, there is no basis for a story. Objects figure in story, but cannot be a character in a story, and when people are reduced to objects, about all one can do is chronicle. The acceptance of narrative as an approach to research depends largely on whether meaning is regarded as the central subject of a career.

As an illustration, consider the career of a fly. In the life cycle of a fly, there are four stages: egg, larva, pupa, and adulthood. Each stage involves definite tasks, so to speak. For example, a larva eats and if it does not eat enough, there will be a deficiency later. An adult fly is not built for eating, and can only supplement its food store a little. The energy of the adult fly depends on food consumption in the larval stage. The career of a fly is difficult to distinguish from stage theories of career development. In Super's (1957) theory, for instance, there are five stages. Each stage is characterized by life tasks that must be accomplished before progressing to the next stage. The adequacy with which a task is accomplished bodes well or ill for future stages. Both stage conceptions are useful. Through identifying critical tasks, one could facilitate the development of a fly or a person. Both involve clear research agendas such as identifying stage tasks and clarifying what enables tasks to be done well. However, is there really no basic difference between a fly career and a human career? Is nothing lost when a human is reconceived as an organism with attributes?

What is lost is the meaning of a career as lived, the interior significance that is peculiarly human and that would allow us to form a story rather than a chronicle. In pursuing a career, we live meanings, and lived meanings make a career narratable, intelligible, and coherent. All that would captivate us in a good autobiography, for instance, would be neglected. Meaning (self-concept, values, etc.) enters as an attribute of an organism, not as the living of a story that endows life with significance or insignificance. Dividing people, for instance, into those with high and low meaningfulness is at best merely preparatory. Careers as texts to be interpreted must still be read to understand the reality that supports and authenticates external attributions. Phrased another way, if we are beings who live in story, represent in story, explain through story, understand through story, and have our meaning in story, then chronicle leaves out the most essential part. We must seek ways to go beyond chronicle to fuller, richer narratives.

NARRATIVE RESEARCH

There are two basic divisions of narrative research. The first is concerned with developing a well-founded story that is faithful to life. The second is concerned with drawing out the meaning, plot, or explanation embedded within a story (or set of stories). While each might be conducted without the other, each often complements the other as phases of a single project. First, one develops the story, and then, one draws out what is of significance in it. The first division might be called narrative construction. The second division might be called narrative criticism (in honor of literary criticism, from which so many methods and ideas stem).

Narrative Construction

The researcher's problem is to construct narratives that are sound and trustworthy. There is no one solution to this problem, nothing like a standard method, and for good reason. There are differences in research aims and resources that require different approaches. A life history might involve past records, letters, journals, photographs, and interviews with the person as well as with friends, relatives, and significant figures, among other things. An ethnographic study might involve participant observation, interviews, and videotaping, among other things, and one can expand the investigation as one goes along (Hammersley & Atkinson, 1983). In general, case study is probably the preferred approach to narrative construction largely because an investigator can gather divergent sources of evidence and rich, compelling detail to support convergence into a narrative description. If there were a troublesome period within the narrative, one could alter the investigation to focus more on that period. However, the aim of narrative construction is not necessarily an individual story.

The aim of dramaturgical phenomenology is to construct a common story that reflects the individual stories of people who have experienced some phenomena such as grief (Cochran & Claspell, 1987). Phenomenological psychologists have developed methods for describing the themes of experience (Giorgi, 1985; Valle & King, 1978; Van Kaam, 1969). Suppose a researcher interviewed several people and gained rich descriptive accounts of how they personally experienced being indecisive. Following Colaizzi (1978), the transcripts of these accounts would first be read and dwelled upon. Essentially, one strives to gain sensitivity to and command of the material. Second, one extracts from each transcript every phrase or sentence that is directly relevant to the experience of indecision. If a transcript contains repetitions, these can be eliminated. Further, statements that are phrased so specifically that they could only bear on the person's unique situation are formulated more generally. Rather than retain a specific statement such as "Dad was upset that I would consider going into commercial art," one would phrase it more generally as "A significant other was upset by one of the decider's options." All such phrasings are provisionally marked as it were to become more specific or general later. For example, if the significant other were always a parent, then *parent* would replace *significant other* in the final description. Third, the meaning of each statement is formulated more clearly. Frequently, the meaning of a statement is partially implicit, drawing from the context in which it figures. For example, the rejection of an option by a parent might also contain a threatened rejection of the decider. In my experience, formulating meanings more clearly is mostly a matter of sharpening the person's statement through reordering, deleting awkward and distracting phrases, and drawing out intended connections. It is not a matter of theoretical or ideological imposition. One's task is to draw out, not to put in. Fourth, the formulated meanings of each transcript are aligned with the formulated meanings of every other transcript. Aligning the meanings is a way to search for common clusters or themes, a movement from individual description to aggregate description. Once themes are formulated, they are referred back to the original transcripts to determine if there were distortions or neglects. Fifth, the themes are woven into a complete descriptive account. Last, the description is presented to each participant to determine if there are significant distortions or neglects.

As the method has evolved in my research and collaborations with graduate students, we usually interview participants after themes are formulated, using their comments to sharpen and enlarge descriptions. Sometimes we are able to elicit new statements, but what is of particular importance is that we are able to see if all participants agree on every theme. Only when the themes are trustworthy reflections of experience do we write a complete description, which is then taken back to the participants for further discussion. In fuller studies we keep adding participants until no new statements are being made or until a saturation point is reached (Glaser & Strauss, 1967). Often we use and compare two methods for arriving at themes such as Colaizzi's (1978) and Giorgi's (1985). We have not found enough difference to justify continuing the laborious effort required, but it has certainly helped to persuade us of the rigor of the general approach. However, the major difference in our conduct of phenomenological research is that our approach is thoroughly dramaturgical from beginning to end.

The stated aim of phenomenological investigations is to reveal the meaning structure of phenomena, a task that is analogous to reconstructing Wagner's composition *The Ride of the Valkyries* on the basis of several performances of it. While phenomenological procedures seem rigorous in identifying parts or themes, the construction of a whole seems much more questionable because there has been no holistic form to guide synthesis. Indeed, many studies merely end in a list of themes with no attempt at integration. While there might be other structures concerned with static description, there is also ample reason for descriptions over time to take the form of a narrative, and many phenomenological descriptions already are narratives although they have not been recognized as such. Story form supplies what phenomenology lacks, namely a descriptive structure for integrating themes into a whole.

With a full story as the aim, the interview is not an open-ended request for an account or description but a request for a narrative description. Particular attention is paid to the beginning, the end, and the middle as a bridge between the two. In extracting meanings and developing themes, there is no restriction to pre-reflective aspects of being. People think, feel, and act as persons. Thus one strives to grasp reflective and action patterns along with feelings. The narrative description begins with an organization of themes into those that bear on the beginning, middle, and end. With this organization, the beginning can be reflected on to sharpen the meaning of the end, and vice versa. Themes of the middle take on significance as extensions of the beginning and as movements toward the end. The opposition between beginning and end establishes a dimension that allows one to judge significance and consequently the degree of emphasis. Themes take on proportion as they find a place in the thematic movement that makes up a story. In general, I have found story form to be of immense value in shaping a rough set of themes into a whole. Story sets a context that allows a whole to sharpen parts and the sharpened parts to clarify the whole, facilitating a version of the hermeneutic circle.

Dramaturgical phenomenology is not the only approach that we have developed, largely because other approaches had to be devised for other types of questions. For example, a Q-sort (Stephenson, 1953) was designed to help clarify dramatic role structure in preparation for interviews (Chusid & Cochran, in press; MacGregor & Cochran, 1988). Ingenuity is more important than standardization at this time, but it is ingenuity tied to the necessity of checks and balances within one's approach to narrative construction. For example, for any theme in Cochran and Claspell's (1987) study of grief, one could offer as evidence statements from each individual story, agreement among statements, consensus between two investigators, validational comments from each participant, and place within a narrative whole that requires that kind of theme. For the Chusid and Cochran (in press) study, each dramatic portrait was supported by Q-sort data, individual statements, agreement between qualitative and quantitative data, agreement of collaborators, agreement from independent reviewers, and agreement from the participants themselves, among other things. Perhaps this degree of convergent sources of support is overdone, but it seems important at this time to temper the sheer richness of narrative construction with as much credibility as possible.

Narrative Criticism

With a story or set of stories, there are numerous questions that can be investigated. What is the plot? What is the meaning of the story? How does the story explain change from beginning to end? What kind of characters figure in the story and how are they aligned? These are only a few examples. Beginning with Dilthey (1976), many qualitative methods to answer such questions have been developed or borrowed from the humanities. On psychological topics of particular relevance to a career, Cochran (1986) has illustrated the way in which several methods might be adapted to the study of lives. Sullivan (1984) integrated many qualitative strands into a critical psychology devoted to the interpretation of personal worlds. Action theory (Harré, Clarke, & De Carlo, 1985) has shown vigorous development and some impressive results. Currently, there is an abundance of methods that can be used to interpret a story. However, in this section, one little-known approach will be described.

Suppose one has a story that is baffling in some way, in need of interpretation to make it intelligible. For example, in Milgram's (1963) famous studies of obedience, some people seemed to be willing to shock another person to the point of physical danger, even when the person (who was acting) writhed and screamed. Apparently obedient to the authority of the researcher in a laboratory situation, these people experienced considerable stress in carrying out their task, but did it nevertheless. The experiment is baffling and sobering because the people seemed to be easily led to violate their own moral codes. What they did was disgusting and reprehensible. Now, how does one make sense of this?

Mixon (1972) developed a dramaturgical form of experimentation that uses imagination and role playing to clarify puzzling aspects of a story. Given a scenario or script, a person might be asked to imagine what he or she would do. Given a scenario and a setting, people reenact the story, taking the roles of the various participants. After an enactment, performers are interviewed to understand more fully the basis of their performance. How did they interpret the situation? What were their motives? What influenced them to perform as they did? A basic scenario such as Milgram's obedience study can be systematically altered to examine pivotal features of plot. For example, Mixon found scenarios in which 100 percent of the people in a subject role obeyed instructions to shock another person. He also found scenarios in which 100 percent refused to obey. One of the crucial features of the story was the behavior of the experimenter. If the experimenter appeared confident and unconcerned about the person receiving shocks, those in the role of subject felt assured that safeguards had not broken down and continued to shock. In contrast, if it became clear that the experimenter believed that the victim was being harmed, subjects refused to administer more shocks.

In Mixon's dramaturgical experiment, the story is filled out by taking different roles in a scenario and altering aspects of that scenario. Mixon went through each role himself before designing a script for others. He perused details of the original experiment as a scriptwriter trying to straighten a story, treating ambiguities and omissions as poor scripting. What to the outside observer seemed clear and obvious was very unclear and uncertain to participants, and the major points of ambiguity became foci for systematic variation in his role-playing scenarios.

Hermeneutics, thick description, structural analysis, phenomenological reflection, and the like are powerful ways to enhance interpretation, and they are certainly much more rigorous than the kind of interpretation found in most quantitative studies. Often they are accused of being "armchair" speculations in contrast to the active testing of experimenters, but there are no more compelling instances of armchair and threadbare theorizing than can be found in the way most experiments are interpreted. The ingenious work of Mixon shows one way in which a researcher can slide out of the armchair, so to speak, and embark on a more active and elaborate reconstruction to straighten the story.

THE SIGNIFICANT QUESTION

Tiedeman and Miller-Tiedeman (1985) have argued that career theory and research have been distorted and restricted by an unexamined adoption of a positivistic stance on research, a myopic focus on current practice, and the materialistic and mechanistic worldview of scientism. Research questions are curtailed by method, focus, and worldview (a worldview, I might add, that seems alien to many if not most counseling psychologists). As in other fields, the result has been a division between research and practice, the cult of the paltry question, and inattention to foundations.

Career theory and research is supposed to inform the practice of career counseling, and career counseling is intended to improve the careers or lives of people. To improve a life course presumes that one knows or at least has some criteria for what a career ought to be. Practice is intended to facilitate this very movement from what is to what ought to be, but without some idea of good and bad careers, there is no way to know what would count as an improvement. A fundamental question then would be: What is the nature of a good life, a good career? Phrased practically, how should one live? Like any fundamental question, an indefinite number of questions flow from it. What are the false paths of life, the temptations to avoid, the obstacles to overcome? What is the proper stance on adversity? What is the role of plans and decisions in life? There are others. As fundamental as this question is to the field of career guidance, it is simply not asked seriously, and worse, it is not recognized as fundamental. Were it taken seriously, we would be studying Aristotle, Kierkegaard, and others who have tried to answer it, and certainly, we would be examining exemplary lives much more intensely to gain inklings of an answer.

The effect of this failure to recognize, ask, and investigate a fundamental question is that the field remains significantly unfounded. The significance of any question cannot be properly evaluated, and one question does not relate clearly to others. There is a collection of research, but not necessarily any integration or clear sense of mission. One person thinks values clarification is important, as if any value will do. Another thinks career maturity is the answer, but maturity for what? Still another thinks that person-environment match is critical, but if this were all, perhaps we could not tell the difference between the career of Margaret Mead and that of anthropologists generally. Without a center in great questions, research flounders haphazardly in isolated and partial answers to a question that has been forgotten.

Along with other qualitative methods, the great advantage of narrative research is that it offers the possibility of a greatly expanded scope for questions that are of direct significance to practice. Fundamental questions can not only be asked, but also investigated. What is the meaning of life? This question is apt to be as embarrassing now as sex was in the Edwardian age. However, it is clearly a fundamental question and can be directly investigated through lives. What is the meaning of the life of Margaret Mead? This can be examined in the way her experiences took a certain shape and came to a certain point. Having investigated many lives, one can investigate the plot of lives that are pervaded with meaning and those that are bereft of it (Cochran, in press). One can examine common values, differences in decision making, the role of story telling to oneself, and so on. Furthermore, answers to such questions are quite practical. To find out how meaning seems to radiate in some lives is to understand more about how to cultivate meaning in one's own life and the lives of others. While it would be premature to promise anything like definitive answers to fundamental questions, it is not premature to state that narrative research offers a frame in which such questions can at least be seriously asked and seriously investigated.

REFERENCES

Arendt, H. (1978). *The life of the mind: Thinking*. New York: Harcourt, Brace, Jovanovich.

Augros, R., & Stanciu, G. (1986). *The new story of science*. New York: Bantam.

Barthes, R. (1977). *Image music text*. (S. Heath, Trans.).New York: Hill & Wang.

Bateson, G. (1979). *Mind and nature*. New York: E. P. Dutton.

Brissett, D., & Edgley, C. (1974). *Life as theater*. Chicago: Aldine.

Britton, J. (1970). *Language and learning*. Baltimore: Penguin.

Brooks, P. (1984). *Reading for the plot*. New York: Knopf.

Bruner, J. (1986). *Actual minds, possible worlds*. Cambridge: Cambridge University Press.

Burke, K. (1957). *The philosophy of literary form*. New York: Vintage.

Burke, K. (1965). *Permanence and change: An anatomy of purpose*. New York: Bobbs-Merrill.

Burke, K. (1969). *A grammar of motives*. Berkeley: University of California Press.

Carr, D. (1986). *Time, narrative, and history*. Indianapolis: Indiana University Press.

Chusid, H., & Cochran, L. (in press). The meaning of career change from the perspective of family roles and dramas. *Journal of Counseling Psychology*.

Cochran, L. (1985). *Position and the nature of personhood*. Westport, CT: Greenwood.

Cochran, L. (1986). *Portrait and story*. Westport, CT: Greenwood.

Cochran, L. (in press). *The sense of vocation: A study of life and career development*. Albany, NY: State University of New York Press.

Cochran, L., & Claspell, E. (1987). *The meaning of grief*. Westport, CT: Greenwood.

Colaizzi, P. (1978). Psychological research as a phenomenologist views it. In R. Valle & M. King (Eds.), *Existential- phenomenological alternatives for psychology* (pp. 48-71). New York: Oxford University Press.

Crites, S. (1971). The narrative quality of experience. *Journal of the American Academy of Religion, 39,* 319-411.

Danto, A. (1985). *Narration and knowledge*. New York: Columbia University Press.

Dilthey, W. (1976). *W. Dilthey: Selected writings* (H. Rickman, Ed. & Trans.). Cambridge: Cambridge University Press.

Forster, E. (1927). *Aspects of the novel*. New York: Harcourt, Brace, & World.

Frye, N. (1957). *The anatomy of criticism*. Princeton: Princeton University Press.

Gardner, J. (1985). *The art of fiction*. New York: Vintage.

Giorgi, A. (1985). *Phenomenology and psychological research*. Pittsburgh: Duquesne University Press.

Glaser, B., & Strauss, A. (1967). *The discovery of grounded theory*. New York: Aldine.

Hammersley, M., & Atkinson, P. (1983). *Ethnography: Principles in practice*. New

York: Tavistock.

Harding, D. (1937). The role of the onlooker. *Scrutiny, 6,* 247-258.

Hardy, B. (1968). Towards a poetics of fiction: An approach through narrative. *Novel, 2,* 5-14.

Harré, R., Clarke, D., & De Carlo, N. (1985). *Motives and mechanisms.* New York: Methuen.

Harré, R., & Secord, P. (1973). *The explanation of social behavior.* Totowa, NJ: Littlefield Adams.

Homer (1946). *The Odyssey* (E. Rieu, Trans.). Baltimore: Penguin.

Kermode, F. (1967). *The sense of an ending.* New York: Oxford University Press.

MacGregor, A., & Cochran, L. (1988). Work as enactment of family drama. *Career Development Quarterly, 37,* 138-148.

MacIntyre, A. (1984). *After virtue.* Notre Dame: University of Notre Dame Press.

Mandler, J. (1984). *Scripts, stories, and scenes: Aspects of schema theory.* Hillsdale, NJ: Erlbaum.

McCall, G., & Simmons, J. (1978). *Identities and interactions.* New York: Free Press.

Milgram, S. (1963). Behavioral study of obedience. *Journal of Abnormal and Social Psychology, 67,* 371-378.

Mink, L. (1970). History and fiction as modes of comprehension. *New Literary History, 1,* 541-558.

Mink, L. (1978). Narrative form as cognitive instrument. In R. Canary & H. Kozick (Eds.), *The writing of history* (pp. 129-149). Madison: University of Wisconsin Press.

Mixon, D. (1972). Instead of deception. *Journal for the Theory of Social Behaviour, 2,* 145-177.

Norris, W., Hatch, R., Engelkes, J., & Winborn, B. (1979). *The career information service.* Chicago: Rand McNally.

Pindar (1976). *The odes of Pindar* (R. Lattimore, Trans.). Chicago: University of Chicago Press.

Polkinghorne, D. (1988). *Narrative knowing and the human sciences.* Albany: State University of New York Press.

Prado, C. (1986). *Rethinking how we age.* Westport, CT: Greenwood.

Ricoeur, P. (1984). *Time and narrative* (K. McLaughlin & D. Pellauer, Trans.). Chicago: University of Chicago Press.

Sarbin, T. (1986). *Narrative psychology.* New York: Praeger.

Spence, D. (1982). *Narrative truth and historical truth.* New York: W.W. Norton.

Stephenson, W. (1953). *The study of behavior.* Chicago: University of Chicago Press.

Sullivan, E. (1984). *A critical psychology.* New York: Harper & Row.

Super, D. (1957). *The psychology of careers.* New York: Harper & Row.

Tiedeman, D., & Miller-Tiedeman, A. (1985). The trend of life in the human career. *Journal of Career Development, 11,* 221-250.

Turner, V. (1974). *Dramas, fields, and metaphors.* Ithaca, NY: Cornell University Press.

Valle, R., & King, M. (1978). *Existential-phenomenological alternatives for psychology.* New York: Oxford University Press.

Van Kaam, A. (1969). *Existential foundations of psychology.* Garden City, NY: Image.

Walcut, C. (1948). The naturalism of Vandover and the brute. In W. O'Connor (Ed.), *Forms of modern fiction* (pp. 255-273). Minneapolis: University of Minnesota Press.

Weston, H. (1970). *Forms in literature: A theory of technique and construction.* Edinburgh: Edinburgh Press.

White, H. (1981). The value of narrativity in the representation of reality. In W. Mitchell (Ed.), *On narrative* (pp. 1-23). Chicago: University of Chicago Press.

Whitehead, A. (1967). *Science and the modern world.* New York: Free Press.

6

Action Theory Approaches
to Career Research

Donald E. Polkinghorne

A premise of this chapter is that the career field currently draws on two conflicting models of human behavior. Whereas career counseling treats human beings as agents responsible for making informed choices, career research essentially puts them in the same category as other natural objects. Because of this discrepancy, conflicts and misunderstandings arise regarding the usefulness of research results for those who counsel human beings, the subject of the field career. In one attempt to overcome the split, behavior modification called on counselors to adhere to the research position and to change human behavior by varying the client's environmental stimuli. In this chapter I suggest an alternate approach to unifying the field—the adoption of a human agent model by career researchers.

Career counseling agrees with the commonsense understanding that people are agents responsible for and capable of making informed decisions by freely choosing from among alternatives. In his review of counseling practice, Ivey (1980) reports that counselors use the "model of freedom" and that "all counseling approaches and techniques are ultimately concerned with freeing people from immobility" (p. 413). According to Zunker (1986), the career counselor's role is to increase client self-awareness and thus lead to rational career choices: "Individuals are being encouraged to consider many aspects of themselves in the career decision-making process, including abilities, interests, personalities, values, past work and leisure experiences, and total lifestyles" (p. 1). Career counselors thus assume that human beings are able to choose among options; the counselor's function, then, is to assist clients in making choices by clarifying their options and helping them to gain more information about themselves and the marketplace.

Career research has adopted the stance of human science disciplines in outlining the proper approach to the generation of knowledge, including the assumption that behavior is governed by environmental and genetic influences. Its approach limits knowledge to theories that can be confirmed by experimentally elicited observations or by generalizations inductively produced from sets of measurements. This research model confines career inquiry to the influence of nonvolitional factors on human behavior.

The career field thus embraces two conflicting views of knowledge and epistemology. One view is based on the ordinary assumptions of human freedom and responsibility; the other, accepting the tenets of natural science, sees human behavior as analogous to the movement of natural objects, both being governed by the regularity of law.

Action theory, supporting the assumptions that inform counseling practice in the career field, is a clarification of the commonsense notion of human freedom and responsibility. Because it also questions the adequacy of the natural science research methods for understanding human action, it encourages the development of an alternate process capable of generating knowledge that includes human agency. The fulfillment of this promise would unify career research and practice in making basic assumptions about human behavior.

It is my thesis that action theory can serve the career field by (a) explaining and clarifying counselors' assumptions about human action, and (b) providing an alternative epistemology for career research in which human agency is included. Action theory can thus serve as the basis of a unified career field in which counseling practice and research methods would see clients as agents capable of free and responsible actions.

THE ACTIONS OF THINGS AND PEOPLE

Although the term *action* refers primarily to the doings of human beings, it also encompasses the actions of things, such as the action of machinery or the action of an acid on metal. The assumptions common to the Western world include a distinction between the actions or movements of things and the purposive actions of human agents. A core tenet of our religious, legal, and philosophical traditions is that human beings have the capacity to make free choices about their actions. This freedom makes us morally and legally responsible for our actions and for shaping our lives.

It is also commonly recognized that not all actions of humans are freely chosen; some of them depend on circumstances beyond our control. Aristotle, for example, reflected this point of view in differentiating an action—what a person does (poiesis)—from what merely happens to him (pathos). A distinction is made between people's conduct when they "couldn't help" what they did and their conduct when they "could have helped" by choosing to do something else. Dan White, who shot and killed the mayor and a councilman of San Francisco, was judged to have been in a state of diminished capacity at the time and thus not fully responsible for his actions.

Although the distinction between the actions of things and the actions of humans has been maintained in the common stock of knowledge, the understanding of the former has undergone significant transformation. The early notion that the actions of things resulted from their animistic spirits was modified by the Aristotlian concept that things moved in order to achieve an end. The teleological explanation for a rock's falling to the earth was that, as the essence of a rock was "earth," it moved toward the earth in order to arrive at its appropriate resting place. The Middle Ages retained Aristotle's explanation but embellished it with the idea that God sometimes intervened in order to accomplish his own ends.

With the rise of modern science in the seventeenth century, the teleological explanation of the movement of objects was supplanted by the notion of laws and efficient cause. Francis Bacon's *Novum Organum* (1620) was intended to replace Aristotle's *Organum*. The new idea was that things move according to specific patterns or laws and that these patterns could be discovered by using the inductive-experimental method. Things moved not to accomplish some purpose but to comply with the preestablished natural order. Humans could uncover and describe this order by employing, as a special kind of reasoning, the formal logic of mathematics. Issac Newton, in fact, maintained that by examining nature he had ascertained that it was written in the language of mathematics.

This new, "enlightened" understanding of why objects move meant that humans could uncover the secrets of nature and use the resultant knowledge to gain control over the movements of things. Knowing how nature will act in response to a designed intervention would enable people to make nature act in certain ways. The progressive revelation of the patterns governing nature's movements, along with its application, produced the Industrial Revolution and the improvements in the quality of life that we presently enjoy.

During the Enlightenment and the concomitant era of scientific progress, the idea that human actions differ from those of nature was retained. Human actions were not felt to be governed by laws as are the movements of nature. René Descartes' theory of two substances—mind and matter—reserved a place for human freedom of choice alongside the law-determined movements in the material world of nature.

In the mid-nineteenth century, the notion of a separate human substance began to erode. A school of thought led by Auguste Comte and John Stuart Mill sought to apply the methods that had revealed the laws governing the movements of things to the study of humans and their actions. Charles Darwin's *Origin of Species* (1859) gave support to the idea that human beings and their actions should be investigated as merely another aspect of nature. Despite the reservations of Wilhelm Dilthey and others, the methods of natural science were deemed applicable to the study of human beings, and the human sciences had their inception (sociology in 1834, anthropology in 1859, and psychology in 1879).

Natural science methodology assumed that movement was caused by laws and that a particular action could best be understood as part of a preordained natural pattern. Under this assumption, the human sciences had to abandon the common-sense belief that human beings are free to choose and are responsible for their actions. History, whose origins preceded the development of the natural sciences, was the last scholarly discipline to retain this notion. Hemple (1965), in a 1942 article, "The Function of General Laws in History," called for history to become a "true" science by adopting the deductive-nomological form of explanation, which would account for a human behavior by a deduction from a general law and a set of initial conditions. Although some historians have resisted the tendency, in the main history has become a natural science of human behavior (Atkinson, 1978).

The purpose in adopting natural science methods for the study of human beings was to overcome the "backward state of the moral [human] sciences" (Mill, 1953, p. 255) and to eliminate capricious and biased opinions from such studies. Philosophers of the Vienna Circle sought to reconstruct and explain scientific thinking in order to determine the boundary that separated its language and logic from the language and logic of ordinary subjective thinking. They assumed that their version of scientific thinking was the sole avenue to truth and protection from error. It is their concept of science that has influenced ideas about the generation of knowledge in the human sciences.

Their system of inquiry was based on the following canons:

1. Knowledge, as opposed to opinion, is contained only in descriptive statements based on direct observation.
2. The goal of science is to form a network of knowledge statements linked together by deductive logic derived from a few axiom statements and grounded in observation statements.
3. The only kinds of statements free from metaphysical overtones and personal bias—that is, the only kinds of statements ensuring certainty—are those based on observation and belonging to the axiomatic system. All sciences must limit their assertions to these kinds of statements. Statements about human "intention," "purpose," "reasons," and "actions," which are not so limited, cannot be included in the body of true knowledge.

Career research, in borrowing its approach to knowledge from psychology, its base discipline, stands within the epistemological tradition of positivism. Thus, human action is outside the purview of its methodological assumptions.

ACTION THEORY

Action theory is primarily identified with ordinary language philosophy. In this chapter I am using the term to include all epistemological efforts that acknowledge the necessity to include human agency and purposefulness in systems or inquiry that study human phenomena.

Ordinary Language Philosophy

The positivist plan called for developing a purified language for science that would be limited to observation statements and logical connectors. Ordinary language philosophers, however, were interested in the language of everyday speech. They found that ordinary speech, unlike the purified speech proposed for science, contained expressions that describe, appraise, and direct human action. In ordinary usage people explain an action by giving the purpose or end it was designed to accomplish, not by giving the law of which it was an instance.

I will not detail here the various studies of human action prepared by ordinary language analysts (see Polkinghorne, 1983). Much of their research was stimulated by Ludwig Wittgenstein, who in his later work posited the notion of a plurality of irreducible language games. A basic thrust of the argument of these analysts is that a direct relation between language and reality, including the so-called purified language of positivist science, does not exist. The meaning of an expression is dependent on its use in a language game, not on an external referent. Science, as merely one type of language game, is no more revealing of the essence of reality than the language used in ordinary conversation. Whether human actions are understood as purposeful behaviors or as instances of laws determined by initial conditions depends on the language game one is using rather than on a correspondence to reality. Experience itself is a construction of one's language system in interaction with sensation.

One response to the effort of the ordinary language philosophers to undermine the belief that language represents reality has been the poststructuralists' skepticism that *any* representation of reality is possible. Their work is based on two themes: (a) critical rejection of the scientific tradition that a picture of reality can be derived from an epistemological foundation of observation statements; (b) nonbelief in a need for knowledge of truth.

The poststructuralists characteristically hold that discussions about knowledge, science, and values take place within language networks that reflect ungrounded assumptions (Lyotard, 1984). They believe that the foundations used to support notions of truth and science are grounded not in reality, but in constructions of language systems. This idea challenges any attempt at a grounded science, including qualitative research.

Richard Rorty, a leading U.S. pragmatic philosopher, suggests that because language is opaque and prevents experience from being a "mirror of nature," the philosophic enterprise should turn toward participation in conversation rather than inquiring into ultimate truths:

> To see keeping a conversation going as a sufficient aim of philosophy, to see wisdom as consisting in the ability to sustain a conversation, is to see human beings as generators of new descriptions rather than beings one hopes to be able to describe accurately. (1979, p. 378)

Rorty understands that the idea of a correct method of approaching knowledge has been acknowledged as self-deceptive and illusory; it is simply a tenet of the scientific tradition. His major effort is to deconstruct this belief by demonstrating that the concern to establish foundations on which to build truth is faulty. Instead of building a new and improved theory of knowledge, he wants to dismantle the entire epistemological project (1982). He thinks that all the traditional scientific arguments over the correct theory of reference or meaning, the necessary conditions for what constitutes knowledge, and the proper solution of the mind-body problem are based on a misunderstanding. These problems are not the perennial or eternal ones that arise from reflection; rather, they are merely the artifacts of a historically conditioned way of framing issues. The source for the erroneous belief that there is a foundation on which truth can be established lies in the ideas of René Descartes, John Locke, and Immanuel Kant, the founders of Enlightenment philosophy.

The notion of incommensurate language games developed by ordinary language philosophers sowed the seeds of poststructural skepticism about the possibility that any true knowledge is achievable. They proposed that we are prisoners of language and that penetration through language to a nonlinguistic reality is not possible. Even the ideas of human intention, purpose, and action are mere artifacts of the word meanings developed in a language game.

Existential-Phenomenological Philosophy

Existential-phenomenological philosophers, like ordinary language philosophers, have argued that the view of human existence developed by natural science overlooks the unique human characteristics of freedom and responsibility. Unlike ordinary language philosophers, phenomenological and existential writers—such as Edmund Husserl, Martin Heidegger, and Maurice Merleau-Ponty—believed that experience includes an immediate knowledge based on the interaction of cognitive schema and sensation. This knowledge achieves its expression in ordinary language and is the underpinning for the structures of ordinary expression. Thus, an articulated experience that is the referent of discourse underlies language.

Language, rather than being opaque and impenetrable, functions as a lens that brings experience into clear and explicit focus. It serves as a medium for the display of original experience. The existential theory of action locates freedom, intention, and purpose at the level of originary experience of human existence, not at the level of a language game. A full understanding of the freedom within which action takes place must come from an examination of experience itself; action is inaccessible to any analysis that is restricted to the level of language. As Paul Ricoeur puts it, the "methodological decision to know experience only in public expressions implies the forgetting of the question of the originary, the obliteration of the question of the origin of meaning" (cited in Thompson, 1981, p. 61). Linguistic analysis may provide a laudable introduction to descriptive discourse on action, yet, according to existential-phenomenologists, action discourse can be justified only through phenomenological investigation into the essential structures of experience.

NARRATIVE ACTION

In his extensive phenomenological investigations of the experience of action, Ricoeur (1984, 1985a, 1985b) proposes that humans, through a preunderstanding, can recognize that human actions are of a different order than the movement of things (see Davis, 1979). They also know that actions are experienced not as isolated events, but as events unified into meaningful episodes. The connecting of single acts into episodes occurs through a noetic operation of narrative emplotment.

The capacity to recognize which events are human actions is similar to the linguistic capacity to recognize which groups of words produce meaningful sentences in regard to organization, linking together of words, and understanding. The capacity to recognize which events are human actions focuses on events that can be gathered together into a plot through temporal ordering.

The competence to determine which bodily movements are human actions is called practical understanding, the basic unit of narration. Ricoeur identifies six components of this competence:

a. Actions imply goals; they are carried out to achieve results or to accomplish an end.

b. Actions refer to motives that explain why someone does something, an explanation that clearly differs from the one that shows the causative effect of one physical event on another.

c. Actions are carried out by agents, that is, by persons who can be held responsible. The question "Who did it?" can be answered within the competence of practical understanding.

d. As actions take place in closed physical systems (Wright, 1971, pp. 63-64), agents recognize that the circumstances in which actions occur place limits on what can be done and set the favorable or unfavorable conditions affecting the outcome of actions.

e. Actions take place as cooperation, competition, or struggle in interaction with other persons, who can either help or hinder the accomplishment of an act.

f. The outcome of an action may bring about a change in one's fortunes or feelings. In short, we recognize that it is appropriate to ask the questions "what?" "why?" "who?" "how?" "with whom?" and "against whom?" in regard to human actions but not in regard to ordinary physical movements.

Besides Ricoeur's recognition of the role of narrative in human action, cognitive psychologist Jerome Bruner has proposed that narrative ordering is crucial for understanding action. Bruner (1986) holds that narrative is one of the two basic modes of cognitive functioning; the other is the logico-scientific mode (which he calls the "paradigmatic" mode):

> There are two modes of cognitive functioning, two modes of thought, each providing distinctive ways of ordering experience,

of constructing reality. The two (though complementary) are irreducible to one another. Each of the ways of knowing, moreover, has operating principles of its own and its own criteria of well-formedness. They differ radically in their procedures for verification. (p. 11)

Bruner says we know "precious little" about how narrative processes work, and that this meager knowledge stands in contrast to the extensive knowledge we have of the workings of the paradigmatic processes used in formal science and logical reasoning. The two processes function differently, and each mode uses a different type of causality to connect events. The paradigmatic mode searches for universal truth, whereas the narrative mode looks for particular connections between events. The special subject matter of narrative consists of the "vicissitudes of human intentions" (Bruner, 1986, p. 16)—that is, the changing directions and goals of human action.

The Narrative Scheme

The narrative scheme is the intellectual process that relates human activities to one another and makes them meaningful. It reveals purpose and direction in human affairs and makes individual human lives comprehensible as wholes. We conceive our own and others' behavior within the narrative framework and through it we recognize the effects that planned actions can have on desired goals. The narrative scheme also connects imaginary people (Snow White, for example) and events (actions in novels) into cohesive stories. Although narrative intelligibility is grounded in everyday actions of human beings, it can be projected by analogy onto the behavior of animals (the three bears in Goldilocks, for example) and of superhuman characters such as the Greek god Zeus or the computer Hal in the motion picture *2001*.

The ordering of relationships by the narrative scheme results from its power to bind a sequence of events into a unified happening; it makes individual events comprehensible by identifying the whole to which they contribute. The ordering process links diverse happenings along a temporal dimension and identifies the effect of one event on another, and it integrates human actions and the events that affect human life into a temporal gestalt. As the number of gestalt operations that produce recognizable perceptual configurations is limited, so also is the number of narrative structures that produce coherent stories. By inclusion in a narrative, individual actions become significant through contributing to a completed episode. In this sense, narrative can retrospectively alter the meaning of events after the final outcome is known. For example, the significance of running out of gas may be enhanced by an ensuing friendship with the person who stops to help. The means by which specific events are made to cohere into a single narrative is the plot or story line, which shows how an individual action contributes to the whole experience. In the example just cited, the plot is the emergence of a friendship. Narrative thus organizes events and human actions into a whole, making individual actions and events significant by showing their effect on the whole. A narrative is different from a chronicle, which simply lists events and acts according to a time line, whereas a narrative connects actions into a unified temporal whole.

Narrative assumes that both the narrator and listeners can understand and use terms like *agent, goal, means, success, failure,* and so on. It adds the structure of a plot to simple action statements. The rules for narrative composition determine the ordering of such statements into the sequence of a story. Because of the sequential linking of sentences into a plot, the agents and their deeds take on a deepened meaning.

The cultural settings within which human action occurs maintain symbolic narrative forms for use in the articulation of action (Harré, Clarke, & De Carlo, 1985). These forms have a public character and are not the private preserve of a particular actor, so an act is undertaken with the knowledge of what it will mean to the community at large. The act of bowing before another person, for example, is a means of expression and will be so understood by the community. This communal significance of actions gives them an initial "readability." Social manners, customs, and the like evaluate actions in terms of their conformity to moral norms, whether they are good or bad, better or worse. Tellers of tales assume that their audiences can properly evaluate the actions in a story. According to Ricoeur (1984), the narrative records "no action which does not give rise to approbation or reprobation, to however small a degree, as a function of a hierarchy of values for which goodness and wickedness are the poles" (p. 59). Likewise, Aristotle held that it is the ethical quality of the characters in a story gives rise to the hearer's emotional response, expressed, for example, in pity for the good character who has unmerited misfortune.

The narrative also assumes that the audience will understand human temporality. Time, rather than being a series of instant nows passing through the slit of a present moment, implies an understanding that actions have to do with future consequences, whether intended or unintended.

In summary, narrative is the form or noesis in experience in which human action is understood and given meaning. Action is the living narrative expression of a personal and social life. As the ability to understand a group of words as a meaningful sentence informs our own speaking of sentences, the ability to understand a series of episodes as a story informs our own action in making episodes composing a whole that is greater than any single action. The length of this whole may range from a short adventure to the time between birth and death, or even to the length of generations of humankind. Nonetheless, the understanding of narrative is as close to our existence as the understanding of a sentence. To define a narrative as a linked series of episodes contributing to a single adventure with a beginning, a middle, and an end—or as the presentation of a problem that is solved by a series of actions—is to describe in simple terms what is already part of our ordinary knowledge.

Action and Narrative

Recognition of the connection between action and narrative has been part of the Western tradition since Aristotle. In *Poetics,* Artistotle (1954) identified narrative as an imitation *(mimesis)* or a representation of human action. The plot *(muthos)* of narrative is the organization of events, not as a static structure but as a synthesis. (Ricoeur prefers to use the term "emplotment" for the gathering up of events into a whole.) *Poetics,* then, deals with the composition of narratives, identified as an interpretive or hermeneutic activity in which the relationship among parts is revealed.

In Aristotle's conception, plot has the features of wholeness or completeness. "Now a thing is a whole if it has a beginning, a middle, and an end" (Aristotle, 1954, page 233). The poet, or narrator, locates the beginning, not as the place where nothing has happened before it, but as the origin of the events that are of importance for what follows. The middle is the succession of events, and the end is marked by the poet's decision that the events contributing to the resolution of the story are complete. The plot must also have the appropriate magnitude, which is determined by the poet. Narrative is concerned not merely with recording all the events that have happened over a period of time, but with creating a dramatic or hermeneutic unity. Emplotment is concerned with drawing out from the flow of events those that significantly contribute to the story and give them coherence. Again, according to Aristotle (1954):

> It is evident . . . that the poet must be more the poet of his stories or plots than of his verses, inasmuch as he is a poet by virtue of the imitative element in his work, and it is actions that he imitates. And if he should come to take a subject from actual history, he is none the less a poet for that; since some historic occurrences may very well be in the probable and possible order of things; and it is in that aspect of them that he is their poet. (p. 235)

In cohering acts into a plot, the degree of freedom is limited. Not any plot will produce a meaningful episode; it must put together the individual actions. In this way, the production of meaning in a plot is similar to the production of meaning in a sentence. The meaning of a sentence is not simply imposed on the individual words that make it up. Rather, the composite of the words gives the sentence its particular meaning. It is possible that the same group of words can make up several meaningful sentences. For example, the words *flying planes can be dangerous* can be interpreted in two ways and, depending on which meaning is intended, the significance of the word *flying* changes. Similarly, the same set of events can be comprised by different plots, thus changing the meaning of particular events. Just as groups of words sometimes allow multiple interpretations, so sets of events can sometimes be emplotted in multiple ways. As in sentences, the temporal order of events is crucial if they are to contribute to the meaningful whole of the plot. The two sentences *The mouse chased the cat* and *The cat chased the mouse,* although containing the same words, produce different meaning because the order of the words is different. Moreover, not just any group of words will produce a meaningful sentence. For example, although the sentence, *Colorless green ideas sleep furiously,* is grammatically correct, it is not a meaningful whole.

Acting may be understood as analogous to writing a poem, with the comprehension of action being like the interpretation of a poem. Narrative is the particular kind of poetic text that gives representation to action; it is the gathering together of events into a plot that gives them significance as they relate to the theme of the story and makes them a whole. The events are transformed from serial, independent happenings into meaningful happenings that contribute to the whole. As the meaning and the function of a single word become clear when the sentence of which it is a part is understood, so the significance of a single event becomes apparent when one knows the plot of which it is a part. Because the creation of a meaningful plot from a set of events employs the same processes of interpretive or hermeneutic reasoning that are used to form a meaningful sentence from a set of words, examples drawn from sentences illustrate the narrative process.

The poet creates plots and represents action. By the same token, the human actor expresses his or her existence through action and through understanding that action is part of a larger configuration of meaning. Action is the poetic expression of human existence as it moves toward valued ends. These ends are not simply the fulfillment of personal desires; they also represent commitments to ethical standards and the fulfillment of promises. When action is seen as movement caused by other physical or mental events and determined by logically structured, unchanging laws, or when it is regarded as expressive of a generative formal organization, the richness and fullness of its meaning as an expression of a hermeneutic existence are missed. The experience of action must be understood in objective terms, without the illusions and projections of subjectivity. The programs that force human action into formal frameworks, however, have not produced valid statements of logically ordered and mathematically described behavior or even statements that capture the human experience of acting. A narrative based on understanding of human action as an expression of existence can produce far more authentic and useful descriptions for a science of the human realm. The concept of human action derived from a narrative approach holds that action is an expression of existence and that its organization manifests the narrative organization of human experience.

LIFE SPAN DEVELOPMENT

Although a narrative understanding of action has widespread implications for career theory and practice, I concentrate here on its possible effect on career planning. Super (1957, 1980) and Zunker (1986) have expanded the career field to include the emergence of and changes in vocational choices throughout the life span. Thus, career choices are constantly evolving as people and their social environment develop and change; the choices are influenced by the theoretical and research progress in the field of life span development.

The life span perspective recognizes the need to search for a sequence of change over one's entire life course, even though there are no biological maturational markers (the menopause in women is considered the only universal biological maturational change in adulthood) and even though social roles in a pluralistic society are extremely diverse. The developmental sequence is controlled by some givens; for example, one cannot become a parent before puberty or, under our legal system, one cannot contract a marriage independent of parental consent before reaching the age of legal majority.

Within these broad bounds, however, there is much possible variation and no single sequence of roles. A first marriage and parenthood may occur at age 20 or 40. A career will peak early for some (professional athletes, musicians, mathematicians) and later for others (artists, writers, social scientists). The sequence of roles may also vary: The first marriage may be followed by a second; career peaks may be followed by career changes. Thus, consideration of one's entire life cycle is complicated by the absence in adulthood of a biological maturation timetable and by the wide variety in social roles.

One of the most influential early works propounding the concept of development over the life cycle is Erik Erikson's *Childhood and Society* (1963; first published in 1950). Erikson, recognizing the individual's interaction with the social context, expanded Freud's ontogenetic sequence of childhood stages of development to include the entire life cycle. Erikson's description of additional stages added new concepts to life span theory: identity-versus-role-confusion, when the young adult finds a place in society; generativity-versus-stagnation, when responsibility for the next generation is assumed; and ego-integrity-versus-despair, when one accepts one's own life cycle and can look at it in retrospect without despair.

Despite Erikson's theoretical work, life span developmental psychology has had difficulty in describing continuity across the life course. The complexity of the variables makes it hard to predict the changes an adult will encounter in the life cycle. Gergen (1977) has proposed that attempts to account for stability and ordered change in adult development are unsuccessful because of the role of chance. He suggests an "aleatoric" perspective, that is, one based on change and chance rather than prediction and control, is most appropriate for understanding human development. "Human behavior will not generally display the same type of stability characteristic as phenomena within the physical sciences" (p. 154).

Freeman (1984) proposes that, rather than attempting to predict what sequences adults will move through, investigators of life span development should explain in retrospect why a particular development occurred. He points out that when one looks forward to what will happen, events seem to occur with a kind of stochastic unraveling in time, but when one looks back over those events, they seem to have been inevitable and not the result of chance.

> That intrinsically different forms of knowledge can be derived
> retrospectively [more] than is possible prospectively is "just" an
> ontological fact. Therefore, given the inevitable variability inher-
> ent in human development owing to the multiplex determination
> of our intentions, it seems evident that a viable science of the life
> course must admit the necessity of adopting a fundamentally
> retrospective perspective for at least a portion of the questions it
> addresses—a willingness to entertain the possibilities of apos-
> teriority. (p. 2)

The retrospective analysis of life events as carried out by historians requires a narrative structure if the analysis is to be an explanation instead of a mere chronological listing. Of two critiques of the retrospective approach to life span investigations, the first concerns the temptation to go beyond merely recounting a person's past by attempting to systematize life events. In response, Freeman points out that aposteriority need not be unsystematic, summoning as evidence numerous historical investigations that have been highly systematic. Because the life span researcher is dealing with more recurrent phenomena than history at large, it is reasonable to assume that systematization is possible. The second critique raises the questions of interpretation and of the validity of the generalizations that can be drawn. Freeman sees this problem as no different from a problem arising in prospective research, as the task of choosing categories in gathering and systema-tizing data is always interpretive. In any event, although no one method of systematizing data can be regarded as purely objective and correct, the researcher is free to choose the likeliest one from among the plausible alternatives. Despite the absence of certainty, an intersubjective consensus minimizes the likelihood of arbitrariness or even outright falsity in interpretation. According to Freeman, it is important to note that "the study of the life course is, of necessity, not only a historical form of inquiry, but one which demands the acknowledgement of its narrative structure. . . . It is, in a distinct sense, an ongoing story to be told" (1984, p. 4).

Historical narrative looks back on past events to discover a pattern in their unfolding. Although narrative can be used in other ways—for example, to give form to personal identity or to imagine a future narrative about events one may carry out in the present—it is basically a retrospective exercise. Its datum is what has actually happened, and its analysis is the configuration of past events into a meaningful theme. Thus, it differs in approach from formal science, which primarily seeks to explain and predict future events (see Baltes, Reese, & Nesselroade, 1977). In formal science, explanation of the past is merely the "turning upside down" of predictions of the future. Just as events will occur because of the lawfulness of behavior, so they have occurred in the past because of the same lawfulness. In contrast, narrative explanation deals with patterns in events that could not have been predicted in advance simply by looking at initial conditions and empirical generalizations.

Freeman uses an example from Michael Scriven, a leading philosopher of science, to illustrate the kind of explanation that is uncovered through retrospective narration. Only when a man has murdered his wife do we know something especially significant about him. We may well have detected an instability, or even a proclivity toward aggressive action, but we do not necessarily claim that his violent act was predictable, even with our retrospective knowledge. After murder has been committed, however, we are not left completely confused: Reasons may be offered for the historical as well as for the immediate genesis of the act. We may cite his cruel upbringing, the recent loss of a job, and so on. However, this narrative explanation requires, in addition to the past facts, an act of judgment that orders the items of evidence in degree of significance into a coherent account of how past events have led to murder.

In the same manner, we can understand human lives by organizing the events that have made them what they are into a pattern of intrinsic relationships. The criterion for narrative explanation is its acceptability or its intelligibility, rather than its predictability. Understanding a narrative explanation is like following a story, where themes and patterns are retroactively detected among arrays of contingencies.

Freeman addresses the question of the kind of cause narrative uses in retroactive explanation. Having a good reason for expecting an event, he says, is not the same thing as explaining why it happens according to law. The singling out of historical connections requires examining their rational (not law-like) necessity within a certain context, as a sequence of related events that are delimited by the field of expected action. In a narrative reconstruction one can understand that, given the circumstances, it is reasonable that things have happened the way they did. Freeman refers to Mandelbaum's proposal to do away with David Hume's explanation of cause, wherein events are isolated and bounded (the colliding pool balls model) (see Beauchamp & Rosenberg, 1981). Narrative explanation does not focus on how one event is predicted or deduced from another, but on how change from beginning to end takes place. Life span events are part of an ongoing process that culminates in the effect to be explained. Although the reason for the occurrence of an event does not flow from a deduction of formal logic, the perception of the patterned totality described by narrative carries with it the experience of causal "power." The subjective need to know why something has happened is satisfied when all the events leading up to the occurrence are brought together in a narrative statement.

If life span development is to be explored by retrodictive study, how is information gathered and how are conclusions reached? To construct a narrative explanation, one needs to know to which later events certain actions are related. The actor, unable to describe these events at the time of an action, can only say what is expected to occur and what consequences are hoped for. However, situational complexities and unanticipated consequences enter into the final narrative explanation. Freeman recognizes the problems inherent in using information based on memory, which often represents less an accurate reproduction than an imaginative reconstruction including distortion, wishful thinking, and "outcome interference."

He poses two options: (a) a "depth hermeneutics," such as psychoanalysis; and (b) juxtaposition of the data of an immediate experience—for example, diary entries—with the data of recollection. The first option attempts to unmask the self-deception of recollection by bringing out repressed thoughts through free association. Because Freeman sees both theoretical and practical problems for life span investigators in this approach, he supports the second option, which he describes as a dialectic between interpretation of life's events as they are happening and the additional meaning they acquire when viewed in light of their consequences. Another option is to collect data from other sources, such as newspaper accounts, written records, and interviews with acquaintances and relatives.

A life span psychology based on a retrospective narrative understanding of an individual's past might reveal a systematic understanding of the general patterns of people's experiences. Such knowledge would not, however, produce predictive laws that would determine what life would be like for everyone. In Freeman's words:

> Although narration moves inescapably backward in its concern with the understanding of the past-in-the-present, the view of development that derives from it can retain a focus on the forward movement that is rendered in the texts provided. Thus, perhaps paradoxically, it is out of retrospection that a project, an approximation toward desired ends, can be revealed. The shape that emerges out of the past extends itself into the future. It is this temporal dialogue which can lay the foundation for a new conceptualization of life span developmental knowledge. (1984, page 17)

Two exemplary studies related to life span narrative by Kenneth and Mary Gergen demonstrate investigative strategies. The first (M. M. Gergen & K. J. Gergen, in press) explores the ways in which two U.S. subcultures—adolescents and the elderly—have characterized their life histories. Twenty-nine persons between the ages of 19 and 21 were asked to chart their life histories along a general evaluative dimension; 72 persons ranging in age from 63 to 93 were interviewed about their general sense of well-being during various periods of life. The data revealed that the young adults hewed to a romantic story line: on the average they "tend to view their lives as happy at an early age, then beset with difficulty during the adolescent years, but now on an upward swing that promises well for the future." In contrast, the typical narrative of the elderly was a rainbow: "The young adult years were difficult, but a progressive narrative enabled a peak of well-being to be achieved somewhere between the ages of 50-60"; thereafter, the quality of their lives had declined. Gergen and Gergen are cautious in their interpretation, pointing out that the findings resemble the typical narrative forms given in our society for these age groups.

The second study (K. J. Gergen & M. M. Gergen, in press) addresses the issue of the social embedding of self-narrative: "Although the object of self-narrative is the single self, it would be a mistake to view such constructions as the product or possession of single selves." To test their thesis, the Gergens analyzed conversations that began with an expression of emotion (for example, "I am angry at you"). They found that the ensuing mutually constructed story at each choice point followed a typical pattern of choosing among the three alternatives of remorse, reframing, and anger. If remorse was chosen, it led to a compassionate or cautious response; if reframing was chosen, the scenario usually continued; while if the choice was anger, hostility escalated. The Gergens's investigation sought to identify the socially accepted patterns that inform the stories that people produce together. In summarizing their findings about lived narrative, they write:

> First, we found that the actor's capacities for intelligibility are embedded within a socio-historical context; in the telling of a story the actor is relying on certain features of a pre-existing social order. In this sense it would be plausible to say that the culture is speaking through the actor, using the actor to reproduce itself. Further, we found that self-narratives depend on the mutual sharing of symbols, socially acceptable performances, and continued negotiation. Finally, we found that narratives typically require the interweaving of identities, and thus, the support of others within the social sphere of interaction.

People use self-narratives to interpret and account for their lives. The basic dimension of human existence is temporality, and narrative transforms the mere passage of time into a meaningful unity, the Self. The study of a person's own experience of the life span requires attention both to the structuring of the narrative form and to the interrelationships between one's life story and those of others.

CASE HISTORIES

A widespread view of personality research holds that its primary goal is

> the development of generalizations of ever increasing scope, so that greater and greater varieties of phenomena may be explained by them, larger and larger numbers of questions answered by them, and broader and broader reaching predictions and decisions based upon them. (Levy, 1970, p. 5)

Runyon's (1983) suggested alternative structure for research in the life span field is based on Clyde Kluckholm and Henry Murray's dictum that "Every man is in certain respects (a) like all other men, (b) like some other men, (c) like no other men." Although Runyon proposes that research be carried on at all three levels, he points out that the third level—the study of particular individuals—has often been neglected. What is true of an individual is often not explainable or predictable in terms of what is true for all people or true for groups of people:

> Explanation at the individual level often occurs, not through the deductive application of universal generalizations, but through processes such as searching for the individual's reasons for acting in a particular way, through collecting as much information as possible about the individual and looking for idiographic patterns within it, and through organizing information about the case into an intelligible narrative. (p. 418)

In agreement with Runyon, I am proposing that the understanding of career life planning can be greatly assisted by the study of particular individuals in the form of narrative life histories. Efforts to describe the career development of particular individuals as White (1952) does will provide examples that can establish an appropriate knowledge base for career counselors. Schön (1983) has proposed that the creation of a formal network of theoretical propositions for application by professionals does not supply the kind of knowledge required for successful practice. Practitioners use their experiences with particular clients as a heuristic guide in their approach to new clients. Abstracting from individual lives to develop empirical generalizations or predictive theories may deform one's original understanding of human action and decision making. There is a nonpredictive knowledge base undergirding the wisdom and skill needed by professionals to assist clients with career development. Consisting of individual's developmental life narratives, this knowledge base is passed on from supervisors of interns and master counselors to beginning counselors through the telling of case stories. As practitioners gain experience, they supplement their original repertoire of life stories with those of their clients. Although life narratives do not provide the kind of knowledge that allows the counselor to predict or control career choices, they do deepen his or her appreciation of the conflicts and complexities facing clients.

Approaching career research from the perspective of action theory necessitates an acknowledgement of the human capacity to freely choose from among alternatives. Choices, however, are not completely open, nor are they isolated events; rather, they are made within the context of other life choices, social structures, and the environmental given. A collection of case histories can enable the career counselor to understand the complexity of career development as it unfolds in individual lives. This kind of understanding is different from that put forward by developmental theories. At the level of particular lives, agency and choice appear at the fore. Human action retreats to the background when generalizations are abstracted from individual lives. Decision and game theories based on purely rational or probability considerations miss the emotional and moral dimension of the choices confronting individuals. The understanding of lives and of life span career development requires attention to the uniqueness of each life.

To understand the meaning attached to career choices, the counselor must be aware that the meaning of actions is constituted by their narrative configuration. The significance of career decisions is seen in their contribution to an unfolding personal and communal episode, or to a life story. The meaning of human actions and career decisions, then, is best understood and explained through the use of a narrative perspective.

If the career field is informed by action theory, research efforts will be refocused on generating case histories of career development in individual lives. Emphasis will shift from developing empirical and theoretical generalizations about group behaviors to producing rich and deep narratives about particular people. If such a change is implemented, the career field will abandon its aspiration to resemble a natural science with precise categories and generalizations capable of accurately predicting human behavior. Instead, it will strive to produce knowledge that shares the characteristics of its object of inquiry, human beings. That knowledge will be suggestive, not predictive, and will take into account the creative, unique, and unexpected actions of individuals.

REFERENCES

Atkinson, R. F. (1978). *Knowledge and explanation in history*. Ithaca, NY: Cornell University Press.

Aristotle (1954). *The poetics of Aristotle*. In I. Bywater, (Trans.), *The rhetoric and the poetics of Aristotle* (pp. 219-266). New York: Modern Library.

Baltes, P. B., Reese, H. W., & Nesselroade, J. R. (1977). *Life span developmental psychology: Introduction to research methods*. Monterey, CA: Brooks/Cole.

Beauchamp, T. L., & Rosenberg, A. (1981). *Hume and the problem of causation*. New York: Oxford University Press.

Bruner, J. (1986). *Actual minds, possible worlds*. Cambridge, MA: Harvard University Press.

Davis, L. H. (1979). *Theory of action*. Englewood Cliffs, NJ: Prentice-Hall.

Erikson, E. H. (1963). *Childhood and society* (2nd, enlarged ed.). New York: W. W. Norton. (Original work published in 1950)

Freeman, M. (1984). History, narrative, and life span developmental knowledge. *Human Development, 27*, 1-19.

Gergen, K. J. (1977). Stability, change, and chance in understanding human development. In N. Datan & H. W. Resse (Eds.), *Life span development psychology: Dialectical perspectives in experimental research* (pp. 135-158). New York: Academic.

Gergen, K. J., & Gergen, M. M. (in press). Narrative and the self as relationship. In L. Berkowitz (Ed.), *Advances in experimental social psychology*. New York: Academic.

Gergen, M. M., & Gergen, K. J. (in press). The self in temporal perspective. In R. Abeles (Ed.), *Life span social psychology*. Hillsdale, NJ: Erlbaum.

Harré, R., Clarke, D., & De Carlo, N. (1985). *Motives and mechanisms*. New York: Methuen.

Hempel, C. G. (1965). The function of general laws in history. In C. G. Hempel (Ed.), *Aspects of scientific explanation* (pp. 231-244). New York: Free Press. (Original work published 1942)

Ivey, A. E. (1980). *Counseling and psychotherapy*. Englewood Cliffs, NJ: Prentice-Hall.

Levy, L. (1970). *Conceptions of personality*. New York: Random House.

Lyotard, J. (1984). *The postmodern condition: A report on knowledge*. (G. Bennington and B. Massumi, Trans.). Minneapolis: University of Minnesota Press.

Mill, J. S. (1953). On the logic of social sciences. In P. P. Wiener (ed.), *Readings in the philosophy of science* (pp. 255-280). Charles Scribner's. (Original work published 1843)

Polkinghorne, D. E. (1983). *Methodology for the human sciences: Systems of inquiry*. Albany, NY: The State University of New York Press.

Ricoeur, P. (1984). *Time and narrative: Vol. 1*. (K. McLaughlin and D. Pellauer, Trans.). Chicago: University of Chicago Press. (Original work published 1983)

Ricoeur, P. (1985a). *Time and narrative: Vol. 2*. (K. McLaughlin and D. Pellauer, Trans.). Chicago: University of Chicago Press. (Original work published 1984)

Ricoeur, P. (1985b). *Temps et récit: Vol. 3*. Paris: Seuil.

Rorty, R. (1979). *Philosophy and the mirror of nature*. Princeton, NJ: Princeton University Press.

Rorty, R. (1982). Overcoming the tradition. In R. Rorty (Ed.), *Consequences of pragmatism* (pp. 37-59). Minneapolis: University of Minnesota Press. (Original work published 1976)

Runyon, W. M. (1983). Ideographic goals and methods in the study of lives. *Journal of Personality, 51*, 413-437.

Schön, D. A. (1983). *The reflective practitioner*. New York: Basic Books.

Super, D. E. (1957). *The psychology of careers*. New York: Harper.

Super, D. E. (1980). A life span, life-space, approach to career development. *Journal of Vocational Behavior, 13*, 282-298.

Thompson, J. B. (1981). *Critical hermeneutics*. Cambridge: Cambridge University Press.

White, R. W. (1952). *Lives in progress*. New York: Holt, Rinehart & Winston.

Wright, G. H. von (1971). *Explanation and understanding*. Ithaca, NY: Cornell University Press.

Zunker, V. G. (1986). *Career counseling: Applied concepts of life planning* (2nd ed.). Monterey, CA: Brooks/Cole.

7

A Theory of Goal-directed Action in Career Analysis

Ladislav Valach

In this chapter the possibilities of an action theory approach to career analysis will be explored from a theoretical as well as a methodological perspective. Action theory refers to an actor's consciously goal-directed, planned, and intended behavior, which is cognitively and socially steered and controlled. It is multidimensionally organized in hierarchy, sequence, and parallelity. In making this exploration, a new approach to and new methods for the analysis of career processes will be suggested. In addition, the limitations of action theoretical approaches in addressing middle- and long-term individual or group processes will be addressed.

Two problems lead me to propose an action theory approach to career analysis. First, the explanation of career by classical personality and other dispositional approaches, particularly when tied to the classical psychometric methodology, has been increasingly criticized (Collin & Young, 1986). Once we give up these personality and dispositional explanations, the psychological and social psychological understanding of career processes are underexplained. A general explanation in which only personality and social structure variables are considered in interaction is no longer possible. Although it is appropriate to call for more specific models, situational specification represents only a small part of the issue. A conceptual specification needs to be established as well. Trying to improve the explanatory power of a career model through introducing increasing numbers of variables, particularly those concerning the conditions under which certain relations are valid (situational specification), can only be partly successful. The discrepancy between such differentiation and the relative conceptual simplicity of the target processes calls for additional conceptual work (conceptual specification).

Secondly, in recent social psychological analysis of individual, as well as group goal-directed behavior, subjective processes have been rediscovered and analyzed with rigorous methods (Ericsson & Simon, 1984; Kalbermatten & Valach, 1985). It became evident that in empirical research based on elicited biographical stories, the criteria for an analysis of the communicative situation from which these stories stem should be explicated. In other words, we know now that it is possible to gain access to linguistic encoding of cognitive processes that are relevant to action through subjective reports, but the conditions under which this is valid are very restrictive and do not include retrospective biographical stories. The data gained in these narratives are relevant in biography and career research, but are related to concepts on different levels. As a result, elicited retrospective stories about career are not identical with cognitive processes that steered the career course. However, this does not mean that such stories lack place in career research. Their action relevance lies in being told again in an interactive situation; for example, the story of unemployment told in an employment interview or a patient career as reconstructed in a patient-doctor interaction.

THEORETICAL FEATURES OF ANALYSIS OF GOAL-DIRECTED ACTION

Theoretical Roots

Empirical research on goal-directed action and its conceptualization is based on extensive theorizing that has become very strong in psychology and social psychology in the last 15 years (Cranach & Harré, 1982; Tajfel, 1984). As the action theoretical approach differs substantially from the mainstream theorizing and empirical research in psychology and social psychology, extensive conceptual work was necessary. The theory of individual goal-directed action (Cranach et al., 1982; Cranach, Mächler, & Steiner, 1985; Cranach & Valach, 1984) and the theory of group action (Cranach, Ochsenbein, & Valach, 1986) are the bases of this conceptual work. These theories are founded on a phenomenological view of action, on systems conceptualization, and on theories of social control.

Phenomenological approaches to the study of action. In all theories of action or goal-directed behavior, the classical phenomenological approaches (A. Schütz, Edmund Husserl, Maurice Merlau-Ponty, Fritz Heider, and others) played a significant role in conceptualizing situated, intended, planned, and conscious everyday human behavior. In particular, the theories of naive psychology (Heider, 1958) supplied a series of concepts used for understanding intentional action. The phenomenological stance also influenced the methodological approach to the analysis of action.

In addition to the phenomenological approaches to action that are invariably individualistic conceptions, our everyday view of action allows us to see a group of people following a task as an acting unit with a shared goal. Although this approach has not often been theoretically formulated, it is regularly used in pragmatic or applied analyses of group behavior.

System theoretical influences. Another important influence on action theory and research was exercised by general system theory (Bertallanffy, 1971; Laszlo, 1972) and the systemic theory of planned action (Miller, Galanter, & Pribram, 1960), as well as by the theory of working activity (Hacker, 1973; Volpert, 1974) and the conception of active and self-organizing systems (Maturana & Varela, 1975; Prigogine, 1979).

System theoretical thinking not only exercised its influence through its general view, it also supplied a number of concepts, for example, processes of steering and regulation, information processing, hierarchical organization, heterarchical organization, three dimensional organization, active systems, goal directedness, plan, strategy, execution, operation, evaluation, resolution, and feedback. Some other concepts were influential through the special treatment they received in system theoretical thinking (for example, intention, will, consciousness, and values).

In addition to the system processes of individual action, a group is conceived as an active system performing group actions. It also relies on goal-directed behavior as a means of adaptation. Thus, the systems approach had the strongest influence on the formulation of the theory of group action since the conception of a group as a system has already been formulated.

Social control of individual action. A social psychological theory of goal-directed action must include concepts of social control. The theories of goal-directed action and of group action draw, among others, on the work of Mead (1934), Goffman (1959b), Harré and Secord (1972), and Berger and Luckmann (1966). Action is based on psychological processes that are determined by social processes (Cranach & Valach, 1984). The most important of these social processes are rules, conventions, norms, and social representations. A group action is a social process at its best. Social representation is the group's process of monitoring (Moscovici, 1987).

The Theory of Goal Directed Action

The notion of goal-directed action refers to consciously goal-directed, planned, and intended behavior. It is socially directed and controlled. The essential features of the theory of goal-directed action that I will argue is an appropriate framework for the consideration of career, have been presented by Cranach and colleagues (1986).

Briefly, goal-directed action occurs in specific settings. It is frequently performed in the execution of a task or task structure that is a socially represented knowledge of "how things should be done." Goal directed action has three dimensions: sequence, hierarchy, and complexity. Sequence refers to the temporary order in an action such as cooking Beef Stroganoff: I will cut the meat, coat the meat strips, brown them, chop the onions and mushrooms, make the sauce, and finally put it all together with cream and sherry. Hierarchy refers to the order of relative subordination and superordination. As I want the Beef Stroganoff to be successful (my goal), I will not only make sure that I brown the meat after coating the strips and not before (action steps) but I will also make a smooth sauce by bringing it to the boil slowly while stirring it regularly (elements of action steps).

Complexity refers to the simultaneous organization of different action processes on the various levels of organization. While simmering the onions and mushrooms, I consult the cook book on what to do next or answer my four-year-old's question, "Why doesn't copper rust?"

Actions are consciously represented. Conscious cognition is the highest self-monitoring system in human information processing, but other self-monitoring systems, such as pain and the emotions, are involved as well. Volitional processes, for example, concentration, attention, and self-control, also direct cognition. The individual represents these underlying cognitions through the use of language, which is the closest we can come to an external representation of cognition. When this view of goal directed action in the individual is applied to group action processes, information processing and action execution proceed on two levels. At the individual level, they proceed as described above. At the group level, information is processed through action related communication and group action is executed through the cooperation of group members.

Theoretical Influence on Career Processes

Naive psychology. A career is understood here in the very broad sense as used in various sociological and social psychological approaches in over the last 30 years (Goffman, 1959a; McKinlay, 1971; Twadle, 1981; Williams, 1981). The following appreciation, for example, can be understood from a phenomenological perspective: interrupting someone during everyday action that does not require full intensive concentration and attention and asking what the person is thinking about will result in reports of career-relevant cognitions of various kinds. They will either be cognitions related to actions that are a part of a career or cognitions related immediately to a career ("I want to go to the library on Monday... ." and "I have to take the upcoming exam, otherwise I cannot finish my studies in two years."), or evaluation or emotion-related cognitions ("I did not like the lecture on Thursday" and "I have been in this job much too long").

Other people observing someone else's action will invariably ask "What is she [or he] doing this for?" meaning "Of what career is this action a part?" An understanding of an action and its life relevance will be achieved if its relation to a career is understood or if it is attributed to a particular career. These examples underline the closer relation of action to career in their common-sense basis.

The following is a list of everyday descriptions of career concepts. The list is by no means complete, but it recognizes that career is an everyday concept beyond the professional trajectory.

Concepts concerning the career trajectory:
— career beginning, taking up a career;
— career end, giving up a career;
— a step in a career;
— career progress (moving forward in a career);
— career regress (set back);
— career speed (quick, slow, speeding up, slowing down);
— career stagnation.

Concepts concerning levels of career organization:
- career goals;
- career strategy;
- career duration (short or long);
- relation of superordination or subordination between career goals and necessary career steps.

Concepts concerning goals of career:
- career goal (what do I want to pursue as a career?);
- preference order of career goals;
- career intention (intention to follow a career/to choose particular steps in a career);
- choice of career goal;
- career success (successful career);
- career failure (failure to make a career);
- developing a career goal.

Concepts concerning internal steering:
- career change (change of career);
- career decision (node);
- career plan (number and series of career steps);
- career strategy (hierarchically ordered number of plans);
- career evaluation (evaluation in/of career).

Values and attitudes in career:
- career value (value in career: personal choice for particular values either because they are unconventional or because they are referred to in a discourse as a norm but are not followed in performance);
- career attitude.

Concepts concerning social steering of a career:
- career rules (rules in career to keep up);
- career norms (expected and sanctioned performance);
- career's convention (consensual and expected performance).

Career-relevant knowledge:
- career knowledge.

Career emotions:
- like/dislike of a career;
- emotions because of the relevance of a particular action or event for a career.

Volition in a career:
- stamina in a career;
- carriage or boldness in a career.

Other career-related cognitions:
- career expectation;
- career anticipation;

> — career attempt (attempt of a career/attempt in a career): used
>   either when giving up or interrupted, unsuccessful, when diffi-
>   cult (discrepancies between resource and task);
> — career step (intentional phase);
> — achievement of career goal;
> — consideration of and in a career;
> — alternatives in and of a career;
> — career persistence;
> — career resolution.

Career in a system of several careers:

> — main career;
> — second career;
> — side career;
> — parallel career.

Career and actions:

> — concept of career-decisive actions;
> — concept of career-relevant actions;
> — concept of career-accompanying actions;
> — individual career action;
> — collective (group) career action.

Career participants

Causes of a career

In the analysis of action, we learned a great deal from everyday descriptions of actions that were brought to our attention by several phenomenologically oriented psychologists such as Schütz (1932), Heider (1958), and Laucken (1973) (Valach, Cranach, & Kalbermatten, 1988). In the study of career phenomena we can learn from naive as well as scientific reports on careers. As we cannot analyze psychological and social phenomena without relying on their meaning, we must include these concepts in our analysis.

Naive observers of ongoing behavior not only describe an action but also infer processes of higher order from their observation as long as the observed action is of biographical relevance (past, present, or future). This is particularly the case when several consecutive actions of the same actor(s) are presented with a time lag between them. Viewing a series of episodes in which a student is buying some books, attending a lecture, reading late in the night at his desk, taking a test, and, finally, celebrating in a restaurant, the observers will infer a student's career. Naive observers and naive participants interpret a series of actions as a part of a career (patient's career, study, marriage, professional career).

A number of actions that are parts of a task differ from a series of actions as a part of a career in a number of points. For example, although a career, particularly as seen by the actor, could be interpreted as a task, it will seldom reach the order that actions show, and cannot, therefore, be considered as just another type of action. The clarity of goal and the conscious control of the individual steps in constructing a market stall for my son cannot be identified with long term processes of being a student or an employee.

Understanding career in terms of discrete actions would mean a reification of social psychological processes that is not in all instances justified. Nevertheless, it is heuristically meaningful to consider the phenomenology of a career as a methodological and conceptual device and to utilize naive concepts of career analysis. It is important to realize that a career is only exceptionally an individual concept. In the majority of cases it is a unit carried with individual as well as group goals.

Systems theory. Some of the classical issues of systems theoretical thinking and their consequences for theorizing on a career can be considered now.

Entropy, negative entropy: The system of physical order shows a tendency toward loss of energy and toward coincidence or disorder. The open systems that are analyzed in psychological, social psychological, and sociological research, on the other hand, can be identified in their tendency toward order and energy absorption. This is termed *negative entropy* or *information*.

A career should be conceptualized as an open system. An order should be assumed. This will stand against time sampling procedures in career analysis that rely on the assumption of coincidence as the underlying order. The units of analysis cannot be chosen by coincidence sampling as a career is organized in a meaningful order. The unit we choose to analyze must be selected according to meaningful criteria.

Goal directedness: A number of system theoretical authors point out that open systems are goal-directed systems (Ackoff & Emery, 1972). Thus, a social psychological conceptualization, methods of analysis, and data evaluation must consider intentionality and orientation toward a future state or future processes.

Theories of career should also consider intentionality and orientation toward a future states or future processes. Conceived to understand the processes of relations between the self and the social institution, a career should nevertheless be understood as an intentional system. The consideration of intentionality and future orientation seems appropriate for a career in professions but should also apply for a "negative" career, such as a career in prison. However, the intentionality is often carried as in the latter case by other agents.

Hierarchy: Systems are organized in a hierarchical way. Although other, more complex forms of system organization have also recently been discussed; for example, triarchy and heterarchy (Turvey, Shaw, & Mace, 1978) an analysis of psychosocial processes must nonetheless involve several levels that are related to each other in a subordinate or superordinate way.

Career as an action system is also organized as a hierarchy. It contains several levels of organization, which are related to each other. The levels of organization differ in quality, extent, and function. The intentional development of career can be seen as the highest level, the career steps which are functional to the career goal as a mediating level, and the career features, which can be characterized in a structural way, as the lowest level of the system. The consequence for an analysis would imply that we have to analyze a career on several levels in order to gain an adequate picture.

Sequence: Systems are processes. Their course and evolution can be captured on several levels in the form of a sequence. Social psychological theories should conceptualize sequences, methods should be designed to describe them, and data analysis must maintain the sequential order of data.

It is generally recognized that a career involves a sequence of units, mostly understood as phases. However, sequences need to be followed at several levels of the career organization.

Complexity: It is obvious from the discussion thus far that simplicity is not the leading concept in an analysis of living systems. Complexity needs to be accounted for as well. A career is a complex phenomenon. It consists of a system career and a subsystem of career related actions. From our own everyday experience, we know that we follow several careers and even perform several tasks at the same time. Thus, a multiplicity in the organization of a career implies a relation of system (career) and its subsystems (actions) as well as any form of parallelity of careers.

Feedback: The inclusion of the concept "feedback" is used to mark the differences between causal-linear and controlled processes of adaptation. Its presence identifies the systemic conceptualization of open systems. Graphically this feature seems to be adequately represented in social psychological writing, but only a few statistical procedures are able to integrate it.

Feedback processes in a career are seldom recognized as a constructing principle and methodological requirement. Rather, they are generally accepted as phenomenological process. An evaluation of existing conditions and desired states as well as following changes or corrections of the course of career are often described.

Feed-forward: An orientation to future states is an important and classical feature of open systems. Feed-forward processes are decisive steering processes. Their inclusion in an analysis leads to substantial changes of research questions. The issue of causes will be supplemented by teleonomical research questions.

This issue is also relevant for a career conceptualization. There is no career without an orientation toward future states. The consequences of introducing individual and joint feed-forward processes for career analysis are significant. Studying causes of a career, particularly social structural variables, should not be the only way of looking at these processes.

Dynamic interaction: The assumption of interactive processes of system-environment relation, external and internal, are a necessary condition of any thinking about social psychological phenomena. The complexity and holistic character of these interactions makes the use of a number of common methodological and statistical procedures, such as the analysis of variance, questionable. The extensive use of popular statistical packages in data evaluation hinders the development of appropriate procedures.

Processes: Thinking in a systemic approach works with concepts about processes. Systems have to be described and analyzed as processes and not as static formations lying behind any changes. This dynamic conceptualization must depart from static and dispositionally conceived methods of analysis and data evaluation, such as factor analysis or multidimensional scaling. Careers are processes. Their description as *becoming* is heuristically more useful than the search for external variables explaining the variance of their outcome.

Information: The relevance of *nonmaterial* processes, either in the form of the classical conception of information-processing theories or as a basis of holographic iconization is particularly stressed in system approaches. Cognitive processes do not have to be considered as an epiphenomena of neurological processes, and processes of information do not have to be thought of as a linear order of elements.

Information processing is a central part in career conceptualization. As cognitive processes, it mediates between an action system and a career system. Communication among group members furnish the information processing in a group action in a career. These communication processes mediate between the career feedforward as represented by others and cognitive processes of the career agent.

Energy: Energy processes of energizing are also a part of systemic conceptualization. Nevertheless, this does not require a dualistic view of nonmaterial information and material energy. Monism, as well as some solution to this question in the form of a systemic order in which the concepts are unified on higher level, is also represented.

Energy and energizing are inseparable parts of career and career actions. Getting up early in the morning after only a few hours of sleep makes us aware of that fact. Walking up a mountain or finishing a task for which the original motivation ceased a long time ago also require some additional energizing. Other actions will mobilize enough energy and motivation for the rest of the day. Processes of energizing are complementary to processes of directing. After the overwhelming influence of cognitive approaches in psychology and social psychology, the role of emotions again become an important research subject. Energizing is one of the processes that should be studied in this context.

Integration: The systemic view is an integrative outlook, not gained through unclear, all-embracing terms, but due to the assumption and conceptualization of a comprehensive organization of psychological and social psychological processes. Thus, some of the knowledge gained on the basis of a narrow theoretical reasoning can be integrated as long as the relevant assumptions are not violated.

An action theoretical conceptualization of career processes may bring about some new views, but its power lies in integrating previous knowledge and insights into a comprehensive model. Biographical, functionalistic, and interactional approaches to the study of a career, to name but a few, can be unified. Descriptions of a career, such as provided by Goffman (1959a), can be integrated with some functionalistic postulates of categorizing of subprocesses, such as those known from structural functionalist approaches in sociology, and with subjective views.

Emergence: A system theoretical view usually assumes an emergence of phenomena of higher forms of organization. It opposes the reductionistic procedure that reduces processes to one level, usually of a lower order.

A career is a multileveled process and must be studied as such. In career analysis, all levels have to be considered and used for description and explanation.

Meaning and intentions, individual steps as well as structural properties of career contribute to its understanding and explanation in a complementary way.

Methods: The systemic approach is not bound to one particular research method. Nevertheless, there are several demands that need to be respected. For example, analyzed processes should be viewed from different perspectives. More than using alternative tests, an analysis of a career can utilize a wide range of methods, which have to be supported by an appropriate conceptualization.

System-environment interaction: The definition of analyzed phenomena must relate to the system-environment interaction. This warrants an embedding of processes in environment which must also be considered in an analysis and data evaluation. The situational specificity is accounted for here and it consequently demands adequate methodological and statistical treatment.

Although a career is often analyzed as a typical process of a statistical group, it has to be considered in its individual occurrence and its situational specificity. It can be analyzed neither from the perspective of the environment only or without any relation to it.

Subject-object relation: In a systems theoretical view, the analysis instrument and the object of an analysis are not considered as being independent as is required by classical measurement theory. There are several conceptual possibilities to support this notion, with extensive methodological consequences.

Careers are more frequently analyzed in a supporting, accompanying interrelationship. In prospective studies, an interviewer sees his partner several times. The independence of individual measurements points is, therefore, not given. Moreover, in analyzing a career, categories of shared social meaning are used.

Organization: The tendency to order in an open system leads to the concept of an organization. The contingency on which a normal distribution is based, for example, is not an open system. It is a meaningful order and not a probabilistic one.

A career is an organized phenomenon. A system career with its subsystems *actions* are processes on several levels and are ordered in hierarchy, sequence, and complexity. These are some of the organizational features of a career.

Wholeness: Holism plays a special and partly defining role in a systemic understanding. It represents an attempt to abolish any atomistic view of the research undertaking. The holistic proposition finds its expression in the conceptualization and analysis of career as a socially meaningful unit, as a system that must be analyzed on several levels, and as a process carried out by intentions of individual and group action.

Development: Processes are considered in system thinking as becoming and not only as consequences of being. The goal of research under this assumption changes substantially.

A number of theoretical approaches to career analysis support this view. Nevertheless, only a few analyses were performed in which the system development was considered appropriately. There are also several methodological problems. In the single-case studies approach, some of them are treated, but a great majority of these questions still remain unanswered.

Epiphenomenality: Also connected to several other assumptions, the position of epiphenomenality can be contrasted to a systemic view. Social psychological processes of a higher order are considered in their own right as a part of a systemic organization and not as epiphenomena of an underlying structure or process. Group processes do not have to be reduced to individual processes, nor cognitive processes to neurological processes. This requires a conceptualization and methods of analysis directed at several levels of the studied phenomena.

Our understanding of career relies on the assumption of cognitive processes, of socially meaningful wholes and system organization with qualitative different levels. Therefore, the view of epiphenomenality is seldom theoretically proposed. However, the way a great number of researchers choose and define the variables in study often shows the underlying view of epiphenomenality in regard to several processes.

Conceptual Features of Career Processes

Several conceptual features of career processes can now be considered from an action theory perspective. Among them, career as a twofold system and the cognitive processes and communication in a career stand out as most important. Career as a socially defined task and perspectives in career will also be discussed.

A career is a twofold system. A twofold system is required to study career phenomena from the action theory perspective. First, a long-term process of an actor or a group of actors in an institutional or informal social setting is a phenomenon of distinct quality and social relevance, and should be studied in its own right. There is no need to reduce it to individual or social structural processes or to consider it an epiphenomenon thereof. Second, as these processes must also be lived "here and now" and as there is no long-term process without action, subsystems of concrete situated actions would have to be assumed. This action could be an individual or group action. In the case of the latter, again a twofold system would have to be analyzed. Obviously, a career could be an individual or a group process; for example, the long-term development of a therapy group could be seen as a group career.

Consider a young person progressing from a beginner through an established student and later to an advanced student of psychology as an example. This student is seen by herself or himself and by others in a student trajectory or career, and goes through various stages, exams, and seminars which are the manifest sign of studying progress. She or he must not only manage the important exams (actions) but also have to consider her or his student goals in everyday decisions. She or he will also partly change her or his everyday actions and interactions and become a recognizable student.

This example points out three types of action and their embeddedness in a career: first, action that marks important steps in a career, for example, initiation, exams, and so on; second, actions that are functional for the career, for example, studying, participating in lectures, buying books, writing essays; third, actions that are not functionally oriented toward the career are influenced by the involvement in the career, for example, a particular mannerism in informal discussion, or a change in social situation because the career influences the actions of the person in a group action and the group structure.

Cognitive processes and communication. Our understanding of cognitive processes and communication is basically the same for action as for career. The orientation, however, is different, as cognitive processes and communication can be either related to action of which they are part or to a career. However, the most important feature of a career is its embeddedness in a social organizational or institutional setting. Thus, decisive points or nodes in a career path are interactive or group actions. Accordingly, the conception of a twofold system of information processing as in a group action will apply in most instances. Moreover, depending on the structure of the relevant group action, the career steering cognitions of the next step of career can sometimes be found only by the other actor of the relevant common or group action. For example, being sent to university and supported by his or her parents, a student might know what to do as a student but not necessarily what his or her father has in store for him or her after final exams. In another example, a patient wants to be healthy again and knows what she or he is going to do after being released from hospital but has only a vague idea how his or her doctor is going to treat him or her and what the next steps are.

The cognitive processes and communication gain a particular importance in their function of inward adaptation. Action, on the other hand, can be seen in the function of outward adaptation. In relating a career to an action and action to a career, complex reflective and interpretative processes are required. As the twofold structure of career process has been neglected in theory and research, the role of these reflective and interpretative processes in an action or in a career is virtually unknown. In studying these processes, the problem of situated values and of the self concept could be partially resolved.

A career is a socially defined task. At this point, it is important to consider the social nature of career. First, career is a social phenomenon. It is a process of a socially categorized group of people. Second, it is never an individual phenomenon in a sense that it always contains interactive or group actions. Young (1984) formulated a similar view in the concept of vocation as relationship. Furthermore, the role of family in vocational development has recently been pointed out (Schulenberg, Vondracek & Crouter, 1984). Third, a career is not a process that is always bound to or dependent on a particular actor such as an individual or a group. Several persons acting in a position in succession could form a career. Consider the career of the position of a president of a theater club. At the beginning, the position was a post for the founding member who could draw new outlines and bring ideas into the club, having been freed from club work by the secretary. Subsequently, it became an honorary position with the duty to chair annual general meetings. Later, it was understood that the president would look after the organization of the current production while the secretary would look after the general communication in the club. Also connected with these changes were some ups and downs in the prestige of the function of president. Thus, as a person could have several careers, several people could have a career as a group, and several people could participate in one career. A similar approach is also formulated by Wicker for behavioral settings (Wicker & King, 1988).

Because of the essential social nature of a career, the intentionality and its goal character were overlooked for a long time. Goal directedness was attributed only to an individual actor whose career was considered. The further progress of this person in a career was then carried out and facilitated through the social situation and social structure of an organization of which this career was a part. This was particularly the case in a "negative career" or an illness career as well as a career in a closed institution. However, with the rising of importance of intentionality in the under-standing of individual and collective human behavior, the career nearly lost its attractiveness as a descriptive concept for developments outside the professional setting. Instead, coping processes, for example coping with illness, were analyzed. Coping is an action concept and was considered as most useful in a "difficult" life situation. However, in dropping the notion of a career and using only an action concept for long-term processes such as patient career, the complex relation between an actual genesis of an action and long-term processes were overlooked. This explains the number of studies collecting data on subjective understanding of a coping action whose function is known neither in a concrete action nor in the long-term career process. In these studies people are asked how they coped with their problem. However, it is not known whether and how these described processes influence their everyday life or the whole career to which they are related. Also, the individual understanding of the coping process hinders us in gaining relevant insights into career processes. Remember that models of coping are models of cognitive-emotional processes and not of general information processing including communication. The concept also fails to account for a group action and for the sequence of a group and an individual action.

Perspective in a career. Career can be approached from several perspectives. We have seen, for example, that career can be considered as a naive biographical concept. Similarly, we have used several concepts, such as manifest career, cognitive steering, and social meaning, to describe career. This stance has been promoted and practiced in career studies for a long time. The concepts of a subjective career, a career pattern, and an individual objective career were intro-duced by Stebbins. "A career pattern is a consensually recognized course of movement through recognized stages with a beginning and an end" (1970, p. 37). "The individual-objective career is . . . the process of an individual (or cohort of individuals) through a career line. It is an observer's view of the patterns of movement stage to stage. . . . . The subjective career is . . . a personalized image of the career pattern as the actor relates its ramification to himself" (p. 39). This perspective is the most neglected in career research (Collin, 1986).

However, it seems that neither the career pattern nor the subjective image of the career are related to the immediate experiencing of action by action in an ongoing career. Considering the empirical work in which this distinction was used, we can assume that we are dealing here with images and stories as told on one occasion either by the career agent or an observer. Only the concept of individual objective career can be related to the empirical course of career as unfolding action by action in time.

This empirical course of a career can be further differentiated. We can distinguish between subjective representation of processes in career and the subjective career discussed above. While the subjective career is a description by the career agent of his or her career and how he or she sees it, the subjective representation of a career implies subjective monitoring of the course of career, the minute-by-minute experience of a career and not a subjective conception of it. Goffman addressed in the concept of *moral career* a similar concept to subjective (or self-) representation. It is "the moral aspects of career—... the regular sequence of changes that career entails in the person's self" (Goffman, 1959b, p. 123).

Another aspect is the social representation of a career as a sequence of naive descriptions. It is the view of naive observers as collected at several (decisive) points of the career in which several perspectives can be distinguished.

Finally, the last view is the integrative stance of a researcher. Having a range of empirical research methods at hand, the researcher cannot fully identify an approach to the study of career with one method only. A career is more than we can infer from subjective data of a biographical interview; it is more than we can observe, and it is also more than we can see from the reports of other participants in the institutional setting. However, the relevant data on a career can be gained in the comparison of these perspectives. It is not the "mean" of this information that matters but the compatibility and differences of these data sets that give us a comprehensive picture of the studied processes.

Another differentiation we wish to make is between a career as we talk about it (our own, someone else's) and as we experience it. We use a number of career concepts to talk about the course, the future, and the past of our own or someone else's career (these are career related judgments). However, they may not necessarily be valid in a particular career-relevant action in which career-relevant cognitions will be processed. This issue presents a methodological problem and we believe that if the methods of action analysis are used, some of its pitfalls can be avoided (Valach, 1986).

As a part of its guidance system, every system must solve a number of universal tasks and perform a number of functions. The application of these functional subsystems to a career-relevant action and a career system follows:

Monitoring the environment
> — In a career-relevant action: In consideration of goals of a career-relevant action, an unemployed person will monitor his or her environment in order to make the job interview a success.
> — In consideration of career goals: A student will be sensitive to any changes that are relevant to his or her student career (such as a new examination schedule, new possibilities in subject specialization) and will always try to be well informed.

Self-monitoring
- — In a career-relevant action: A person at a job interview shows apprehension because of the relevance of this interview for his or her occupational career.
- — In a career: During the preparation for exams, a student has insomnia and digestive problems and shows tension for several weeks.

Selecting aim
- — In a career-relevant action: Considering the short time before exams a student sets a goal for the evening to study instead of going out.
- — In a career: After buying a computer and hearing about the good employment possibilities, a student changes the second emphasis of his studies from philosophy to computer science.

Adopting a program
- — In a career relevant action: During an oral examination, the examiner and the student have to work out a strategy so that the examiner can judge the student's performance and the student can present his or her knowledge.
- — In a career: A student chooses a series of lectures and seminars as she or he intends to write a final essay on a particular problem and wishes support from a particular professor.

Transformation into behavior
- — In a career-relevant action: The examiner formulates a first question for which she or he assumes the students are prepared in order to reduce their anxiety.
- — In a career: A student takes the necessary steps in changing the subject of his or her study.

Execution control
- — In a career-relevant action: A student and his or her examiner are making sure that they do not lose their mutual understanding in the process of their discourse.
- — In a career: A student makes sure that the choice of the subject of his or her studies and the selected lecture will facilitate employment possibilities.

Stopping the behavior
- — In a career-relevant action: As the examination is limited in time, the discourse of the examiner and the student will finish at the time limit. However, it is the examiner who declares the session closed and gives the closing signal.
- — In a career: a career is an institutionalized unit and, therefore, its beginning, its important nodes, and its end are well marked and often stressed with particular action such as rituals or examinations.

Final examination and storing of essential features of the whole behavior

— In a career-relevant action: The examiner and the student evaluate the performance during the examination either in a discussion or by a grade (or grade expectation in the case of the student).

— In a career: An examination is an institutionalized evaluation of a career or a career step. The outcome of an examination will be understood as an evaluation of the student's achievement in his or her whole student career or part thereof. The student considers improvements for the next step.

METHODOLOGICAL FEATURES OF THE ANALYSIS OF GOAL-DIRECTED ACTION

The authors of the theory of goal-directed action maintain that the theory unites three classes of concepts (manifest behavior, cognitive processes, and social meaning) and that therefore, three different methods must be used in order to collect data on the appropriate processes without violating any of the theoretical assumptions. These methods are systematic observation, naive observation, and a self-confrontation interview (Kalbermatten & Valach, 1985). In studying the role of social representation in action, the biographical interview was also used. In an analysis of organizational action, documents were studied (Cranach, Ochsenbein, & Tschan, 1987).

The methodological approach is characterized by two important rules. First, the processes of data collection should be compatible with the target processes. Manifest behavior is not a subject of an interview but it is observed; action-related cognitions are collected as close to the action as possible, attributions are monitored while the naive observers face the action, and organizational processes are studied from documents. Second, the assumption of equality of all variables is abandoned. The combination of several instruments for data collection does not allow a simple correlational approach to the data analysis. Data have to be related according to qualitative criteria, such as the individual episodes. Moreover, within the individual sets of data, an organization is constructed that corresponds with the assumed organization of the target processes. Thus, in data comparison, the levels in a hierarchy have to be respected.

An action analysis is based on the analysis of action execution, and systematic observation is an important method of data collection. The most important rule for systematic observation concerns the organization of an action (hierarchy, sequence, complexity). It means that the observational system of categories has to be constructed accordingly. Assumptions about each level of the organization of action have to provide the basis for the definition of observational units.

Human action is steered and regulated on several levels of organization. The highest level is a level of purposeful instances; at the medium level, it is the course of action organized through plans and strategies; and at the lowest level, the system functions through self-regulation. The highest level, the action level, is characterized by goals. Observational units are socially meaningful and relate to molar behavioral units. The observation starts with the segmenting of ongoing actions into action units through an attribution of a goal. The observer works out the sequence of goals of the actor, for example, to set up a toy animal farm, to quarrel over a toy, to pack a parcel. On the intermediate level of analysis, action steps are observed. The units of observation here are functional categories designed to identify a step of an act in its function, for example, functional group *unload:* put aside, empty out, put down, set up; communicative steps to organize interaction: proposition, command, contradiction).

On the third level of analysis, the structures of action steps are analyzed. An action step can be performed in different ways. On this level analysis proceeds in terms of movements and positions, and in terms of speech qualifiers.

In the analysis of an action in a career, systematic observation will proceed in the same way. Observing at the career level, similar strategies should be used. However, it can be assumed that because of the long-term character of career processes, in the reconstruction of ongoing processes additional data sources would have to be used such as document analysis, time budget studies, and so on.

In addition to the verbal utterances, data on cognitive processes in action should be analyzed. The method used in action analysis is labeled "self-confrontation interview," comprising an open systematic interview on a particular action in which the actor views a video recording of this action immediately after its execution. The actor is asked to report on his cognition, emotion, sensations, and so forth. These reports are transcribed and systematically analyzed. The self-confrontation interview should be used more frequently in career analysis; first, in the analysis of career-relevant action and, second, in actions that are the everyday processes of a career. If it is not possible to use video self confrontation, alternative methods should be employed. Any interview that aims at action-relevant cognitive processes must be modeled on the self-confrontation interview. A number of alternatives can be used, such as diary methods, self-confrontation interview with audio recordings, experience sampling method, and other techniques. They are not fully comparable with the video self-confrontation interview, but they are, nevertheless, much closer to action accompanying cognitions than any other forms of interview.

Actions are social processes. Their social embeddedness also requires that, in an analysis of action, data on its social meaning have to be collected. Attribution by naive observers of a particular socially categorized group of people supplies information on the interpretative frame of reference from various perspectives which should also serve as a basis for a systematic interpretation by a scientist.

The information gained from these naive observations is interpreted as a part of the processes of social control. Conventions and social representation of particular groups are not only descriptive concepts on a socially emergent level but also data on influences of action processes.

Collecting attributions and data on social representation is even more important in career studies (Young & Marks, 1986). Careers live from their social definition and, therefore, are empirical material that must be gathered. A patient's career has often been defined from the view of a doctor but seldom from the view of the patient's family members. The discrepant views on professional career could also be considered as relevant data in studying the problem of equality of chances.

Naive observation should be performed, like the other two data collections, very close to the actual ongoing activity. It is not a problem to perform it in career relevant actions, but in collecting data on the career level, other methods and techniques would often need to be substituted.

SUMMARY

Several features of action theory were presented and their relevance for career conceptualization and analysis discussed. Phenomenological and systems theory influences were particularly stressed. In formulating an action theory approach to an analysis of career processes, the twofold nature of career and action, information processing, the social character of career, and the perspectives of analysis were further explicated.

In the methodological part of this chapter, it was suggested that researchers use systematic observation, self-confrontation interviews and naive observation more often in career analysis not only in the analysis of career-relevant actions but also for the analysis of the career process itself.

When analyzing a career, various levels should be reconstructed and described. Relevant actions could be analyzed and the accompanying cognitions, particularly career-relevant cognitions, could be collected. Finally, naive interpretation of people from career relevant groups should be analyzed.

REFERENCES

Ackoff, R. L., & Emery, F. E. (1972). *On purposeful systems.* Chicago: Atherton.

Berger, P. L., & Luckmann, T. (1967). *The social construction of reality.* Garden City, NY: Doubleday.

Bertalanffy, L. von. (1971). *General systems theory.* Harmondsworth, England: Penguin.

Collin, A. (1986). Career development: The significance of the subjective career. *Personal Review, 15,* 22-28.

Collin, A., & Young, R. A. (1986). New directions for theories of career. *Human Relations, 39,* 837-853.

Cranach, M. von, & Harré, R. (Eds.). (1982). The analysis of action. *European studies in social psychology.* Cambridge: Cambridge University Press.

Cranach, M. von, Kalbermatten, U., Indermuehle, K., & Gugler, B. (1982). *Goal directed action*. London: Academic.

Cranach, M. von, Mächler, E., & Steiner, V. (1985). The organization of goal directed action. In G. P. Ginsburg, M. Brenner, & M. von Cranach (Eds.), *Discovery strategies in the psychology of action* (pp. 19-61). Orlando, FL: Academic.

Cranach, M. von, Ochsenbein, G., & Tschan, F. (1987). Action of social systems: Theoretical and empirical investigation. In G. R. Semin & B. Krahé (Eds.), *Issues in contemporary German social psychology—History, theories and applications* (pp. 119-155). London: Sage.

Cranach, M. von, Ochsenbein, G., & Valach, L. (1986). The group as a self-active system: Outline of a theory of group action. *European Journal of Social Psychology, 16*, 193-229.

Cranach, M. von, & Valach, L. (1984). The social dimension of goal directed action. In H. Tajfel (Ed.), *The social dimension of social psychology* (pp. 285-299). Cambridge: Cambridge University Press.

Ericsson, K. A., & Simon, H. A. (1984). *Protocol analysis: Verbal reports as data*. Cambridge, MA: MIT Press.

Goffman, E. (1959a). The moral career of the mental patient. *Psychiatry, 22*, 123-142.

Goffman, E. (1959b). Presentation of self in everyday life. New York: Anchor.

Hacker, W. (1973). *Allgemeine Arbeits—und Ingenieurpsychologie*. Berlin: Deutscher Verlag der Wissenschaften.

Harré, R., & Secord, P. F. (1972). *The explanation of social behavior*. Oxford: Blackwell.

Heider, F. (1958). *The psychology of interpersonal relations*. New York: Wiley.

Kalbermatten, U., & Valach, L. (1985). Methods of an integrative approach for the study of social interaction. *Communication and Cognition, 18*, 281-315.

Laszlo, E. (1972). *Introduction to systems philosophy*. New York: Harper Torchbooks.

Laucken, U. (1973). *Naive Verhaltenstheorie*. Stuttgart: Klett.

Maturana, H. R., & Varela, F. (1975). *Autopoietic systems* (Biological Computer Laboratory Report No. 9.5). Urbana, IL: University of Illinois Press.

McKinlay, J. B. (1971). The concept of 'patient career' as a heuristic device for making medical sociology relevant to medical students. *Social Science and Medicine, 5*, 441-460.

Mead, G. H. (1934). *Mind, self and society*. Chicago: University of Chicago Press.

Miller, G. A., Galanter, E., & Pribram, U. H. (1960). *Plans and the structures of behavior*. New York: Holt.

Moscovici, S. (1987). Answers and questions. *Journal for Theory of Social Behavior, 17*, 513-529.

Prigogine, I. (1979). *Vom Sein zum Werden*. Munchen: Piper.

Schulenberg, J. E., Vondracek, F. W., & Crouter, A. C. (1984). The influence of the family on vocational development. *Journal of Marriage and the Family, 46,* 129-143.

Schütz, A. (1932). *Der sinnhafte Aufbau der sozialen Welt.* Vienna: Julius Springer.

Stebbins, R. A. (1970). Career: The subjective approach. *Sociological Quarterly, 11,* 32-49.

Tajfel, H. (Ed.). (1984). *The social dimension of social psychology.* Cambridge: Cambridge University Press.

Turvey, M. T., Shaw, R. E., & Mace, W. (1978). Issues in the theory of action: Degree of freedom, coordinative structures and coalitions. In J. Requin, (Ed.), *Attention and performance VII: Proceedings of the Seventh International Symposium on Attention and Performance* (pp. 557-595). Hillsdale, NJ: Erlbaum.

Twaddle, A. C. (1981). Sickness and the sickness career: Some implications. In L. Eisenberg & A. Kleinman (Eds.), *The relevance of social science for medicine* (pp. 111-133). Dortrecht, the Netherlands: D. Reidel.

Valach, L. (1986). *An action theoretical conception of career processes.* Paper presented to the Annual Conference of the British Sociological Association, Loughborough.

Valach, L., Cranach, M. von, & Kalbermatten, U. (1988). Social meaning in the observation of goal directed action. *Semiotica, 71,* 243-259.

Volpert, W. (1974). *Handlungsstrukturanalyse als Beitrag zur Qualifikationsforschang.* Köln: PahlRugenstein.

Wicker, A. W., & King, J. A. (1988). Life cycles of behavior settings. In J. E. McGrath (Ed.), *The social psychology of time: New perspectives* (pp. 182-200). Beverly Hills, CA: Sage.

Williams, R. (1981). *Career management and career planning.* London: HM Stationery Office.

Young, R. A. (1984). Vocation as relationship. *Counseling and Values, 28,* 169-178.

Young, R. A., & Marks, S. E. (1986). Understanding attributional processes in cross-cultural counselling. *International Journal for the Advancement of Counselling, 9,* 319-330.

8

Field Research
and Career Education

Donald Fisher

Educational institutions are complex interactional areas, which are held together through intersecting moral, political, and social orders.[1] What occurs within these institutions emerges from what respective interactants bring to them. There is a web of interactions. Educators and students are not passive but rather are self-conscious and active. These participants construct lines of conduct in the face of outside and internal forces. To understand this world, which is essentially shifting, researchers must enter it as *participant observers*. This is vital if they are to avoid the fallacy of objectivism, that is, the imputing of motive from the observer to the subject. Only through participation can the researcher focus on the process whereby behavior is constructed, and not simply the means or the ends. By situating themselves in the institutional settings, researchers can confront the educational experience over and through time, document the process, and, in the words of Herbert Blumer "lift the veils" off the "silent language" of the culture (Blumer, 1969). The objective for field researchers is to enter the world of those whose behaviors we wish to understand and thereby access the possibilities for grasping the motives, the values, the beliefs, and the forces that lie underneath and behind the actions of research subjects.

The general intent of this chapter is to provide an overview of the ways in which field researchers have approached the study of career education. Career education will refer to the explicit institutional attempt to educate people for and into careers. In addition, this concept will include the more general socialization for work that is part of most educational experiences whether inside or outside formal educational institutions. The chapter will be divided into four sections: first, a discussion of what is meant by "field" research—a rather limited definition will be posited that is housed primarily in the discipline of sociology and the perspective known as symbolic interactionism; second, a summary of some of the classic studies of career education that have utilized a field approach; third, an analytic summary of the current work in this genre, and finally, the chapter will conclude with a discussion of the advantages and disadvantages of the field approach for studying educational experiences.

A DEFINITION OF FIELD RESEARCH

Fieldwork is a generic term that refers to what is a long and established research tradition within the disciplines of sociology and anthropology (Burgess, 1984, 1985). The focus is on participant observation and the use of ethnographic techniques to record these observations.[2] The approach is clearly nonexperimental and in part emerged in opposition to the spread of natural scientific procedures into the social sciences. In the sense that statistics are not used to convert social process into variables, so the approach is nonquantitative. Fieldwork is a craft rather than a technology. Because the research is the measuring instrument, it rests with the individual to learn the craft through reading and doing.

As noted in the introduction, I am going to focus on the field research that has been done by sociologists. Further, while this approach in sociology has roots in ethnomethodological and phenomenological perspectives, my intention is to limit my discussion to the work that has been motivated primarily by symbolic interactionism. This latter perspective can be seen as an unbroken line of thought that began with John Dewey and George Herbert Mead providing a challenge and an alternative to the predominant stimulus response model in the social sciences. It is a unique perspective that offers substantial insights into the meaning of our world. Mind, body, and environment are linked not in an abstract formula that is capable of providing categories and positive results, but rather in a meaningful way for individuals reflecting on their own actions, thoughts and behaviors. The key concepts *society, mind, self, objects*, and *act* are linked together so that the emphasis is always on *interpretation, understanding,* and *meaning* in the social process. Symbolic interaction is both the medium for the development of human beings and the process by which human beings associate (Manis & Meltzer, 1967; Mead, 1934; Rose, 1962).

This perspective does not separate the empirical world, theory and methodology. Instead, they are all part of the same quality. The act of research is just as much a part of symbolic interaction as the relations being studied. The implications for the researcher who adopts this perspective is to focus on the process of social interaction as it is, not as it might, should, or could be. The research actively includes all the situational and contextual influences rather than attempting to control for them. Whereas in experimental work the objective is to control parts of a given segment of social reality, in field research the objective is to search for understanding and explanation by concentrating on the "natural" complexity of empirical reality. It follows that the field researcher is constantly struggling to maintain a holistic gaze rather than a fragmented one.

Blumer (1969) contrasts his methodological approach with those of the "idealists" and the "realists," both of whom impose their view of the world on reality. For Blumer:

> Empirical science is an enterprise that seeks to develop images
> and conceptions that can successfully handle and accommodate

> the resistance offered by the empirical world under study. . .
> [Therefore, methodology] refers to, or covers, the principles that
> underlie and guide the full process of studying the obdurate
> character of the given empirical reality. (pp. 22-23)

In attacking mainstream sociological analysis, Blumer points to the fallacies that surround the classifying of processes as variables. The assumption that the independent variable predetermines the outcome of the dependent variable has no foundation in reality. The process of interpretation is ignored so that the product is substituted for the process. For Blumer, the whole approach is flawed precisely because one cannot classify the act of interpretation, which is a shifting and unpredictable entity, as a variable.

According to Denzin (1970), there are six methodological mandates associated with symbolic interactionism (p. 19).

1. Both symbols and interaction must be brought together before an investigation is complete. The researchers must view human conduct from the point of view of those they are studying. They must get inside the process of interaction. Researchers must gain firsthand knowledge if they are going to avoid the imposition of external second-hand images of social reality. For Blumer, the person who seeks to describe reality objectively is the most subjective and can see from the point of view of his or her images.

2. Blumer describes two processes that help the researcher to "get close", and "be a part" of the social action under study. (a) Exploration: The approach is flexible. The researcher begins with a large range of images and theories which are gradually narrowed down, and are capable of complete alteration depending on what is in each situation. There is a deliberate attempt not to operationalize concepts so as to allow for the emergence and grounding of meaning. (b) Inspection: This process involves both examination and analysis. For Blumer, "inspection is flexible, imaginative, creative and free to take new directions" (Blumer, 1969, p. 44). The nature of analytical elements are developed through the examination of the empirical world rather than being set in advance of the study. The relation between elements is also a developing process that requires scrutiny.

3. Methods must move at the individual and social level simultaneously. Linkages between the conceptions that people have of themselves and the group(s) of which they are a part, must be observed.

4. The researcher must consider the "situated aspects" of human conduct. The aim is to understand how people act toward their objects. The method focuses on the meaning of objects (the environment) for individuals. There is the need to train and cultivate the act of "taking the role of the other."

5. Methods must be capable of capturing the process elements of human interaction. The concern must be with understanding the objects of the society or groups as they arise from action. Through this understanding the nature of

the social act in question will become clearer. This is particularly important when considering a new joint act. To understand and explain joint action it must be situated both horizontally and vertically. The research must, therefore, capture both the sychronic and the diachronic aspects of social interaction.

6. The very act of engaging in research must be seen from the perspective of symbolic interaction. The concept and method are inseparable, and act as a sensitizing influence on one's perception. Researchers must, therefore, guard against letting their own objects interfere in the process. The researcher becomes a "reflexive" practitioner.[3]

Classic Studies in Career Education

Following the methodological mandates, researchers who adopt this perspective make the strategic decision to try and understand the educational experience from the perspective of the social actors. They decide not to impose their own "definitions of the situation." The most consistent and successful researcher in this category is Howard S. Becker, who with various colleagues has been working in educational settings since the early 1950s. His early work utilized the concept of *identity* to explicate the career patterns of teachers (Becker, 1952; Becker, 1956; Becker & Carper, 1956). The study that is generally regarded as the most important methodologically is *Boys in White* (1961) which Becker co-authored with E. C. Hughes, B. Geer, and A. Strauss. The authors chose to look at the Kansas Medical School through the eyes of the students. They focused primarily on the problem of discovering what the medical school did to medical students in addition to giving them a technical education. The researchers assumed that the way these students conducted their lives was a product of their interaction with each other when faced with the day-to-day problems of medical school. The research method was participant observation. The participants focused on different groups of students at different stages in their education. Part of the time was spent observing the students in a continuous and total way, so that, for example, the observer would spend all day with a group, sleep in the dorm, and so on. Some 50 members of the staff were also interviewed, but these data were only used in a sensitizing manner. The emphasis was on how the students saw their world. As Becker and colleagues (1961) put it:

> We studied those matters which seemed to be of importance to the people we studied, those matters about which they themselves seemed interested or concerned. Second, we studied those matters which seemed to be the occasion of conflict or tension between the students and the other social categories of persons with whom they came into contact in the school. (p. 20)

The fieldnotes were indexed under coded topics as the observation was in process, yet there was a constant interplay between searching for particular things while at the same time being aware of the importance of "emergence." The researchers were constantly aware and consciously looking for the unexpected. As they noted:

> In short, what appears in our field notes depended in part on the hypotheses we were attempting to explore, but our fieldnotes also contain material not bearing on any hypothesis under consideration at the time, on the premise that we might later wish to construct hypotheses on points of which we were not yet aware. (Becker et al., 1961, p. 28)

Students were interviewed both formally and informally. The informal interviews were conducted with individuals and groups, the focus being on their class and educational background and on future professional plans. While some of the early interviews were conducted with groups, the researchers found that the social dynamics inhibited some individuals and, therefore, they decided to concentrate on single interactions where sympathetic questions were asked. A more formal structured interview was conducted with a random sample of students for each school year. In addition, a sample of the staff were interviewed about their careers, their aspirations, their attitudes toward students, and their educational philosophy.

In the analysis of the data, the researchers took note and quantified whether statements were voluntary or directed by the observer. These categories were crosstabulated to take account of whether the statements were made to the observer alone or to others in everyday conversation, and whether these were individual or group activities (See Becker et al., 1961, table p. 43). In the process of analysis, the researchers looked not just for positive items of a particular theme or pattern, but also for negative items that might then contradict and suggest a new line of inquiry. Three main concepts emerged from the data: (a) group perspectives; (b) student culture, which emerges from the consistency of perspectives concerning the level and direction of academic effort between students and in relation to the "role of student"; and (c) organization and institutional setting.

The researchers see a "perspective" arising when people face choice points, that is, "problematic situations." For these authors, "perspectives differ from values in being situationally specific" (Becker et al., 1961, p. 36). They also distinguish between immediate and long-range perspectives, so that one can identify changing perspectives in the short and the long range. These students entered medical school with a long range "idealist" perspective in terms of their future practice and profession. In the short range, they became "cynical" and concerned with the day to day problem of getting through school. They soon realized that they could not learn all the material and had to make choices. This meant finding out "what the teacher wanted." The most important thing was to "get through school," a view that united the whole class. In the clinical years the students presented a collective front to their superiors to protect each other, and to gain the knowledge and practice needed to get a license. Patients were defined in terms of the student culture. This meant that the students were concerned with doing well and passing. They were not concerned about the patients as individuals. Towards the end of school, the students are once again openly idealistic about the practice of medicine. Even so, their idealism was different. The students were more informed, more specific, more knowledgeable, and more professional.

The authors conclude that the students had collectively set the level and direction of their efforts to learn. The various perspectives had combined into a whole, which was a complex of mutual expectations. To this whole, the researchers gave the label *student culture*. In effect, the students had formed a "community of fate." The culture had a clear and substantial impact on the sorts of careers and the vocational and professional identities that were developed in this educational setting.[4]

As indicated earlier, there is a close association for these writers between the concepts of career and identity. Indeed, for Everett Hughes, who pioneered the sociological study of careers and occupations, to study career was to study identities (Hughes, 1952). For Hughes,

> The career includes not only the processes and sequences of learning techniques of the occupation, but also the progressive perception of the whole system and of possible places in it, and the accompanying changes in conceptions of the work and of one's self in relation to it. (Hughes, 1971, p. 295)

It follows that as a person's career unfolds, then changes in structural position are necessarily constitutive of changes in identity. For Becker and Strauss (1956), in their analysis of adult socialization, career is unpredictable. The journey that is a career moves people "up, along and down" into unexpected and novel places even though in some ways the destinations are foreseen. In dealing with this reality, adults "must gain, maintain and regain a sense of personal identity. . . . Identity is never gained or maintained once and for all" (p. 263).

The other study that deserves special mention is the monograph *The Educational-Decision Makers* by Cicourel and Kitsuse (1963). The study centered on the administrative process through which students in a high school were processed and distributed into categories of either college-qualified or non-college-qualified. The authors approached their task as phenomenological interactionists. The focus was on the way in which the organizational personnel had constructed the ongoing social organization in which the students were defined, recorded and treated as instances of the college and non-college categories. The researchers divided their research tasks into two areas. First, they examined the "rate-producing-process." The aim here was to explore the "vocabulary and syntax" of the language used by personnel to identify types. In other words, the researchers wanted to explore the "common sense constructs" used by these actors. Second, they examined the consequences of these identification and classification processes for the development and direction of any given student's career in school. The concept of *career* was utilized as a method of describing and charting a sequence of organizational directions and actions taken toward students.

Preliminary fieldwork emphasized counselors as strategic because they identified talent and dealt with any students who displayed discrepancy between tested ability and achievement. The fact that problems were interpreted in psychological and clinical terms had important consequences. This orientation served to deflect administrators from examining the organization and methods of the school system, including the counselors, as sources of academic problems. Another consequence was the creation of a category of students that needed therapeutic treatment. There was an increasing stress on social and mental judgment in this process. It followed that the researchers decided to examine the counselor's position of authority/power as a validating agent of the students' future career.

The researchers did not set out to test hypotheses but rather to explore general notions about the impact of organizational procedures and professional ideologies on the careers of high school students. They were interested in the categories by which the actors on a daily basis organized their thoughts and experiences. They were concerned with how situations were defined, the criteria for these definitions, and with the commonsense manner that was used to place students in these categories. To accomplish these objectives, the researchers open-ended interviews. In an effort to get at the actors' definitions, these interviews were made difficult for the actors because the interviewer was constantly probing. With the use of a technique of annoying the respondent by following initial questions with probing questions like "How's that?" and "Could you tell me more about that?" the researchers hoped to get at the deeper information.[5] The interviewer asked the question and then carefully avoided giving the subject any help at first, but then gradually let the subject "off the hook." These probes followed standardized limits. There was a specific number of questions on each point.

The research design included three groups: a student sample of 100, the parents of the students in the sample, and 22 counselors. Open-ended interviews were conducted with everyone. As Cicourel and Kitsuse (1963) noted:

> The questions were designed to pinpoint the social processes whereby students and parents made decisions on the choice of curriculum and future aspirations, their knowledge of the curriculum, and their interaction with the school. The counselors were interviewed to investigate how students are differentiated by various official and unofficial criteria. (p. 29)

Some social workers were also interviewed to examine the possibility of further differentiation.

The researchers first looked at organizational differentiation by asking: How are college-going intentions of students articulated within the organizational processes of the high school? Three course programs were available: (a) college-prep, (b) possible college, and (c) non-college. Participation in these streams was not simply dependent on student's choice, or School and College Ability Test scores, or grade point averages. When there were discrepancies in a student record, the counselor was called in to evaluate. Evaluations were done periodically. From these data the researchers concluded that

> the characteristic interpretation made by the counselors and other school personnel of SCAT/grade point discrepancies is that students perform below or above their tested ability as a consequence of motivational, personal, and social "problems," not methods of teaching, preparation (readiness), or aptitude. (Cicourel & Kitsuse, 1963, p. 62).

The researchers asked the counselors to describe their categories of assignment (achievement types) and found definite discrepancies (considering individual students) between these assignments and the objective tests. Types of students were produced that the organizational personnel expected to have "problems."

The researchers (Cicourel & Kitsuse, 1963) followed up by exploring the social class categories that the counselors used. The counselors were asked the following questions:

a. How many social statuses, that is, social class groups, would you say there are here at Lakeshore High School?
b. How would you describe, in general, each of the groups you mentioned?
c. How would you place each of the students named on these cards [handing him a set of cards with the names of all the students in the sample] into each of the groups you mentioned? (p. 66).

The questions were designed so that respondents would interpret these categories in their own terms.

The researchers found that the social types identified were not strictly hierarchical as in the conventional social class scale. The types were pluralistic and seemed based on a combination of aspiration and the rejection or withdrawal of students from participation in school and off-campus activities. The materials suggested that achievement classification (objective tests) did not account for the majority of achievement types identified, and that the conventional social class categories were no better.

The next focus was on the bureaucratization of the counseling system. To identify the professional perspective, the researchers interviewed an outside sample of 19 counselors who were taking courses at Northwestern University. In order to further explore the organization of counseling activities, the researchers asked the study sample the following question: "How do students come to your attention?" Finally, the researchers explored how the differential identification and classification of student problems was affected by bureaucratic organization. They found that the professionally oriented counselor would seek out students with problems and attempt to "probe" for the underlying causes. For the counselor-teacher, the main preoccupation was with the underachiever. They found that "the implementation of the college-going aspirations is made more problematic by the ways in which they are interpreted and reinterpreted by professionals in a bureaucratically organized system" (Cicourel & Kitsuse, 1963, p. 101). Cases were defined in a commonsense manner into two principal types: *disciplinary* and *poor academic performance*. With increasing bureaucratization and professionalization, there was more of a search for underlying problems. This led to the "managed student," about whom the counselor had information that covered all aspects of life. The record keeping increased and became more professional. There was a continuing tension for counselors concerning their occupational identity and whether they should be "talent scouts" or should be more concerned with individual adjustment.

In conclusion, the researchers identified what they labeled *organizational sponsorship*. This is a different form of the ascription or sponsorship principle of placement which is implemented by the bureaucratic set of procedures. As Cicourel and Kitsuse (1963) put it:

> The characteristics that determine placement by this principle would not be the traditional attributes of caste, kinship, race, sex, or other biologically or culturally determined traits of individuals or groups, but the data of test score records, biographical history of family or personal problems, childhood accidents and traumas, academic difficulties, adjustment problems, and the like. (p. 141)

The contingencies of social mobility were controlled within a bureaucratic setting where professional education doctrines, policies, and practices were fused with clinical and commonsense conceptions which allowed for the interpretation of information and for the counselor to differentiate between potential success and failure. The authors concluded their study by noting that "the effective realization of equal opportunity is a problem of organizational implementation" and not of better, more objective tests.

CONTEMPORARY STUDIES OF CAREER EDUCATION

There is a dearth of field research on career education. Searches of the social science abstracts and the use of an education data base produced a mere handful of articles. Nonetheless, in the last two decades there has been an enormous expansion in the number of "interactionist" studies in the sociology of education. The "new" sociologists adopted this methodological perspective as the essential and most appropriate technique. Building on the community study tradition in British sociology, researchers like Hargreaves and Lacey provided new insights into the school as a community (Hargreaves, 1967; Lacey, 1970). The work since the early 1970s has focused on what happens inside the classrooms. We now know a great deal about the form and shape of the educational experience and how knowledge in educational settings is managed, organized, and distributed.[6] Titles like "Interaction in the Classroom," "Life in School." "Sociology and the School: An Interactionist Perspective," and "The Negotiated Order of Schooling" give some sense of what has become almost an industry (Delamont, 1983; Hammersley & Woods, 1984; Martin, 1976; O'Keefe & Faupel, 1987; Woods, 1983). The studies that contribute to our understanding of career education provide a general orientation rather than detailed sociological accounts of these practices. The work on sex socialization (Delamont, 1980), on learning "women's work" (Deem, 1980)[7], on race/gender stereotyping (Fuller, 1980), and on the reproduction of social class divisions (Anyon, 1981; Sharp & Green, 1975), provides a general framework for studies of the ways in which education socializes people for work. Similarly, more recent studies of the culture of schooling such as the work of Everhart (1983) on adolescent culture provide general signposts about the context of career education.[8] Everhart spent two years doing fieldwork in a junior high school where he focused on the lives of approximately 10 students. While he began with a symbolic interactionist outlook, Everhart consciously attempted to take account of the structural regularities in the setting. Drawing on the work of Jürgen Habermas, this author concluded that 'technical interest' is the dominant cognitive interest that is reinforced in most schools. This leads to a knowledge mode that Everhart calls "reified knowledge" (for Habermas, "empirical-analytic") and social action that is predominantly instrumental (Everhart, 1983, pp. 239-275).

While there are no studies in this genre that approach the study of career education using the narrow definition, there are a number of fine studies that contribute to our understanding of the construction of what we might call vocational or occupational identities. Knowing that the majority of participants in education regard the experience as being for the most part about vocation and career, that is, a socialization for life, it makes sense to include some of these more broadly focused studies. Once again, the concept *identity* and the related concept *status passage* are particularly useful.[9] Fuller (1980) was able to show that the superficially bad behavior of black females in class enabled them to mask their academic and job aspirations from black males who they felt would have rejected and ridiculed them (Fuller, 1980). Helen Roberts's (1986) case study of the transition from school to work for girls who leave school without any credentials shows how they end up in low-paying jobs with little training and few opportunities for promotion. Sallie Westwood in *All Day and Every Day* (1984) went the next step by doing her fieldwork in the type of factory in which the Roberts's subjects were likely to work. As a participant observer, Westwood was able to venture inside the lives of these women workers and provide insight into their sources of identity. The analysis goes beyond the immediate contexts of family and factory and places these events in the structural reproduction of male and female labor.

Two studies stand out as the modern classics in this genre. The first is Paul

Willis's field study of working-class boys, *Learning to Labor* (1981). Willis set out to find an answer to a deceptively simple question: How do working-class kids get working-class jobs? He chose participant observation as his method and decided to provide an ethnographic account because "without always knowing how, [this way of presenting material] can allow a degree of the activity, creativity and human agency within the object of study to come through into the analysis and into the reader's experience" (Willis, 1981, p. 3).[10] The main case study focused on 12 nonacademic, working-class boys who were attending a nonselective secondary modern school in a West Midlands, England, industrial town. These boys were selected through friendship networks and because they belonged in some way to an oppositional culture within the school. Five comparative studies were undertaken during the same period: (a) a group of working-class conformist boys in the same school; (b) a group of working-class conformist boys in a nearby mixed secondary modern school which had the reputation of being "rougher"; (c) a group of working-class nonconformist boys in the single-sex grammar school; (d) a group of working-class nonconformist boys in a comprehensive school that was near the middle of the larger conurbation in which the original town was housed; and (e) a group of mixed-class nonconformists boys in a high-status grammar school in the most exclusive area of the conurbation. As Willis noted, "As far as possible, all groups were in the same school year, were friendship groups, and were selected for their likelihood of leaving school at the statutory minimum leaving age of sixteen" (1981, p. 5).

The main group was studied intensively. These boys were observed in class, around school, and during their leisure activities. Willis conducted regular recorded group discussions, did informal interviews, and maintained diaries. Willis participated in classes as a student which cut across the whole timetable and sat in on a run of "career" classes. He taped long conversations with the parents of the main group boys, with senior teachers in the school and with teachers in the junior school who had been their main contacts, and with the career officers. In addition, Willis followed the main group and three selected boys from the comparison groups into the workplace, where he conducted 15 short participant observations working alongside the subjects. Finally, Willis conducted taped interviews with the boys and did selected interviews with foremen, managers, and shop stewards.

Willis documents a counter culture that has as its most "basic, obvious and explicit dimension," an "entrenched general and personalized opposition to 'authority'" (Willis, 1981, p. 11). This culture is a style that is instantly recognized by students and teachers alike. The style and all the elements of interaction that form it take on an almost ritualistic appearance as these boys celebrate their sense of masculine superiority. After the authorities, the next most important target for the "lads" are the conformist boys, who not only ally themselves with authority in the school but are actually enthusiastic about schooling. These conforming students are labeled by the lads as the "ear'oles" or "lobes." The "lobes" are perceived to be effeminate and outside the masculine culture of working-class work. The alliance with authority is a measure of their "softness" and in the opinion of the lads it illustrates that the lobes do not really understand school for what it really is. The lads pity the lobes for their lack of experience and their naiveté.

In contrast, the lads are defiant. They manage to create a culture that sees through the domination of middle-class schooling. They partly penetrate the official versions of working-class culture and celebrate what they take to be a superior oppositional stance, yet at the moment of most penetration these lads have simultaneously deluded and, therefore, damaged themselves. The opposition is part of the process of cultural reproduction, which is folded into the more general relation of social reproduction. The choice of manual labor by these lads is part of the internal contradiction of the relations of production. Willis concludes that for a good proportion of working-class youth, particularly the disaffected, the process of getting a working-class job "is in the form of a partial cultural penetration of their own real conditions and a mystified celebration of manual work which nevertheless preserves something of a collective, rational, though incomplete, logic" (Willis, 1981, p. 185).

The second study is Lois Weis's research on black community college students, *Between Two Worlds* (1985). Building on the earlier work on white community college students by London (1978), Weis conducted a participant observation study documenting the culture of these black students who are between the worlds of work and education. As Weis notes, she adopted this methodology because it allowed her "to explore both the direct experiences of education and the way in which these experiences are worked over and through the praxis of cultural discourse" (Weis, 1985, p. 171). During the academic year 1979-1980, Weis immersed herself in the life of the college by attending classes and conducting in-depth interviews with both faculty and students. A record was kept of all comments and experiences, whether in the classroom, the corridors, the stairwells, the offices, or the cafeteria, coffee shop, or bar. Weis documents the culture of the college and shows that it is neither the product of entirely internal or external forces but rather a culture that the students actively and consciously create and recreate. Weis is able to show how this black student culture "acts primarily to ensure that the vast majority of students will return to the ghetto streets" (1985, p. 159). This is in spite of the fact that the students attend the college in order to escape the under class and become part of the dominant culture, and in spite of the fact that the institution is explicitly designed to help them do just that. As Weis concludes, "it is the culture that students 'produce' within the college that makes a significant contribution to low 'success' rates in traditional academic terms and the reproduction of a social structure that is strikingly unequal by class and race" (1985, p. 159).

CONCLUSION

The four studies that I have highlighted are special methodologically because they follow the methodological mandates referred to earlier in this chapter. First, these studies do synthesize symbols and interaction. The authors focus on linking statements, definitions, and actions into meaningful description. The reporting of conversations as part of the presentation in Willis; the linking in table form of observations, statements, and actions by Becker et al.; and the comparison by Cicourel and Kitsuse of the differentiated students and the definitions of counselors are all indicative of this synthesis. All four studies move at the individual and social levels. Becker and colleagues focused on individual and group interactions and generalized the items into collective perspectives. While Cicourel and Kitsuse concentrated on the three main groups as social entities, they did also use individual expressions of a perspective as the basis for those group interactions. Similarly, Weis traced the constitution of the culture of the community college by bringing together the individual and institutional expressions for both students and faculty. Willis weaves together expressions of individuality, of friendship and of belonging to group, culture, and class so that the reader can feel what it is to be a "lad." All these studies consider the situated aspects of their research. They describe situations in detail and they insist on participating in order to discover how the actors define their situations. Only Cicourel and Kitsuse stepped back from embracing a participant observer role.

Becker and colleagues saw the movement through medical school as a process and they tried to capture the essence of that process by concentrating on groups of students who were at different stages. In Cicourel and Kitsuse's study the primary focus was on the process by which students become defined as belonging to a category. Weis and Willis step inside the process of producing culture. Weis stays very much within the boundaries of the institution whereas Willis is more ambitious as he follows the lads through school into the community, into their homes, and finally into the workplace. All the researchers see their work as symbolic interaction and include themselves in the research design. Concepts like *perspective, career, identity, definition of a category,* and *culture* are used in a sensitizing manner. This evaluation applies equally to the general concepts used in field research such as *definition of the situation, taking the role of the other,* and *commonsense definitions.*

The major criticism that can be applied to the earlier studies by Becker et al. and by Cicourel and Kitsuse is that they were ahistorical and, in a structural sense, atheoretical. The reader was not given sufficient detail of the history of the individual school or college, and the events were not placed in their larger historical context. Similarly, these early studies and the perspective of symbolic interactionism is open to the criticism that they are unable to provide structural, macro-explanations. Determinism is the complete antithesis of the interactionist orientation. Field researchers set out to examine and understand the world of those they study from their subjects' perspective and not from the standpoint of external and abstract concepts. It follows that underlying these studies there is a tension between a deterministic stance, that is, the imposition of hypotheses, and the search for emergent hypotheses from the data. In an attempt to deal with this tension, Glaser and Strauss have proposed what I will label *inductive dialectical theorizing* (Glaser, 1978; Glaser & Strauss, 1967). These authors make a strong plea for what they call "grounding theory" and proceed to describe a series of techniques for practicing this art.

While Willis and Weis are open to the same criticism with regard to historiography, they cannot be accused of theoretical insensitivity. In line with current developments in the sociology of education, both authors take a neo-marxist perspective on their work. Both contribute to the debate on reproduction and give insight into the role of contradictions in the production of consciousness. Willis uses the concept *partial penetration* as a tool to draw the reader inside the nexus between the lads culture and the structural conditions in which they are housed. Similarly, Weis uses the concept *limitation* to refer to the way in which the process of producing the culture involves in itself the seeds of its own domination.

Future Directions

We clearly need more studies like the ones discussed in this chapter. Specifically, we need field research that is longitudinal and that cuts across the boundaries of education and work. These studies should focus on career education in all its forms so that we can better understand the production of work roles in the family, in educational institutions, and in the workplace. The topics/institutions that might be studied are endless, but some interesting work has already been done on the career education of teachers (Hanson & Herrington, 1976), work experience in schools (Moore, 1976), and the culture of the workplace (Deem & Salaman, 1985). However, as noted at the beginning of this chapter, the quantity of work is minute particularly when one compares field studies to the enormous literature on career/vocational education that continues to be churned out using quantitative psychologically based methodologies (Garbin & Stover, 1980). If, as many writers suggest, vocational/career education is the means by which some kids are given a second-class education in order to maintain the class stratification in our society (Grubb & Lazerson, 1975; Wagner, 1980), then the need to "get inside" these processes is even more pronounced. There is a need for a complete overhaul, both conceptually and empirically, of the relation between education and work. The best starting point I would argue for such an overhaul is with a field research perspective. As Becker (1983) points out, only by digging under the surface of social reality can we hope to truly understand and explain social phenomena. This means that we must take on the role of participant. The best field research holds out the prospect of bringing description, understanding and explanation together in and through time. This means that fieldwork at its best should be simultaneously historical, theoretical, particularistic, and generalizing.

NOTES

1. For the full explication of this description, see Waller (1967), *Sociology of Teaching* (New York: Wiley). An indication of the complexity of the emergent social reality is the report by Jackson that classroom teachers engage in approximately 1,000 interpersonal exchanges each day (1968, p. 11). On average, Smith and Geoffrey estimated that classroom teachers initiate 80 individual interchanges with students each hour (1968, p. 5).
2. For many researchers, the label *ethnography* has become synonymous with what in this chapter is being called fieldwork. Whereas Hammersley and Atkinson 1983) want to use ethnography to refer to both a general approach and a technique simultaneously, I prefer to make a distinction between these two aspects.
3. See Hammersley and Atkinson (1983) for a discussion of reflexivity. For an overview of fieldwork in education, see Bogdan and Biklin (1982).
4. To explore the more general questions of what it was like to be a university student, the researchers did a follow-up study of Kansas University, the first part of which was published in 1968. See Becker, Geer, and Hughes (1968).
5. This technique is very similar to the one used by ethnomethodologists as they attempt to expose the deeper meanings in an interaction process. See Garfinkel (1967).
6. For an overview of the development of the sociology of education, see Banks (1982).
7. In Deem (1980), see specifically Katherine Clarricoates, "The importance of being Ernest . . . Tom . . . Jane: The perception and categorization of gender conformity and gender deviation in primary schools." Clarricoates did participant observation studies in four primary schools and shows how teacher views on sex differences produces differential behavior toward boys and girls.
8. This book can be seen as part of a continuing interest within sociology on the adolescent years. See Coleman (1961) and Cuzick (1972).
9. Glaser and Strauss (1971) have characterized the socialization for life aspects of education as "status passage."
10. A study that, in some ways, runs parallel to Willis's work was done by Angela McRobbie (1978) on working-class girls.

REFERENCES

Anyon, J. (1981). Social class and school knowledge. *Curriculum Inquiry, 11*, 3-42.
Banks, O. (1982). The sociology of education, 1952-1982. *British Journal of Educational Studies, 30*, 18-31.
Becker, H. S. (1952). The career of the Chicago public school teacher. *American Journal of Sociology, 57*, 336-343.

Becker, H. S. (1956). The development of identification with an occupation. *American Journal of Sociology, 61,* 289-298.

Becker, H. S. (1983). Studying urban schools. *Anthropology and Education, 14,* 99-108.

Becker, H. S., & Carper, J. (1956). The elements of identification with an occupation. *American Sociological Review, 21,* 341-348.

Becker, H. S., Geer, B., & Hughes, E. C. (1968). *Making the grade.* New York: Wiley.

Becker, H. S., Hughes, E. C., Geer, B., & Strauss, A. (1961). *Boys in white: Student culture in medical school.* Chicago: University of Chicago Press.

Becker, H. S., & Strauss, A. (1956). Careers, personality and adult socialization. *American Journal of Sociology, 62,* 253-263.

Blumer, H. S. (1969). *Symbolic interactionism: Perspectives and method.* Englewood Cliffs, NJ: Prentice-Hall.

Bogdan, R. C., & Biklin, S. K. (1982). *Qualitative research for education: An introduction to theory and methods.* Boston: Allyn and Bacon.

Burgess, R. G. (1984). *In the field: An introduction to field research.* London: George Allan and Unwin.

Burgess, R. G. (1985). *Field methods in the study of education.* London: Falmer.

Burgess, R. G. (Ed.). (1986). *Exploring society* (2nd ed.). London: Longman.

Cicourel, A. V., & Kitsuse, J. I. (1963). *The educational decision makers* [Monograph]. Indianapolis, IN: Bobbs Merrill.

Clarricoates, K. (1980). The importance of being Ernest . . . Tom . . . Jane: The perception and categorization of gender conformity and gender deviation in primary schools. In R. Deem (Ed.), *Schooling for women's work* (pp. 26-41). London: Routledge, Kegan Paul.

Coleman, J. S. (1961). *The adolescent society.* New York: Free Press.

Cuzick, P. (1972). *Inside high school.* New York: Holt, Rinehart & Winston.

Deem, R. (Ed.). (1980). *Schooling for women's work.* London: Routledge, Kegan Paul.

Deem, R., & Salaman, G. (Eds.). (1985). *Work, culture and society.* Milton Keynes, England: Open University Press.

Delamont, S. (1980). *Sex roles and the school* (2nd ed.). London: Methuen.

Delamont, S. (1983). *Interaction in the classroom* (2nd ed.). London: Methuen.

Denzin, N. K. (1970). *The research act.* Chicago: Aldine.

Everhart, R. B. (1983). *Reading, writing and resistance: Adolescence and labor in a junior high school.* Boston: Routledge, Kegan Paul.

Fuller, M. (1980). Black girls in a London comprehensive school. In R. Deem (Ed.), *Schooling for women's work* (pp. 52-65). London: Routledge, Kegan Paul.

Garbin, A. P., & Stover, R. G. (1980). Vocational behavior and career development, 1979: A review. *Journal of Vocational Behavior, 17,* 125-170.

Garfinkel, H. (1967). *Reading in ethnomethodology.* Englewood Cliffs, NJ: Prentice-Hall.

Glaser, B. S. (1978). *Theoretical sensitivity: Advances in the methodology of grounded theory.* Mill Valley, CA: Sociology Press.

Glaser, B. S., & Strauss, A. (1967). *The discovery of grounded theory: Strategies for qualitative research.* Chicago: Aldine.

Glaser, B. S., & Strauss, A. (1971). *Status passage.* New York: Aldine.

Grubb, N., & Lazerson, M. (1975). Rally round the workplace: Continuities and fallacies in career education. *Harvard Educational Review, 45,* 451-474.

Hammersley, M., & Atkinson, P. (1983). *Ethnography: Principles and practice.* London: Tavistock.

Hammersley, M., & Woods, P. (Eds.). (1984). *Life in school: The sociology of pupil culture.* Milton Keynes, England: Open University Press.

Hanson, D., & Herrington, M. (1976). *From college to classroom: The probationary year.* London: Routledge, Kegan Paul.

Hargreaves, D. H. (1967). *Social relations in a secondary school.* London: Routledge, and Kegan Paul.

Hughes, E. C. (1952). The sociological study of work: An editorial forward. *American Journal of Sociology, 57,* 423-426.

Hughes, E. C. (1971). *The Sociological eye: Selected papers.* Chicago: Aldine/Atherton.

Jackson, P. W. (1968). *Life in classrooms.* New York: Holt, Rinehart & Winston.

Lacey, C. (1970). *Hightown grammar.* Manchester: Manchester University Press.

London, H. B. (1978). *The culture of a community college.* New York: Praeger.

Manis, J. G., & Meltzer, B. M. (Eds.). (1967). *Symbolic interaction: A reader in social psychology.* Boston: Allyn and Bacon.

Martin, W. B. W. (1976). *The negotiated order of the school.* Toronto: McMillan.

McRobbie, A. (1978). Working class girls and the culture of femininity. In Women's Studies Group (Ed.), *Women take issue: Aspects of women's subordination* (pp. 96-108). London: Hutchinson.

Mead, G. H. (1934). *Mind, self and society.* Chicago: University of Chicago Press.

Moore, D. T. (1976). Learning at work: Case studies in non school education. *Anthropology and Education Quarterly, 17,* 166-184.

O'Keefe, T. F., & Fuapel, C. E. (1987). The other face of the classroom: A study of ethnography. *Sociological Review, 7,* 141-151.

Piker, J., & Simon, R. (1984, June). *Studying education and work: A dialogue between two research frameworks.* Paper presented at the Canadian Society for the Study of Education, Guelph, Ontario.

Roberts, H. (1986). After sixteen: What choices? In R. G. Burgess (Ed.), *Exploring society* (2nd ed.) (pp. 91-113). London: Longman.

Rose, A.M. (1962). *Human behavior and social processes: An interactionist approach.* Boston: Houghton Mifflin.

Sharp, R., & Green, A. (1975). *Educational and social control: A study in progressive primary education.* London: Routledge & Kegan Paul.

Smith, L. M., & Geoffrey, W. (1968). *The complexities of an urban classroom.* New York: Holt, Rinehart & Winston.

Wagner, K. (1980). Ideology and career education. *Educational Theory, 30,* 195-213.

Waller, W. (1967). *Sociology of teaching.* New York: Wiley.

Weis, L. (1985). *Between two worlds: Black students in an urban community college.* Boston: Routledge & Kegan Paul.

Westwood, S. (1984). *All day and every day: Factory and amity in the making of women's lives.* London: Pluto.

Willis, P. (1981). *Learning to labor: How working class kids get working class jobs.* New York: Columbia University Press. (Original work published in 1977)

Woods, P. (1983). *Sociology and the school: An interactionist perspective.* London: Routledge & Kegan Paul.

Part III

Career Research Studies

9

Parental Influences on Career Development: A Research Perspective

Richard A. Young and John D. Friesen

We have undertaken research intended to map a heretofore largely unexamined area: what parents intentionally do to influence their children's lives (e.g., Young, Friesen, & Pearson, 1988). Our general aim in this research is to understand the process of career development from one ecological perspective, namely that of the family as a major socializing factor in the career development of children and youth. This chapter is concerned with issues of methodology and the study of career as they relate to the intentional activity of parents regarding the career development of their children.

The study of intentional behavior raises specific methodological issues that are addressed in a number of chapters in this book, for example, Cochran (1990), Polkinghorne (1990), and Valach (1990). Clearly some types of research methods that are alternative to traditional, quantitative approaches are appropriate to study questions raised by intentionality. However, it is not sufficient to know about the methods to be used. It is contingent on researchers who entertain alternative methods to ground their study in a thorough review of the research as well as in a theoretical framework. In this chapter, both a review of the literature on parental influence of career development and our ecological perspective are presented. The ecological perspective formed the basis for our research questions and underlies the series of research methods for current and future studies.

REVIEW OF RESEARCH

Family Background and Structural Variables

The influence of parents' social class on a child's educational and occupational attainment is clearly established. Rehberg and Hotchkiss (1979), reviewing socio-logical models and studies that incorporated parental socioeconomic status (SES), found it was a significant predictor of the child's eventual occupational attainment. In their review of the literature on contextual influences, Schulenberg, Vondracek, and Crouter (1984) suggested that socioeconomic status is one of the most powerful and consistent environmental predictors of occupational aspirations and attainment. They concluded that, in general, "SES begets SES" (p. 131). Socioeconomic status certainly appears to be one of the most consistent predictors of males' occupational levels (Brown, 1970). Sons have been seen as inheriting their fathers' occupational levels (Goodale & Hall, 1976).

Goodale and Hall's (1976) suggestion that parental interest and support mediate the relationship of SES to career clarifies the more complex relationship in women's development. This hypothesis has been upheld by other studies. For example, Breton's (1972) results from a large scale Canadian study showed that parental encouragement had the strongest impact on the educational intentions of boys and girls. Both family and school/community encouragement has been reported as a major facilitator of high-school girls' achievement motivation and planning for nontraditional careers (Farmer, 1980, 1985; Haber, 1980; McClure & Piel, 1978). The influence of fathers' encouragement has been noted as particularly important in the development of high achieving and nontraditional career women (Astin & Myint, 1971).

Other aspects of the family environment that have been found to have an impact on career development include maternal employment (Almquist & Angrist, 1971; Hoffman & Nye, 1974), birth order (Weller, Shlomi, & Zimont, 1976), early parent-child interaction (Medvene & Shueman, 1978; Roe & Siegelman, 1964), identification with parents (Hocks & Curry, 1983; Jackson & Meara, 1977; Ridgeway, 1978; Tangri, 1972), parental support (Goodale & Hall, 1976; Lunneborg, 1982), and perceived parental influence (McClure & Piel, 1978; O'Neill, Ohlde, Tolefson, Barke, Piggott, & Watts, 1980).

Studies on background and structural characteristics of families have provided us with a fund of useful information. They do not, however, elaborate on the family process and dynamics involved, except, to some extent, in studies on parental support and encouragement. Researchers still have little information about the ways in which such effects as socioeconomic status and parental encouragement get translated into actual expectations and work choices. Little is known about variables that go beyond the criterion of occupational attainment such as actual parent behaviors or the development of attitudes, values, and skills.

Socialization Influences

An increasing emphasis on women's vocational development has drawn attention to the differential socialization that boys and girls frequently receive in their families. Researchers have called for attention to be given to sex role-related characteristics and sex-role orientation as explanatory variables (Fitzgerald & Betz; 1983; Unger, 1979). Block (1979, 1983), in her reviews of the literature on the parental child-rearing orientation of mothers and fathers, found consistent evidence in favor of sex differentiated parental socialization behaviors. Moreover, the differentiation appears to increase with the age of the child and the sex-related values of the parents. The evidence also revealed a sex of parent-sex of child interaction. Female socialization stresses nurturant and expressive roles and teaches women to strive for approval in the social arena. As a result, women frequently lack characteristics such as instrumentality, assertiveness, and self-esteem, which are required for success in the occupational world today (Gilligan, 1982; Hoffman, 1972; Spence & Helmreich, 1980). Hackett and Betz (1981) suggest that female socialization practices do little to encourage strong self-efficacy expectations in women. This, coupled with external barriers to women's career development, causes their career options to be severely restricted. Gottfredson (1981) proposed that the circumscription of career choice starts very early in children's lives and centers on racial, social-class, and sex-role issues. She suggested that vocational interests are sacrificed to gender and prestige aspects of the social self long before youngsters encounter the job market. As marriage plans and values become more prominent, young women increasingly opt for traditional "feminine" occupations which will offer them less financial security in the future.

Although in the past, the socialization of men has fitted them well to the demands of the world of work, there is increasing evidence that social and economic changes will require equivalent changes in the socialization of young men. As the centrality of the work role diminishes in the current economic and technological climate, and as family roles become more salient and desirable for men (Pleck, 1982), they will need to be able to profit from the psychological protectiveness that multiple roles have been shown to provide (Baruch, Barnett, & Rivers, 1983). With so much evidence pointing to the important consequences of differential socialization of boys and girls, it is imperative that we begin to look in more detail at the ways in which parents prepare their children for life and the understanding that children have of their parents' intentions. Katz (1987), for example, delineated a range of family socialization behaviors, from parental emphasis on gender cues to parental modeling of occupational roles, that may affect children's gender schemata. These specific behaviors warrant investigation.

Ecological Integration

There appears to be a general movement toward recognizing that career development can be more fully understood within a relational perspective that elucidates the dynamic interaction between the developing person in a changing context (Vondracek, Lerner, & Schulenberg, 1986). Farmer (1985) recently designed and tested a multidimensional model to explore the influence of background, personal, and environmental variables on young people's achievement and career motivation. Her results attest to the complex, interactive effects of these three influence sets; she underlined the impact of the changing environment on career and achievement motivation. Super (1980) also recognized the importance of situational determinants and differentiated between remote determinants—that is, social structure and economic conditions—and intermediate determinants—that is, community and family. He proposed that career development takes place as the individual chooses and shapes a variety of work and nonwork related roles in four environments—home, community, school, and workplace. Like Super, Law (1981) also drew attention to the interaction between individual and context. He viewed career development as a process of construing a series of representations of self and situation based on interactions with the individuals in one's community, including the family. Law suggested that interaction processes not only transmit the effects of larger sociological variables, they also modify these effects.

Evidence about the role of the family in career development has not always been clear. The family has traditionally been thought of as an important influence on the career development of children, and studies have attested to this fact (for example, Breton, 1972). Adolescents have relied on their parents for this influence. Sebald (1986) for example, found that adolescents seek their parents' advice regarding their future education and career goals, although this activity declined somewhat in the 1970s. Many adolescents themselves, however, do not acknowledge any significant parental influence in their eventual career or educational choices (O'Neil et al., 1980). Some of this research has been conducted with young adolescents who may report lack of influence for reasons of an apparent desire for independence. As Lerner and Busch-Rossnagel (1981) point out, although individuals are inextricably tied to a group such as the family, they strive to see themselves as individuals. Moreover, the survival of the group depends on a certain adaptive level of variation.

Too often in the past, the agency of individuals has been overlooked. Gillis (1981) pointed to historical evidence to show that young people have a hand in the social construction of youth. They act on society and help create the circumstances in which they live, and they do this in continuity with their elders (Gillis, 1981; Lerner & Busch-Rossnagel, 1981). It is possible that, had studies exploring adolescents' perceptions of parental influence focused more on interactive processes and less on reductionistic outcome criteria such as choice of college major, they may have had more informative results. In their review of the influence of the family of origin on vocational development, Schulenberg, Vondracek, and Crouter (1984) note that the influence of family interaction patterns has been largely ignored by researchers. They conclude that a focus on family processes (that is, parent-child relationships) or socialization practices, would appear to be a fruitful domain within which to explore vocational development.

In the last few years, studies have begun to emerge that conceptualize the family as more than a mere context (Bell & Bell, 1983; Cooper, Grotevant, & Condon, 1983; Powers, Hauser, Schwartz, Noam, & Jacobson, 1983). Interactions between adolescents and parents are seen as shaping both the relationship and the individuals within it—both develop interdependently. As Youniss (1983) remarked, research that conceives of the family not as an abstraction but as a system that is co-constructed with society at large manages both to treat society in an acceptable psychological manner and to fully maintain the agency of the individual. As intentionality is derived from the communication and cooperative relations between two people (Meacham, 1984), studies need to be based on the relations between individuals. Exploring career development as a bidirectional process between parent and child within the context of the family environment enables us to explore how parents structure situations for children so as to make their intentions explicit and capable of guiding behavior.

THEORETICAL FRAMEWORK

As Vondracek, Lerner, and Schulenberg (1983) pointed out, vocational theory has tended, until very recently, to neglect the role of social, economic, and family contexts. The lack of a comprehensive developmental career theory has been an issue of concern to theorists in general as well as to researchers interested in the vocational development of women (Astin, 1984; Fitzgerald & Betz, 1983; Fitzgerald & Crites, 1980; Harmon & Farmer, 1983). The need for a life span perspective has been emphasized (Perun & Bielby, 1981; Vondracek, Lerner, & Schulenberg, 1983). Models have been proposed that attempt to take account of the dynamic interplay between work and nonwork related roles (Rapoport & Rapoport, 1980; Super, 1980) and between a broad array of individual and environmental variables (Astin, 1984; Farmer, 1985). What these models are incapable of addressing is the need for a microanalytic perspective that will enable researchers to truly balance an understanding of causality with one of process, that is, to apprehend not only why but also how and under what conditions.

Ecological and Contextual Constructs

It is now suggested that the adoption of an ecological perspective allows for a worthwhile synthesis between outcome and process variables and provides a means of addressing both objective and subjective reality (Gibbs, 1979). Bronfenbrenner's (1979) ecological model permits development to be understood as occurring in four hierarchically embedded contexts, the microsystem, the mesosystem, the exosystem, and the macrosystem.

Our current work on career development is clearly situated within the microsystem of Bronfenbrenner's model. The microsystem is concerned with the immediate settings containing the developing person in which the person engages in face-to-face interactions in ways that can influence the system as well as be influenced by it. An important feature of the microsystem is that it mediates and transmits the effects of the other systems to the developing person. For example, socioeconomic status (an exosystem variable) is transmitted by interpersonal transactions in the microsystem, some of which occur between the parent and the child. Stafford and Jackson (1983) showed how families (microsystem) mediate the prospect of unemployment (exosystem) for school leavers in an area of high unemployment.

The parental activities that are the focus of our work are, in Bronfenbrenner's (1979) terminology, molar activities; that is, they have a momentum of their own, persist through time, and have resistance to change, rather than being momentary. They also have complex goal structures. As such, they are considered to have the potential to influence the developing person. Bronfenbrenner noted the absence of concepts, methods, and data bearing on the content and interpersonal structure of molar activities exhibited in settings of everyday life by persons at varying stages of development.

The ecological approach consists in treating everything as existing in reciprocal relation to everything else. As Shotter (1983) suggested, what is described is a world-in-the-making and individuals are seen as makers rather than merely finders of what exists. Features of the contextual-dialectic paradigm (Lerner & Busch-Rossnagel, 1981) draw attention to a consideration of the individual in relationship and recognition of the social construction of development (Youniss, 1983, 1984). The process of development is seen as one in which agents cooperate to reach a common understanding (Ford, 1982; Furth, 1983; Youniss, 1980).

Intentionality and Action Theory

In general, research in the area of action theory takes a more microanalytic approach to the study of intentional action and deepens an understanding of the processes involved (Cranach, Kalbermatten, Indermuehler, & Gugler, 1982; Cranach & Valach, 1984; Valach, 1989). Chapman (1984) pointed out that the behavior of human beings is meaningful to them and that intentional action (acting to bring about a desired goal) is one of the most common forms of meaning by which people interpret their behavior. Development is a personally regulated process in which recognition is given to the fact that the development of the person is implied in his or her actions (Eckensberger & Meacham, 1984). Action theory stresses that development occurs within a social context and distinguishes itself from other approaches by its emphasis on the intersubjective nature of intentionality (Chapman, 1984; Youniss, 1984). Intentionality is derived from the communication and the cooperative relations between two people. Intentions within the mind of an individual are fluid and ephemeral; once they have been communicated they become stable and long-lasting. In the social context, intentions persist and are re-membered, and thus have the potential to guide and direct behavior rather than merely reflecting it (Meacham, 1984).

The use of contextualist and action theory constructs within the organizing framework of Bronfenbrenner's (1979) ecological model provides the theoretical basis for our current research. This framework enables us to examine how parents structure situations for children so as to influence their career development. It also allows us to take account of the transactional, interpenetrative relationship that occurs between parent and child. Finally, it permits a sensitivity to both subjective and objective realities, and supports our attempt to understand parents' actions from the subjective viewpoint of the agents involved.

RESEARCH PROCEDURES

To date, we have undertaken two studies in which we have used a number of research procedures that respond to both the issues of parental influence in this domain and our theoretical framework. We envision a third project that we will also describe briefly here. In the first study, we used the interview and the critical incident procedure (Flanagan, 1954). In a subsequent study, we added the Q-sort method (Block, 1978; Stephenson, 1953) and a procedure to elicit personal constructs. In the first and second studies we also collected information regarding family environment by means of the Family Environment Scale (Moos & Moos, 1981).

The Interview and Critical Incident Procedure

In the first stage of this research our purpose was to map the domain of (1) activities that parents use intentionally to influence the career development of their children and (2) interpersonal relations between the parent and young person that characterize these activities. It can be noted here that activities and interpersonal relations are two of three elements of Bronfenbrenner's (1979) microsystem. Our research is based on the assumption that there is inherent value for scholarship and the advancement of science and understanding in careful observation and description.

The critical incident technique is a set of flexible procedures devised by Flanagan (1954) for collecting observations of human behavior. Its essential component involves a request for an event or experience that was helpful in forwarding some aim: in the case of this research, forwarding the child or adolescent's career development. In our use of the critical incident technique, we began with a request for a broad description of the goals, directions, and aspirations of the young person's life, and subsequently sought specific events that were judged as having a significant impact in moving these aims forward. Two examples of incidents from the interviews are presented in the Appendix as Incidents 1 and 2. Eventually, the incidents contributed to the development of categories that represent parental activities and relations in this domain.

The use of the critical incident procedure was imbedded in a longer interview. Both the procedure and the interview fulfilled several of the goals of this research and met most of the 12 modes of understanding for qualitative research interviews proposed by Kvale (1983).

The interview and critical incident procedure allowed parents to describe what they had done to influence the career development of their child or adolescent. Parents were able to describe, from their perspective, intentional and volitional activities. In Incident 1, for example, the parent sets expectations about the prerequisites before an adolescent is allowed to babysit. In Incident 2, the mother advises her son to avoid certain friends. In a subsequent study, young adults were able to describe critical events in which their parents attempted to influence their career development.

The interview allowed a story to be told, several molar behaviors to be explained, and meaning to be ascribed to the activity. The narrative focused on the life world of the interviewees. In Incidents 1 and 2, the parents describe themselves as well as their children. On the average, parents were able to provide eight critical incidents, some of which ran from 500 to 800 words. These fairly uninterrupted descriptions were necessarily retrospective. The parent in Incident 2 began by saying that the incident stood out in her mind even though the an event occurred approximately nine years ago. The incidents also represented a naive understanding of career on the part of the interviewee (Young, 1988). Additionally, by obtaining extensive and rich descriptions of specific incidents, broader meanings could be inferred.

The critical incident interview also met the criterion of specificity (Kvale, 1983). We did not seek general opinions of the parents about what might be helpful in influencing their children or their general attitudes about child rearing. In Incidents 1 and 2, specific parental activities are described, that is, setting expectations and advising. The critical incidents elicited in these studies were also contextually sensitive in that they are about events that happen in specific families, and in a broad sense between two or more individuals. Parents addressed strategies they used with their children.

The interviews were conducted without specific presuppositions, categories, or interpretations. The interviewer remained open to the talk of the interviewee. At the same time there was enough specificity in the incidents to allow for categories to be created later.

Brodsky (1987) raised the issue of whether narratives such as these should be dismissed as hopelessly subjective and outside the interests of science. We propose that the issue of parental influence requires studies of this type. Narratives, as expressed in critical incidents, are not only how life is imagined to be (or how life is) for parents and children, but indeed, how career, in the broad sense, is transmitted. One studies these critical incidents not because they are necessarily true, but because they represent how individuals make sense of their own lives and the lives of those with whom they interact. From them we can learn what parents and adolescents consider worthy of taking into account, what they consider useful to deal with, and what can be avoided.

From the critical incident interview, we were able to construct several groups of categories, the most important of which were interpersonal interaction, parental activities (Young, Friesen, & Pearson, 1988), and parental intentions. In the cases of parental activities and parental intentions, the categories were constructed using the traditional critical incident procedure for creating categories (Flanagan, 1954); that is, incidents were grouped and labels attached until there was a sufficient range of categories to account for all the incidents. For the interpersonal interaction category, the incidents leant themselves to a categorization using Benjamin's (1974, 1984) Structural Analysis of Social Behavior (SASB). Since Benjamin's model was designed initially with parent-child interaction in mind, it was found to be particularly suitable for use in this study. The reliability of rating incidents by categories was averaged at .69 for two raters using Cohen's (1960) Kappa.

Q-Sort Method and Elicitation of Personal Constructs

In order to establish the practical and theoretical significance of the categories, we used the Q-sort method and a procedure for eliciting personal constructs in a subsequent study. A group of incidents from the first phase of this research was selected as representative of the categories. Abbreviated versions of these incidents were submitted to a sample of parents and young adults for ranking using the Q-sort method. The Q-sort method (Block, 1978; Stephenson, 1953) allows for the assigning of scores to items (abbreviated incidents) from a pool of incidents. In the case of this study, the groups of incidents were sorted separately on two constructs, importance of the activity in the career development of children and adolescents, and likelihood that parents would engage in the activity to foster their children's career development. Once the sortings were made, subjects had the opportunity to identify personal constructs for their particular sort of the incidents on each of the two predetermined constructs, importance and likelihood. These data have yet to be analyzed, but we anticipate that we will be able to identify a range of constructs that parents and young people use in understanding parental activities and interpersonal relations in this domain.

Through factor or cluster analyses of the Q-sort scores, we anticipate being able to identify common factors and themes in these categories. One of the strengths of the Q-sort procedure is the opportunity to factor the scores according to persons rather than by items. As Dennis (1986) noted:

> When people load together on the same factor, it is because their Q-sorts are similar and highly correlated. Conceptually, this means that they share a common perspective on the topic of the study and define the categories that emerge as dimensions of the phenomena. (p. 12)

This procedure will enable us to derive dimensions of career influence according to demographic characteristics of the sample, their personal constructs for sorting, and aspects of family environment.

At least one future direction for this research is to attempt to use action theory and methods more explicitly in assessing actual interactions between parents and their children in this domain. The self-confrontational interview proposed by Valach (1986, 1989) may be an appropriate method to consider if we are able to capture on videotape actual parent-adolescent interactions in the domain of parental influences in career development.

CONCLUSION

In summary, we have attempted to argue that the area of parental influence in the career development of children warrants the use of nontraditional research methods if we are to address the range of issues involved, including contextual and intentional dimensions. Our research has used the in-depth, minimally structured interview and the critical incident procedure as methods that are appropriate to beginning an investigation. It was suggested that other methods, including those more psychometrically refined, can be added to this research.

Notwithstanding the argument made for the research methods used in these studies, a number of issues need greater clarification, including the use of retrospective accounts in the study of intentionality, the mix of qualitative and quantitative methods, and the extent to which the construction of categories such as those identified represents a hermeneutical approach to the data.

APPENDIX

Incident 1

Father-Daughter, Age 13
    P: She very much likes being with babies and helping out little kids. This is one of the ways she likes to make money. She hires herself out to babysit. She actually babysits the (inaudible word) children. The first thing that she wanted to do as soon as she was able was to go off to the babysitting class and learn all the things about First Aid and CPR and how to help little kids in trouble.
    I: Do you remember when she first told you she wanted to do that?
    P: As soon as she found out it was available through the school. There was a notice came round to the school, that they would be having for a certain age group of kids—the first day there was an announcement at school and a piece of paper to bring home to get your parents to sign and it was fired home. "I"ve got to get myself in that course."
    I: What was your response to that?
    P: Great, I don't have to get babysitters anymore. It's a great minicourse to take to give them a little bit of confidence. Also it's a good course to give them in terms of what to do about emergencies and how to get a hold of a policeman and the ambulance, what to do with kids that are in trouble and not to panic. Ann (pseudonym) is very much into not panicking. The course is an excellent course to get them started. It was one of our prerequisites that you are not going to go out babysitting until you learn some of the fundamentals. We had heard that there was such a thing around. It sounded like a great idea.
    I: You let her know that she would have to show that she was responsible?
    P: Yes, I think within herself she realized that was one of the things that she had to do, but very much wanted to go out and babysit and make some of her own money and be able to say, "I'm capable enough to look after somebody."
    I: Do you remember talking to her and telling her that she needed those credentials?

P: I can remember talking about the subject, saying it was an excellent idea. Anybody that wanted to get into babysitting should go to this thing.

I: How to you think it has affected her?

P: It seems to fit her whole personality of wanting to help people that are in trouble or seem to be not too happy.

Incident 2

Mother-Son, Age 23

P: One incident stands out in my mind. Not really an incident but a pattern I could see developing—that was about Grade 9, in Junior High. He was beginning to spend more and more time after school and in the evening with certain friends at school that he didn't want to bring home. I knew the boys but not well, just casually. I was a little bit concerned about the kind of kids they were, not that they were doing anything than playing street hockey. But the point was that I wasn't really aware totally of where he was and what was going on. Again it was verbally I discussed the whole situation with him and said to him, "I think you need to think about the type of personality you are." I always thought that he was the type of child who was never very strong in asserting his values to other people. He was more the type who would fall in with the crowd in whatever the crowd was doing so as not to be held up to ridicule. So I said to him:

"At this age in your life," he would have been about 13 or 14, "you're not doing at the moment that isn't right. I know that and I trust." I said, "Look at the people you are associating with and try to think in terms of if you build an association with these kids and strengthen it by keeping on with it, look at yourself and try to project yourself to 18 or 19, and try to visualize what these kids are going to be doing at that age, and whether you're going to be wanting to be doing the same types of things then, and whether you're going to be strong willed enough to say, 'Gee, I don't think I want to be involved with whatever it is, drinking, drugs, whatever.'"

I said, "You think about the friendships you're forming right now and whether you're going to be happy with them later on. Just think about that." I'd say that within a year he had gradually dropped certain friendships and developed other ones where I knew where he was and what he was doing. So I thought that it was the talk that we had where I said, "Try and assess your strengths and your weaknesses and don't try to get into a situation where your weaknesses get the better of you. You're not going to be able to get out later on." And again it seemed to work and it gave him enough to think about that he didn't continue on. Again we didn't have any worry about drugs. I know his values were such that he would never would have wanted to get involved with anything like that. But he had developed strong ties with the wrong types of friends. He might not have been able to pull himself out of it.

I: . . . As a way of making the picture even fuller, I'm wondering how did he react in that conversation, let's say?

P: Very quietly, extremely quietly. He didn't give me any indication at the time that he was agreeing with me. He listened to what I said and that was it, and we really didn't discuss it after that. But obviously it became clear by the end of the school year that he had been thinking about. So I didn't get any indication at the time.

I: How did it affect your relationship with him?

P: I don't know whether this particular instance altered my relationship with him or his relationship with me. He has always been, as I say, very quiet and he has not been one to discuss things with me, just occasionally. He's one of those people who will have the occasional fit of communicativeness, where he will talk for an hour or so, but that's rare. Most of the time he won't have an awful lot to say, and still doesn't. He's a very introverted person. But nonetheless, I wouldn't say it negatively affected our relationship at all.

NOTE

This research was supported by grants from the Social Sciences and Humanities Research Council of Canada, Strategic Grants Program—Family and Socialization of Children, Grant Nos. 498-84-0009 and 498-86-0020.

REFERENCES

Almquist, E. M., & Angrist, S. S. (1971). Role model influences on college women's career aspirations. *Merril-Palmer Quarterly, 17,* 263-279.

Astin, H. S. (1984). The meaning of work in women's lives: A sociopsychological model of career choice and work behavior. *Counseling Psychologist, 12*(4), 117-126.

Astin, H. S., & Myint, T. (1971). Career development of young women during the post high school years. *Journal of Counseling Psychology Monograph, 18,* 369-393.

Baruch, G., Barnett, R., & Rivers, C. (1983). *Life prints: New patterns of love and work for today's women.* New York: McGraw-Hill.

Bell, D. C., & Bell, L. G. (1983). Parental validation and support in the development of adolescent daughters. In M. D. Grotevant & C. R. Cooper (Eds.), *Adolescent development in the family* (pp. 27-43). San Francisco: Jossey-Bass.

Benjamin, L. S. (1974). Structural analysis of social behavior. *Psychological Review, 81,*392-425.

Benjamin, L. S. (1984). Principles of prediction using structural analysis of social behavior. In R. A. Zucker, J. Aronoff, & A. I. Rabin, (Eds.), *Personality and the prediction of behavior* (pp. 121-174). New York, Academic .

Block, J. (1978). *The Q-sort method in personality assessment and psychiatric research.* Palo Alto, CA: Consulting Psychologists Press. (Original work published 1961)

Block, J.H. (1979). Another look at sex differentiation in the socialization behaviors of mothers and fathers. In J. Sherman & F.L. Denmark (Eds.), *Psychology of women: Future directions of research* (pp. 29-87). New York: Psychological Dimensions.

Block, J. H. (1983). Differential premises arising from differential socialization of the sexes: Some conjectures. *Child Development, 54,* 1335-1334.

Breton, R. (1972). *Social and academic factors in the career decisions of Canadian youth.* Ottawa: Manpower and Immigration.

Brodsky, L. (1987). Writing ethnographic narratives. *Written Communication, 4,* 25-50.

Bronfenbrenner, U. (1979). *The ecology of human development: Experiments by nature and design.* Cambridge, MA: Harvard University Press.

Brown, D. (1970). *Student's vocational choices: A review and critique.* Boston: Houghton Mifflin.

Chapman, M. (Ed.). (1984). International action as a paradigm for developmental psychology: A symposium. *Human Development, 27,* 113-144.

Cochran, L. (1990). Narrative as a paradigm for career research. In R. A. Young & W. A. Borgen (Eds.), *Methodological approaches to the study of career* (pp.71-86). New York: Praeger.

Cohen, J. (1960). Weighted kappa: Nominal scale agreement with provision for scaled disagreement or partial credit. *Psychological Bulletin, 70,* 213-220.

Cooper, C. R., Grotevant, H.D., & Condon, S. M. (1983). Individuality and connectedness in the family as a context for adolescent identity formation and role-taking skill. In M. D. Grotevant & C. R. Cooper (Eds.), *Adolescent development in the family* (pp. 43-61). San Francisco: Jossey-Bass.

Cranach, M. von, Kalbermatten, U., Indermuehler, K., & Gugler, B. (1982). *Goal directed action.* London: Academic.

Cranach, M. von, & Valach, L. (1984). The social dimension of goal directed action. In H. Tajfel (Ed.), *The social dimension of social psychology* (pp. 285-299). Cambridge: Cambridge University Press.

Dennis, K. E. (1986). Q-methodology: Relevance and application to nursing research. *ANS: Advances in Nursing Science, 8,* 6-17.

Eckensberger, L. H., & Meacham, J. A. (Eds.). (1984). Action theory, control and motivation: A symposium. *Human Development, 27,* 163-210.

Farmer, H. S. (1980). Environmental background and psychological variables related to optimizing achievement and career motivation for high-school girls. *Journal of Vocational Behavior, 17,* 58-70.

Farmer, H. S. (1985). Model of career and achievement motivation for women and men. *Journal of Counseling Psychology, 32,* 363-390.

Fitzgerald, L. F., & Betz, N. E. (1983). Issues in the vocational psychology of women. In W. B. Walsh & S. H. Osipow (Eds.), *Handbook of vocational psychology: Vol. 1 Foundations* (pp. 83-159). Hillsdale, NJ: Erlbaum.

Fitzgerald, L. F., & Crites, J. O. (1980). Toward a career psychology of women: What do we know: What do we need to know? *Journal of Vocational Behavior, 16,* 83-95.

Flanagan, J. G. (1954). The critical incident technique. *Psychological Bulletin, 51,* 327-358.

Ford, M. (1982). Social cognition and social competence in adolescence. *Developmental Psychology, 18,* 323-339.

Furth, H. G. (1983). Freud, Piaget and MacMurray: A theory of knowledge from the standpoint of personal relations. *New Ideas in Psychology, 1,* 51-65.

Gibbs, J. C. (1979). The meaning of ecologically oriented inquiry in contemporary psychology. *American Psychologist, 34,* 127-140.

Gilligan, C. (1982). *In a different voice: Psychological theory and women's development.* Cambridge, MA: Harvard University Press.

Gillis, J. R. (1981). *Youth and history.* New York: Academic.

Goodale, J. G., & Hall, D. T. (1976). Inheriting a career: The influence of sex, values, and parents. *Journal of Vocational Behavior, 21,* 48-60.

Gottfredson, L. S. (1981). Circumscription and compromise: A developmental theory of occupational aspirations [Monograph]. *Journal of Counseling Psychology, 28,* 545-579.

Haber, S. (1980). Cognitive support for the career choices of college women. *Sex Roles, 6,* 129-138.

Hackett, G., & Betz, N. E. (1981). A self-efficacy approach to the career development of women. *Journal of Vocational Behavior, 18,* 326-339.

Harmon, L. W., & Farmer, H. S. (1983). Current theoretical issues in vocational psychology. In W. B. Walsh & S. H. Osipow (Eds.), *Handbook of vocational psychology: Vol. 1. Foundations* (pp. 39-77). Hillsdale, NJ: Erlbaum.

Hocks, R. A., & Curry, J. F. (1983). Sex-role identification of normal adolescent males and females as related to school achievement. *Journal of Youth and Adolescence, 12,* 461-470.

Hoffman, L. W. (1972). Early childhood experiences and women's achievement motives. *Journal of Social Issues, 28,* 129-156.

Hoffman, L. W., & Nye, F. I. (1974). *Working mothers.* San Francisco: Jossey-Bass.

Jackson, R. M., & Meara, N. (1977). Father identification, achievement, and occupational behavior of rural youth. *Journal of Vocational Behavior, 10,* 82-91.

Katz, P. A. (1987). Variations in family constellation: Effects on gender schemata. *New Directions in Child Development, 38,* 39-56.

Kvale, S. (1983). The qualitative interview: A phenomenological and hermeneutical mode of understanding. *Journal of Phenomenological Psychology, 14,* 171-196.

Law, B. (1981). Community interaction: A "mid-range" focus for theories of career development in young adults. *British Journal of Guidance and Counselling, 9,* 142-158.

Lerner, R. M., & Busch-Rossnagel, N. A. (1981). Individuals as producers of their development: Conceptual and empirical issues. In R. M. Lerner & N. A. Busch-Rossnagel (Eds.), *Individuals as producers of their development: A life-span perspective* (pp. 1-36). New York: Academic.

Lunneborg, P. W. (1982). Role model influencers of non-traditional professional women. *Journal of Vocational Behavior, 20*, 276-281.

McClure, G. T., & Piel, E. (1978). College-bound girls and science careers: Perceptions of barriers and facilitating factors. *Journal of Vocational Behavior, 12*, 172-182.

Meacham, J. A. (1984). The social basis of intentional action. *Human Development, 27*, 119-124.

Medvene, A. M., & Shueman, S. A. (1978). Perceived parental attitudes and choice of vocational specialty area among male engineering students. *Journal of Vocational Behavior, 12*, 208-216.

Moos, R. H., & Moos, B. (1981). *Family Environment Scale Manual*. Palo Alto, CA: Consulting Psychologists Press.

O'Neill, J. M., Ohlde, C., Tolefson, N., Barke, C., Piggott, T., & Watts, D. 1980). Factors, correlates, and problem areas affecting career-decision making of a cross-sectional sample of students. *Journal of Counseling Psychology, 27*, 571-580.

Perun, P. J., & Bielby, D. D. (1981). Towards a model of female occupational behavior: A human development approach. *Psychology of Women Quarterly, 6*, 234-252.

Pleck, J. H. (1982). The work and family role system. In R. Kahn-Hut, A. Kaplan Daniels, & R. Colvard (Eds.), *Women and work: Problems and perspectives* (pp. 101-111). New York: Oxford University Press.

Polkinghorne, D. (1990). Action theory approaches to career research. In R. A. Young & W. A. Borgen (Eds.), *Methodological approaches to the study of career* (pp. 87-105). New York: Praeger.

Powers, S. I., Hauser, S. T., Schwartz, J. M., Noam, G. G., & Jacobson, A. M. (1983). Adolescent ego development and family interaction: A structural-developmental perspective. In M. D. Grotevant & C. R. Cooper (Eds.), *Adolescent development in the family* (pp. 5-27). San Francisco: Jossey-Bass.

Rapoport, R., & Rapoport, R. N. (1980). Balancing work, family, and leisure: A triple-helix model. In C. B. Derr (Ed.), *Work, family and the career: New frontiers in theory and research* (pp. 281-328). New York: Praeger.

Rehberg, R., & Hotchkiss, L. (1979). Career counseling in contemporary U.S. high schools. *Review of Research in Education, 7*, 92-150.

Ridgeway, C. (1978). Parental identification and patterns of career orientation in college women. *Journal of Vocational Behavior, 12*, 1-11.

Roe, A., & Siegelman, M. (1964). *Origin of interests*. (APGA Inquiry Studies No. 1). Washington, DC: American Personnel and Guidance Association.

Schulenberg, J. E., Vondracek, F. W., & Crouter, A. C. (1984). The influence of the family on vocational development. *Journal of Marriage and the Family, 46*, 129-143.

Sebald, H. (1986). Adolescents' shifting orientation toward parents and peers: A curvilinear trend over recent decades. *Journal of Marriage and the Family, 48*, 5-13.

Shotter, J. (1983). Duality of structure and intentionality in an ecological psychology. *Journal for the Theory of Social Behavior, 13*, 19-41.

Spence, J. T., & Helmreich, R. L. (1980). Masculine instrumentality and female expressiveness: Their relationship with sex-role attitudes and behaviors. *Psychology of Women Quarterly, 5*, 147-153.

Stafford, E. M., & Jackson, P. R. (1983). Job choice or job allocation? Work aspirations and job seeking in an area of high unemployment. *International Review of Applied Psychology, 32*, 207-232.

Stephenson, W. (1953). *The study of behavior*. Chicago: University of Chicago Press.

Super, D. E. (1980). A life-span, life-space approach to career development. *Journal of Vocational Behavior, 13*, 282-298.

Tangri, S. S. (1972). Determinants of occupational role innovation among college women. *Journal of Social Issues, 28*, 177-199.

Unger, R. K. (1979). *Female and male: Psychological perspectives*. New York: Harper and Row.

Valach, L. (1986). *An action theoretical conception of career processes*. Paper to the Annual Conference of the British Sociological Association, Loughborough.

Valach, L. (1990). A theory of goal-directed action in career analysis. In R. A. Young & W. A. Borgen (Eds.), *Methodological approaches to the study of career* (pp. 107-126). New York: Praeger.

Vondracek, F. W., Lerner, R. M., & Schulenberg, J. E. (1983). The concept of development in vocational theory and intervention. *Journal of Vocational Behavior, 23*, 179-202.

Vondracek, F. W., Lerner, R. M., & Schulenberg, J. E. (1986). *Career development: A life-span developmental approach*. Hillsdale, NJ: Erlbaum.

Weller, L., Shlomi, H., & Zimont, G. (1976). Birth order, sex and occupational interest. *Journal of Vocational Behavior, 8*, 45-50.

Young, R. A. (1988). Ordinary explanations and career theories. *Journal of Counseling and Development, 66*, 336-339.

Young, R. A., Friesen, J. D., & Pearson, H. M. (1988). Activities and interpersonal relations as dimensions of parental behavior in the career development of adolescents. *Youth and Society, 20*, 29-45.

Youniss, J. (1980). *Parents and peers in social development*. Chicago: University of Chicago Press.

Youniss, J. (1983). Social construction of adolescence by adolescents and parents. In H. D. Grotevant & C. R. Cooper (Eds.), *Adolescent development in the family* (pp. 93-111). San Francisco: Jossey-Bass.

Youniss, J. (1984). Discussion: Single mind and social mind. *Human Development, 27*, 133-135.

10

Help Seeking and Coping
with Unemployment

Thomas Kieselbach

For many of those affected, unemployment represents a stressful life event that significantly changes many everyday routines, relationships, social roles, and central aspects of the perception of self and others (Kieselbach, 1988, in press-b; Kieselbach & Svensson, 1988; Kieselbach & Wacker, 1987; Schwefel, Svensson, & Zöllner, 1987). Furthermore, it leads to forms of psychosocial distress often unanticipated by the individual concerned, which can then develop into a threatening life crisis through the cumulation of "daily hassles" according to the principle of acceleration. In many cases, such a crisis cannot be overcome by the person affected using his or her own coping resources or those of the closer social network, but only by seeking professional help.

In contrast to clinical psychological research, which is mainly concerned with the problem of the effectiveness of the therapeutic intervention, the starting point of research into help-seeking behavior is concerned with those complex processes that precede professional intervention or that hinder the realization of such intervention in spite of an existing need for help. From the perspective of a community psychology construct, such as help-seeking behavior, we are involved in analyzing those natural (nonprofessional) helpers—who, after all, provide a large part of the psychosocial crisis support—as well as the determinants for the acceptance or nonacceptance of professional help (Kieselbach 1985a, 1986, in press-a; Klink & Scherner, 1986).

In the area of unemployment research, only a few investigations of, or reflections on, help-seeking behavior have been undertaken thus far (Buss & Redburn, 1983; Dooley & Catalano, 1985; Finlay-Jones & Eckhardt, 1981, 1982; Liem, 1983; Spruit, 1983). It may be seen from these studies that the unemployed who suffer a psychosocial crisis in association with the loss of their job:

1. Avoid seeking professional help, sometimes in spite of having rather exact information about the availability of such help—to a point which frequently must be viewed as self-destructive—in order to preserve their personal feelings of self-respect, which they believe may be endangered by accepting help (Liem, 1983).
2. Fear that professional helpers might "normalize" their situation, and conse-

quently palliatively persuade them to resign themselves to their unemployment (Spruit, 1983).

3. Tend, because of feelings of shock, stigmatization, or shame due to job loss or continuous unemployment, even more strongly than other people with mental difficulties, to conceal the true extent of their problems from others (Buss & Redburn, 1983, p. 170).

People experiencing a life crisis may demonstrate a natural resistance to being treated as an object of research, either by other people in general, or by scientific researchers specifically. This resistance is frequently indispensable for the maintenance of personal integrity in a psychosocial crisis and can be understood as a healthy reaction. In the research a medium degree of self-disclosure has been found to correlate closely with a positive level of mental health. However, in the subgroup of the unemployed we studied who sought help from the social-psychiatric services, the therapeutic contacts themselves may have led to a proto-professionalization of the clientele that in turn facilitated self-disclosure about mental problems.

The analysis of help-seeking processes in a psychosocial crisis arising from unemployment must take account of the conditions mentioned, if it is not to remain confined to a surface-level view, or, indeed, obscure what are in retrospect very significant aspects of the crisis or other critical life events being investigated. A quantitative survey producing highly reliable results (for example, using questionnaires) would probably miss out on important problems associated with the development of psychological crises and the resultant coping mechanisms. Neither can a qualitative investigation of the kind described below escape the distorting mechanisms of ignoring, denying, or reinterpreting one's own reality. Nevertheless, a research situation that more closely approaches the everyday reality of a conversation offers comparatively more opportunities to react sensitively to the mechanisms mentioned, to remove blocks to the conversation on sensitive issues, or to prevent a breaking off of the interview. Client-centered interview strategies can also facilitate the thematization of psychologically delicate topics.

THE RESEARCH PROJECT: HELP SEEKING OF THE UNEMPLOYED IN SOCIAL-PSYCHIATRIC SERVICES

Selection of the Sample

We conducted 20 in-depth clinical interviews in our investigations of help-seeking behavior and self-disclosure with unemployed people who had come to the social-psychiatric services in search of help. It was determined by the responsible professional in these cases that the problems had been caused by unemployment or at least clearly had been aggravated by it. Further criteria for selection of the sample were a minimum of three years of continuous employment and no more than five years of unemployment, and no psychiatric record before the start of unemployment.

The investigation of self-disclosure and help-seeking behavior of the unemployed set out to analyze those processes which led a particularly vulnerable group of the unemployed to seek social-psychiatric help. In addition, we wanted to examine those circumstances that caused the decision to seek help to be delayed or postponed in each case, and also the individual expectations regarding accessible, acceptable, sensible, and effective help in a psychosocial crisis associated with unemployment.

It became apparent during conversations with the professional helpers in question that clients who precisely met our criteria were not willing to take part in any conversation with us because their psychosocial crisis was too deep. This seems especially worthy of note because it points to a certain underestimation of psychosocial stress during unemployment described in empirical studies based on questionnaires, in-depth interviews, or the reports of those affected. It is precisely those who are most under stress who least often take part in scientific research at all—a point that Warr and colleagues have also made in connection with a study of youth unemployment (Warr, Banks, & Ullah, 1985). Such a tendency to "submerge" is further substantiated by the fact that virtually none of those individuals actually interviewed by us agreed to take part at a point in time considered to be the most intensively critical. It can be concluded from this that studies of the unemployed probably demonstrate a clear selection effect, whereby those under the most stress are excluded from investigation.

To this must be added the following considerations: Individual defense mechanisms can further contribute to a conservative estimation of the psychosocial damage caused by unemployment, because they might involve self-assertion or resistance to individualizing perspectives of one's own unemployment. One of the most dramatic descriptions of a personal crisis brought on by unemployment was obtained from a worker already in new employment, who expressly stated that he would not have been prepared under any circumstances to participate in the study while he had been unemployed. This is corroborated by results obtained by Rostila (1985), who received descriptions from reemployed Finnish workers that were retrospectively much more negative than those given in the first interviews during their unemployment.

Our sample is thus selective vis-à-vis the highly vulnerable unemployed; within this group, however, it was those under less stress who were willing to take part in our investigations.

Field of Research and Methodological Approach

The investigation was aimed at obtaining insights that could be used for better planning and implementation of counseling and other services for the highly vulnerable unemployed. It appears especially important to gain knowledge from the analysis of concrete attempts at coping to be used for the development of reactive preventive programs (for the concept of proactive and reactive primary prevention, see Catalano & Dooley, 1980) which should offer:

— anticipatory counselling;
— possibilities of crisis intervention, and increased availability, acceptability, sensibility, and effectiveness of psychosocial service institutions for the unemployed; and
— outreach concepts for the unemployed, which should include their previous collective working environment and experiences.

Help seeking during a psychosocial crisis as an object of research justifies choosing an approach that guarantees a comparability between the information given by each of those interviewed, on the one hand, and an adequate treatment of the subject matter, on the other: namely, the manner of coping with unemployment on the part of people under extreme strain. These people often had not established contact with professional helpers until after an attempted suicide, and were receiving therapy or psychotherapeutic counseling at the time of the inquiries. With regard to the first requirement, comparability, a semi-structured problem-focused form containing questions on 11 thematic areas was chosen (Witzel, 1982), supplemented by a questionnaire (social data, life event scale, a scale of psychological well-being). A narrative approach was rejected, since this frequently supplies only singular interviews or individual case descriptions, which lack comparability due to the great divergence in the progress of each interview.

The form of the interviews, which in all 20 cases were conducted by the author (assisted by a cointerviewer who went through the questionnaire with the interviewees and asked supplementary questions during the conversation phase) was oriented toward clinical in-depth interviews with a non-directive approach. The guiding line for the conversation, which provided orientation in terms of the sequence of the points to be dealt with, comprised the following complexes:

— social data,
— description of the coping with the unemployed situation to date,
— changes within the social network during unemployment,
— stressful life events,
— determinants of self-disclosure regarding mental problems in general and unemployment specifically,
— help seeking with regard to finding new employment,
— help seeking in earlier stressful life events,
— help seeking with regard to psychosocial crisis associated with unemployment, with, in each case, the sub-points:
— definition of the problem,
— perception of the need for help,
— acceptance of the need for help,

— evaluation of the psychological costs of seeking help,
— results of the process of evaluation,
— determinants of the resistance to seeking help,
— operationalization of help seeking,
— style of help seeking,
— evaluation of the help seeking process, and
— development of personal well-being.

The interviews lasted between two and four hours and were audiotaped and transcribed verbatim. All statements made by the interviewees were independently assigned to the 11 previously selected thematic areas by the two interviewers, and then, after a discussion between them in which divergent interpretations were discussed, corrected, and, where possible, standardized, the statements were compiled into written text form, whereby the interpretative areas provided the points of reference. Quotes from the interviews were included, either in complete form or integrated into the interpretation of the case. Case descriptions of individual coping mechanisms were obtained from these descriptions of the various interpretative areas, whereby the main emphasis was placed on the determinants for help seeking or the resistance to help seeking. In the following pages I will describe some of the results of my as yet uncompleted investigations, with reference to some phases of the help-seeking process.

Self-Disclosure and Help Seeking

The construct of self-disclosure has been defined, based on the work of Jourard (1964) as an interpersonal communication in which the individual intentionally shares or discloses some central, critical, and private part of him- or herself (Goodstein & Reinecker, 1974, p. 70). Thus, the concept of self-disclosure has two aspects:

— as a personal attribute, it characterizes the ability of self-exploration
  and the communication of personal aims;
— as a process, it characterizes the informational exchange within an
  interpersonal relationship.

In the area of clinical psychology, self-disclosure with the therapist forms an important predictor for the success of the therapy (see the survey in Cozby, 1973; also see Goodstein & Reinecker, 1974).

> Persons with positive mental health are characterized by disclo-
> sure to a few significant others and medium disclosure to others
> in the social environment. Individuals who are poorly adjusted
> are characterized by either high or low disclosure to virtually
> everyone in the social environment. (Cozby, 1973, p.78)

The following hypothesis may be formulated concerning unemployment: Existing tendencies to self-disclosure in a situation of psychosocial difficulty are reduced in the situation of unemployment due to the given social and individual evaluations of unemployment (such as stigmatization, withdrawal in shame, individual attribution of blame, threat to self-esteem, and the fear of being viewed as a failure).

The construct of help seeking may be defined as "any communication about a problem or troublesome event which is directed toward obtaining support, advice, or assistance in times of distress" (Gourash, 1978, p. 414). It presents a completion or an alternative to individual coping attempts and, as a rule, is used first insofar as these have failed. A precondition is the self-disclosure or readiness to disclose a private problem to someone who is not concretely affected by this event. The process of help-seeking behavior has been investigated mainly in connection with illness behavior and medical help (Mechanic, 1982; Zola 1964), but its use in the area of help seeking for psychosocial difficulties was developed later (Buchholz, Gmuer, Höfer, & Straus, 1984; DePaulo, Nadler, & Fisher, 1983; Gourash, 1978).

THE PROCESS OF HELP SEEKING
AND ITS PSYCHOLOGICAL COSTS

The process of seeking help has become a subject of social scientific investigation partly as a result of the fact that everyday experience reveals no linear relation between the need for help and the actual seeking and accepting of help. Under certain circumstances people in need are not willing to seek help, while outside assistance is sometimes sought by others who could easily solve their problems on their own. Nonutilization of help, whereby coping mechanisms such as acceptance, ignorance, or denial of the problem are preferred to any active help seeking, can be explained in terms of experiencing actual or anticipating future psychological costs associated with the seeking or acceptance of help (Gross & McMullen, 1983; Gross, Wallston, & Piliavin, 1979; Nelson-LeGall, Gumerman, & Scott-Jones, 1983).

These psychological costs can be classified into two general categories: personal costs, relating to self-esteem and self-concept, and social costs, associated with interpersonal relations and perception by others. The process of help seeking has been conceptualized from the perspective of different theoretical approaches (DePaulo et al., 1983; Fisher, Nadler, & DePaulo, 1983; Nadler, Fisher, & DePaulo, 1983; Wills, 1982).

We can distinguish among the following theoretical frameworks:

— Attribution theory concepts, which emphasize the attributed responsibility of the origin and the solution of one's problems on the one hand, and threat to self-esteem on the other (Tessler & Schwartz, 1972);
— Theories of social comparison, based on the work of Leon Festinger, which especially emphasize the achieving of self-enhancement by

using downward comparison in a situation where help is needed
(Wills, 1983);
— The concept of embarrassment, based on Goffman's (1956-1957)
theory of social interaction and the assumption that help seeking is
affected by feelings of shame and pride, which people experience
depending on their actual or perceived evaluation by others (Shapiro,
1983); and
— Equity and indebtedness concepts based on the assumption that
receiving help that cannot be reciprocated contradicts the deeply
rooted norm of equity in social relations (Greenberg, 1980).

In order to undertake a more precise analysis of those psychosocial factors
influencing help-seeking behavior, various models have been developed that
subdivide the help-seeking process into the following separate phases:

— perception and definition of the problem,
— perception of the need for help,
— decision to seek help,
— identification of potential helpers,
— selection of strategies for seeking help, and
— evaluation of the help-seeking process (Gross & McMullen, 1983;
Nelson-LeGall, et al., 1983; see also Klink & Scherner, 1986).

At this stage of our study, however, we only wish to illustrate, using examples taken
from the in-depth interviews, some problems that seem especially important for the
process of help seeking by the unemployed, without laying claim to providing any
systematic analysis.

SPECIAL PROBLEMS OF
UNEMPLOYED INDIVIDUALS SEEKING HELP

The Principle of Acceleration in the Development of Crises

The unemployment experience is viewed in unemployment research either as a
stressful life event or as a series of "daily hassles" (Kanner, Coyne, Schaefer, &
Lazarus, 1981), which are structured as an accumulation of stressful problems
according to the principle of acceleration (Frese, 1985). Brenner (1980, p. 73)
described such a situation: job loss leads to financial problems and strains within the
marriage and the family that favor a breakup of the family. The loss of friendships
made at work speeds up social isolation, the stressful search for a new job, perhaps
of lower status, and the involuntary move to a new area lead to a further exhaustion
of the available coping resources, which finally results in psychological reactions

to this overburdening situation. I have found evidence in my investigations that supports both approaches to coping with unemployment.

In one case, the subjectively most significant stressful life event for the 37-year-old interviewee before his job loss had been the traumatic experience of being unemployed for six months after completing his apprenticeship, a later repetition of which he constantly feared. This experience had obviously led, not to increased immunization against the effects of unemployment, but rather to an increase in vulnerability, and in this sense had determined to a considerable extent whether he could cope with the present situation. The loss of his job was experienced here as a decisive life event in itself, and as a massive threat. Another interviewee had worked on building sites for 17 years, where he had regularly experienced seasonal unemployment—he had been unemployed for several months each winter. Both financially and with regard to the structuring of his time, he was able to anticipate, plan for, and thus cope with this situation. After an accident at work which left him hampered in walking, his unemployment became more protracted, but he assumed that he would be able to cope positively with this just as he had done before. However his experience was to the contrary, and being unemployed for a longer time than previously caused boredom, which he had never known before. This along with an increasing number of conflicts within the family due to his higher levels of alcohol consumption compared with his previously more normal drinking behavior, led to the problems escalating, which resulted finally in psychiatric intervention on the part of the social-psychiatric services.

The principle of acceleration can be illustrated more fully using the following example: A 29-year-old interviewee had had various jobs as a truck driver after serving four years in the army, without managing, however, to gain a real foothold in job terms. He had been unemployed for the last three years and had been receiving therapy from the social-psychiatric services for nine months.

He described three situations of psychosocial crisis during his unemployment, each clearly separated from the other, that were interconnected and can be interpreted according to the principle of acceleration. The first crisis arose from a conflict with his landlady, who had given him notice to leave his apartment due to his not having paid his rent, which in turn had been due to his benefits being stopped by the labor office. Since he had not managed to find a new, cheaper apartment, he continued to live in the old one. Once, when he was not at home, his landlady packed his things together, ripped the wallpaper from the walls, and took out the door. Even though he was able to obtain an interim injunction against the landlady, he did not move back into the flat, but went back to live with his mother again.

The second crisis occurred after a further change of residence. He had moved into an apartment in a high-rise block, in which he felt very lonely and which he left only rarely during the daytime. In connection with reading mystical literature, he began to hear sounds and voices. The third crisis is linked to his attempts to commit suicide—before the beginning of his treatment with the social-psychiatric services and two months later. While unemployed he made increasing efforts to read literature which might provide him with a foundation on which he could base his further direction in life. He occupied himself with relaxation techniques, yoga, and mystical literature. After two years of unemployment he became increasingly phobic in the high-rise block, fearing "to go down and look in the postbox to see if there was any post" and "afraid to use the lift" (N1/11). The situation became increasingly worse: "I used to have hallucinations up in the flat, I could hear sounds and used to totally crack up." He associated his hallucinations with a book by a Tibetan yogi, which had impressed him very strongly.

> Something just gave way, something or other got unhooked maybe. I kept hearing a kind of click-clack under the polystyrene ceiling, in different corners, but always in the same spot. I remember sitting there with a friend, going half crazy. (N1/11f).

Occasionally he could not stand it any longer in his apartment and stayed the night with friends. He suffered more and more often from paranoid fears, and finally ran out of the apartment in panic. "I thought there was somebody following me who was out to get me." His persecution fantasies become more definite and threatening.

> I thought that the military security services were somewhere, following me, or that someone was using me as a guinea pig and doing experiments with me in the flat, or at least that's how it seemed, because I was always hearing voices. I heard a group, women's voices, men's voices, and this clicking sound in my ears the whole time. And I think I actually did reach the madness stage and all I could do was just get away. I was thinking, this is it, I've had it. All of us unemployed are in for it soon now, know what I mean? Yes, that we here—and not just the unemployed, but the low-paid, the lower ones generally, that they're really being used as guinea pigs, that experiments are being done on them .... How they behave together, when they freak out, when they crack up, how much stress you can put them under, how you can get them. And then I saw something on TV about the CIA, that they pumped people full of drugs and played some tape over and over again until they went out of their minds. (N1/32f).

He talked about his hallucinations to a friend, who advised him to go and see a parapsychologist, on the grounds he might be a "medium." He felt equally misunderstood by other acquaintances, because they saw his problems as a chance for creativity. One positive result of his seeking help was that a friend went with him to see a neurologist. This doctor had only five minutes' time for him. He prescribed some pills and referred the man to a psychiatric clinic.

Subsequently, the interviewee felt relieved as he experienced fewer hallucinations because of the pills. However, he did not follow the recommendation to go to the psychiatric clinic because of opinions he had heard about psychiatry from acquaintances:

> My friends . . . they were giving me examples of people who had
> gone there and who came back really out of their minds, like
> robots.... In any case they painted a totally negative picture of the
> place. That the people there foam at the mouth, just stare the
> whole time, walk like robots and all kinds of things, and I got so
> horrified about going there at all to get help. (N1/31)

When the hallucinations then became more threatening, he tried to get to the source of the voices he heard and tore down the polystyrene ceiling to find out whether there were loudspeakers hidden there. His apartment was in a totally chaotic state when he left, rented a car, and drove to Austria with the express aim of looking for a job. He went to the labor office in Salzburg and asked how he could get a work permit, which he did not get "because they've got so many unemployed of their own" (N1/33). After his attempt to find work in Austria failed, he was afraid to return home, explaining "the humiliation, you can't stand what they're all saying about you" (N1/35). He feared ending up in "the madhouse" or jail (N1/36) or being declared legally incapacitated. At this point, he tried to kill himself by feeding exhaust fumes into the inside of the car. After 15 minutes, however, he abandoned his attempt at suicide, which he now views as an extreme form of self-help: "I just had to do something to help myself" (N1/34).

On his return, he talked to his mother, who encouraged him to go to the social-psychiatric services. Her concern was crucial to his going, as was his own recognition of the fact that he could no longer solve the additional problems that had developed (his apartment destroyed, the invoice for the car rental) on his own. While previously he had had enough energy to try and solve his problems by himself, "now there was nothing left" (N1/37).

The interviewee considered reading mystical literature and his situation of being unemployed both responsible for the development of the hallucinations:

> Yes, they've got something to do with it all right [with his situation
> while unemployed], somehow or other, because I had a lot of time
> alone and got involved with things that maybe nobody else gets
> involved with. And if I hadn't had the time, if I'd had to do
> something during the day, a tight schedule the whole time, then
> maybe I'd never even have run into that sort of thing. (N1/12)

Psychological Costs of Seeking Help

The utilization of professional psychosocial help can lead to the social and emotional isolation and stigmatization of the person receiving help. Unemployed people who anticipate any such stigmatization tend to avoid any utilization of professional help, so as not to exacerbate the feeling of stigmatization already arising from the situation as unemployed person (Kieselbach, 1985a).

At this point, two aspects of this avoidance of help seeking can be described in more detail: the nonacceptance of help as an expression of masculinity, and the stigmatization of social-psychiatric help.

An ex-sportsman had been working in various temporary jobs since he had discontinued his studies. He was drinking increasing quantities of alcohol and as a result getting into more and more difficulties at his place of work. During a longer period of being unemployed, his avoidance of seeking any help can be ascribed to his "masculine behavior" (W1/14), by his conviction that "You can make it on your own, you'll get through it, right?" (W1/14). He did not want to disclose himself to anyone for fear of "being a bit at the mercy of other people" (W1/40), and of thus being open to personal exploitation. He did not turn to potential helpers because he was embarrassed

> that friends could suddenly have quite a different impression of me. Where they would get to know me in all my helplessness and with all my weaknesses, when I was basically someone you could look up to, for a certain circle of friends. (W1/44)

For these reasons, he followed through his strategy for coping "on my own! As a man you've just got to grit your teeth and, no matter how, you'll fall on your feet again" (W1/44f.). During this time he was too ashamed to ask anybody for help, primarily a consequence of his increasing consumption of alcohol. Neither did he apply for the social welfare to which he was entitled for two years.

Another interviewee was well known to his colleagues at work as a "comforter of souls," and, as a matter of course, advised them to seek professional help with their psychological problems. He refused to make use of such help himself when unemployed, even though he was informed about the existence and work of the social-psychiatric services—an acquaintance, employed there as a clerk, had often advised him to go there. When asked for the reasons why he had not tried the social-psychiatric services before his attempted suicide, he replied that "I thought, me? I haven't got a screw loose" (W2/15). Even at the later climax of his crisis, he perceived the social-psychiatric help that he had "had to" accept as socially marginalizing and stigmatizing.

An interviewee sought help from a marriage counselor he had known from earlier consultations when his wife left him after he had been unemployed for six months. When the marriage counselor advised him to go to the social-psychiatric services, he was very sceptical at first, "Because I had always thought that only barmy people go there. I mean, people that really have the shakes or something. Because I never thought that they are also there for normal people who just happened to be a bit down with their nerves" (W3/36). When the counselor advised him to take his troubles to the social-psychiatric services, he replied that he was "not off my rocker, I've just got a touch of the nerves" (W3/36).

Coping attempts by unemployed persons who turn to anonymous counseling services show clearly that fear of "indebting" oneself psychologically by seeking help from their closer social network significantly inhibits any seeking or accepting of nonprofessional help from friends (Gross, Wallston, & Piliavin, 1979). This is compounded by the need to not have to admit publicly to one's psychosocial problems and thus become identifiable as someone who cannot adequately and independently cope.

The avoidance of seeking help can be explained using concepts based on attribution theory (Gross & McMullen, 1982; Tessler & Schwartz, 1972). Proceeding on the assumption that people endeavor to find explanations for their own behavior, it follows that potential help seekers want to know their reasons for needing help. In cases where help seeking cannot be viewed as normal, or as resulting from external conditions or necessity, personal reasons for needing help are usually sought instead. In our culture, seeking outside help is predominantly associated with negative attributions such as failure, incompetence, or inadequacy (Rosen, 1983). Fear of negative attributions on the part of significant others is a further factor that can control one's behavior. Such negative attributions threaten self-esteem, which in turn has multiple effects, including derogation of the helper and the quality of aid, and inhibition of subsequent help seeking (Cohn, 1983; Greenberg, 1980; Nadler, Fisher, & Streufert, 1976).

Feelings associated with seeking and accepting help resemble to a great extent those that can arise in conjunction with long-term unemployment in general. For this reason the acceptance of help during a psychosocial crisis can include a reinforcement of emotions experienced through job loss or due to failure while seeking employment, and thus help seeking might be inhibited. Help that would have been considered acceptable in a more stable life situation is avoided owing to its association with being unemployed.

Covert Help Seeking

Covert help seeking can be seen as a typical way of coping with psychosocial problems due to unemployment. When the unemployed experienced a far greater degree of stigmatization than they do today (see Brinkmann, 1985), it presented an important possibility for obtaining help while concealing the fact of being unemployed.

One interviewee talked about his "deep problems" (N3/23) as if they were those of others and not his own. He described a situation when he was unemployed many years ago and was looking for a chance to talk about unemployment:

> And whenever I would be sitting in the pubs, I'd want to hear what they all thought about unemployment, and in the mid-70s, when it was slowly starting, people said that everybody who wanted work could find it. And I always tried to listen in on what they were saying, but never said that I was the unemployed one. I told them something else, that I worked . . . somewhere or other. I

would say I heard that, or I read this or I saw something. I mean
I never referred to myself, because I was afraid that they would
pick on me. I didn't want to be the only one. (N3/23)

In order to avoid negative consequences of self-disclosure, such as "vile gossip"
(N3/22), he would never talk about his problems with acquaintances or neighbors.
"I'm always very wary, although I'm normally quite open with strangers when it
comes to talking about my problems. By which I mean absolute strangers—having
a conversation and then never meeting again" (N3/22). The purpose of his indirect
form of self-disclosure—his "story-telling strategy"—was to gather ideas or
suggestions (N3/22), but he wanted to keep control over the extent to which he made
"use of this information" (N3/21).

The Relevance of Confidential Relationships

The sportsman identified earlier was not able to seek and accept help until his
girlfriend had given him the ultimatum that he must either change himself or she
would break off the relationship. Only in response to this extreme pressure did he
agree to go to the social-psychiatric services with her. His girlfriend, whom he
described as the "central point to which I always go with my inner problems" (W1/
40), seems to have played an important role in his stabilization. She facilitated his
seeking help from professional helpers, and by accompanying him provided an
example of self-disclosure. It was this close, important relationship that gave him
the chance to actively seek and accept help from institutions such as the labor office
and the social welfare office.

A confidential relationship also made a significant contribution toward overcoming the crisis in the case of the unemployed building site worker. His wife not
only exerted pressure on him to seek help and be able to accept it, she also acted as
a mediator with regard to professional help and facilitated self-disclosure to these
helpers. In so doing, she supported him emotionally to the limits of her own
capacities. His seeking help was principally the result of fear of consequences on
the family, that is, the danger of his wife leaving.

The specific conditions described above that led to the decision to seek help can
be interpreted to mean that the "masculinity" of not seeking help was in this case
moderated by the "femininity" of being willing to do so. The pressure exerted by his
confidante and the threatening of sanctions changed the balance between the
psychological costs of seeking help and those costs arising from the avoidance of
help seeking, and thus facilitated, finally, the acceptance of professional help.

GENERAL CONCLUSIONS FOR
PSYCHOSOCIAL INTERVENTIONS AND PROVISION OF HELP

Individual Expectations Concerning
Accessible, Acceptable, Sensible, and Effective Help

What are the expectations that the interviewees themselves formulate regarding help that would have been capable of preventing the worsening of their psychosocial crisis? On the whole, it is clear that many interviewees have expectations toward those institutions that they view as responsible for matters in connection with unemployment (or employment). They also expect the institutions to provide help with psychosocial problems associated with unemployment.

The interviewee who had regular hallucinations in the isolation of his high-rise apartment after three years of unemployment described his expectations toward institutions concerning effective support in crisis situations as follows, here referring to the social welfare office:

> Well, help would be more effective if it were more mobile. If they would come and have a look themselves. So house visits would be a good idea . . . but it has to be qualified people who are trained somehow, who've got experience in dealing with such things, when someone for example goes strange in the head, who knows that you can get frightened, or that you feel inferior. If someone had come back with me and looked at my flat, maybe somebody would have said, this won't do, we'll have to do something about it. (N1/41)

A second interviewee expressed a similar need for comprehensive outreach offers of help:

> I could also notice [at the labor office] how a lot of people sat there, some virtually crumpled up into themselves and then looking around almost ashamed of themselves, or maybe not even looking at all, y'know. Where nobody even tries standing up straight, basically. (W1/39)

> Well, I would say that of course it's difficult to make what I want to say possible. But there should be a possibility at the labor office—it could also be a social worker [or a therapist, (W1/39)] employed by the labor office, who would go to a person's house if he's afraid of going to the labor office or to the welfare office, someone else you could approach. . . . [F]or me personally that would have been a good thing. (W1/28)

He saw effective help as "cooperation between the labor office, the welfare office and this kind of advice place [the social-psychiatric services]. So that, y'know, there are different places where people can go" (W1/49). In the facilities he envisages

> carefully directed help being given from the very start. . . .
> [I]f people have got problems for example, and to help people get over their fear of going there and accepting help, because everything is interlocked, it extends right into your private life. (W1/49)

A preliminary conclusion can be drawn here: even when different institutions continue to have different functions to perform, closer cooperation between the labor office, social welfare office, and psychosocial agencies could contribute significantly toward a more adequate form of offering help if there were some form of intersectoral networking (Schwefel, 1986).

Another interviewee, who had received psychotherapeutic counseling from the social-psychiatric services following an attempted suicide, stated quite explicitly that help as offered by psychosocial institutions or by self-help groups did not represent accessible or acceptable help as far as he was concerned. The only form of help that he thought, retrospectively, would probably have been acceptable would have been help connected directly to his work in the company, for example, from the trade union. This was, after all, the organization that had represented his interests while he was employed. If the unions had offered counseling, he would sooner have gone there:

> The unions particularly, they can work closely with the labor office and all of that—they could counsel people regarding the work problem, with finding a new job. It might not work out straight away for every single person, but they could give people a future perspective, give people hope, realistic hope as far as employment is concerned, together with the mental side, as well, that would be excellent. . . . [Y]es, something for the mental aspect and then concerning employment, too. (W2/43)

The one institution whose utilization would have involved the lowest degree of stigmatization for him was, from his point of view, the organization he knew from the firm in which he had also been an active trade unionist. The aggravation of his crisis might have been avoided if help had been available and known to him from organizations other than those in the psychosocial field.

No systematic evaluation research has so far been done on psychosocial counseling available at the company or trade union level. Only one investigation was carried out in the United States, which produced rather negative results (Buss & Redburn, 1983). They assessed the utilization of psychosocial help by unemployed individuals in connection with the closing of a large steel plant in the United

States. The services offered were specially conceived as a crisis intervention service for the unemployed and were, as far as can be judged from the description given by the authors, extremely sensitive, closely linked to the company and the trade unions, and set up by experienced professionals. Despite this, the help and counseling offered were barely used by the steel workers who had been laid off. The majority of those who did use it were family members, while only 2 percent of those directly affected made use of the service (p. 143). A drop-in center in a trade union building was a particular failure. The low level of utilization on the part of the potential clientele was explained by one member of the team thus: "Because we are identified with 'you can't do it, buddy: you lost your job and now you are losing your mind'; we are identified with sickness and weakness" (p. 147). Only a general crisis intervention center was used to a greater extent than before by the laid-off workers as a result of the plant closure. However, it is questionable, given the role that unions play in the United States, whether the results of this study are transferrable to other countries.

For certain groups of unemployed people, who strongly fear the loss of control over their conditions of life, this fear can be intensified by accepting help. Anonymous psychosocial help—for example, in the form of a hot-line service—could represent an adequate means of support in coping with a psychosocial crisis arising from being unemployed. In this way, help seekers' fears of being rejected or indebting themselves psychologically, and their need for control over their social identity vis-à-vis the helper, as well as control over the duration, contents, and frequency of the counseling process, would all be addressed. A critical point of this process, however, can be the occasionally necessary referral for personal and professional help.

Compensatory Model of Helping

Psychosocial interventions and measures taken with unemployed persons locate themselves somewhere between the two poles of "blaming the victim" and "social victim" (see Kieselbach, 1985b, 1986; Liem, 1983). Both poles must be judged, however, as inadequate for psychosocial interventions. It is necessary, it seems, to make a fundamental differentiation, as has been done by Brickman, Kidder, Coates, Rabinowitz, Cohn, and Karoza (1983) in their theoretical model of the helping process. The authors developed a general model of helping and identified four different approaches, which differ with respect to recipients' responsibility for the problem (for example, loss of employment) and his responsibility for the solution, such as success in finding work.

In the "compensatory model of helping," the cause of the problem is seen to lie in societal conditions, while the responsibility for solving the problem rests with the person concerned. In this model, recipients of help are considered to be innocent victims of a prior injustice and therefore are not held responsible for the onset of their problem. Once they have received help they are regarded as being responsible for subsequent success but also for subsequent failure. If they fail and need help again they will have difficulty claiming the innocent victim status (Brickman et al., 1983, p. 40).

As far as interventions with the unemployed are concerned, it would appear adequate to modify the compensatory model with regard to the responsibility for solving the problem so that a balance is found between externalization and personal responsibility. A pure internalization may, in the case of protracted unemployment and after conclusion of interventional means, lead to an increase in depressive reactions as a result of personal feelings of blame.

If the compensatory model is applied in the isolated situation of psychosocial counseling, there is the danger that the intervention will focus on the clients' personal assets. If the clients fail, they can only blame themselves for their failure. If, however, such an intervention is embedded in collective action, for example, within the framework of self-help initiatives, the actors may not necessarily attribute personal internal responsibility for subsequent failures because this approach focuses the group's attention on external opposition (Brickman et al., 1983, p. 42).

A pure externalization of the solution, however, would produce helplessness or the mere transfer of individual action to the level of political activity, without any solution to the individual's unemployment. Unemployment still remains a personal problem to be resolved on an individual level. The option of being satisfied with taking over the social role as a "proactive" long-term unemployed person (Fryer & Payne, 1984) might be given only for a very small minority of "psychologically privileged" unemployed (Jahoda, 1982). Thus, a strategy of prevention needs to combine the following two elements:

— counseling with regard to reemployment, qualification, and psychosocial problems on an individual level, and
— a strategy of empowerment in the direction of political action
  (Rappaport, 1981, 1987).

Individual problems are here perceived in their social context and collective solutions for collective problems are undertaken (for more details, see Kieselbach, 1987a, 1987b, 1989).

Concluding Methodological Remarks

Our investigations were conducted with unemployed persons who sought help from social-psychiatric services in a psychosocial crisis and received psychotherapy. We found that those unemployed individuals who had severe problems with unemployment, in the estimation of the professional helpers treating them, were not willing to talk to us. This points to an underestimation of the psychosocial problems within our sample group. Whether such a sample bias weighted in favor of those less under strain is even more marked when using a quantitative survey (Warr, Banks, & Ullah, 1985), or whether in fact the anonymous situation of a questionnaire provides a reduced threshold for self-disclosure with regard to psychologically stressful themes cannot be judged with any certainty.

The discussion of psychologically delicate topics requires an attitude on the part of the interviewer that more closely resembles therapeutic procedures than any other exploratory approach. The interview process often becomes a help-seeking process in itself on account of the determinants of help seeking involved. A number of those interviewed experienced the interview situation as a quasi-therapeutic situation, in the course of which intense emotional reactions to strain occurred, including crying. After the interview was completed, and a transition made to the present situation, however, there were clear statements expressing relief at having had the chance at last to be able to speak coherently about unemployment and the problems associated with it without feeling under any time pressure.

The interview situation was frequently used by those being questioned as part of a help-seeking process in itself, in order to obtain help with special problems associated with unemployment. In such cases, contacts were made with other counselors (psychologists working at the labor office or in special psychosocial counseling services for the unemployed), or to leisure and continuing education organizations, to self-help groups for the unemployed, or to welfare organizations in which the unemployed could gain work experience by doing voluntary work. We later received information that some of those interviewed by us had indeed followed up the suggestions or information supplied by the researchers, and that further continuous developments had arisen from this. We received something from those we had been interviewing. In addition, even though it was not planned at the outset as part of the concept for the research process, we were able to give something in return. This was a relief of sorts, since after having spoken to those affected about what were sometimes extremely stressful mental problems, we were unable to give them hope regarding their central problem of unemployment because of the very serious labor market situation in Bremen (West Germany).

Stressful life events that we asked about in the course of the interview using a list of critical life events adapted from Holmes and Rahe (1967) were often, to our surprise, mentioned by the interviewee much later in the interview, even though they had not been marked when given the list previously. This would appear to us an important indication that the experience of extremely stressful events is often greatly repressed, or simply forgotten owing to the sheer frequency of critical life events. Even the stimulus of a list of critical life events did not suffice in these cases to reverse the tendency to concealing or forgetting. Such information was not brought out into the open until the situation of an intensive dialog provided the appropriate framework. This further underlines the need to critically evaluate the reliability of any quantitative research instruments in connection with particularly stressful mental problems. It would be well justified to validate results so gained by means of intensive qualitative inquiries.

REFERENCES

Brenner, M. H. (1980). Industrialization to economic growth: Estimates of their effects on the health of populations. In M. H. Brenner, A. Mooney, & T. J.Nagy (Eds.), *Assessing the contributions of the social sciences to health* (pp. 65-115). Washington, DC: American Academy for the Advancement of Science.

Brickman, P., Kidder, L. H., Coates, D., Rabinowitz, U., Cohn, E., & Karoza, J. (1983). The dilemmas of helping: Making aid fair and effective. In J. D. Fisher, A. Nadler, & B. M. DePaulo (Eds.), *New directions in helping. Vol. 2: Recipients' reactions to aid* (pp. 39-44). New York: Academic.

Brinkmann, C. (1985). Psychosoziale und gesundheitliche Folgen der Arbeitslosigkeit—Ergebnisse einer repräsentativen Längsschnittuntersuchung des IAB. In T. Kieselbach & A. Wacker (Eds.), *Individuelle und gesellschaftliche Kosten der Massenarbeitslosigkeit—Psychologische Theorie und Praxis* (pp. 186-206). Weinheim, Basel, Switzerland: Beltz.

Buchholz, W., Gmuer, W., Höfer, R., & Straus, F. (1984). *Lebenswelt und Familienwirklichkeit*. Frankfurt: Campus.

Buss, T. F. & Redburn, F. S., with Waldron, J. (1983). *Mass unemployment. Plant closings and community mental health*. Beverly Hills, CA: Sage.

Catalano, R. & Dooley, D. (1980). Economic change in primary prevention. In R. H. Price, R. F. Ketterer, B. C. Bader, & J. Monahan (Eds.), *Prevention in community mental health: Research, policy and practice* (pp. 21-40). Beverly Hills, CA: Sage.

Cohn, E. S. (1983). Effects of victims' and helpers' attributions for problem and solution on reactions to receiving help. In A. Nadler, J. D. Fisher, & B. M. DePaulo (Eds.), *New directions in helping: Vol. 3. Applied perspectives on help-seeking and -receiving* (pp. 46-70). New York: Academic.

Cozby, P. C. (1973). Self-disclosure. A literature review. *Psychological Bulletin, 79*, 73-91.

DePaulo, B. M., Nadler, M. A., & Fisher, J. D. (Eds.). (1983). *New directions in helping: Vol. 2. Help-seeking*. New York: Academic.

Dooley, D., & Catalano, R. (1985). Why the economy predicts help-seeking: A test of competing explanations. In G. Westcott, P. G. Svensson, & H. F. K. Zoellner (Eds.), *Health policy implications of unemployment* (pp. 205-230). Copenhagen: World Health Organization.

Finlay-Jones, R., & Eckhardt, B. A. (1981). Psychiatric disorder among the young unemployed. *Australian and New Zealand Journal of Psychiatry, 15*, 265-270.

Finlay-Jones, R., & Eckhardt, B. A. (1982). *Survey of psychiatric disorder among the young unemployed of Canberra*. Final Report submitted to the Research and Development Grants Advisory Committee, Australian Department of Health.

Fisher, J. D., Nadler, A., & DePaulo, B. M. (Eds.). (1983). *New directions in helping: Vol. 1. Recipient reactions to aid*. New York: Academic.

Frese, M. (1985). Zur Verlaufsstruktur der psychischen Auswirkungen von Arbeitslosigkeit. In T. Kieselbach & A. Wacker (Eds.), *Individuelle und gesellschaftli-che Kosten der Massenarbeitslosigkeit—Psychologische Theorie und Praxis* (pp. 224-255). Weinheim, Basel, Switzerland: Beltz.

Fryer, D. M. & Payne, R. L. (1984). Proactive behaviour in unemployment: Findings and implications. *Leisure Studies, 3,* 273-295.

Goffman, E. (1956-1957). Embarrassment and social organization. *American Journal of Sociology, 62,* 264-271.

Goodstein, L. D. & Reinecker, V. M. (1974). Factors affecting self-disclosure: A review of the literature. In B. A. Maher (Ed.), *Progress in experimental personality research: Vol. 7* (pp. 49-77). New York: Academic.

Gourash, N. (1978). Help-seeking: A review of the literature. *American Journal of Community Psychology, 6,* 413-423.

Greenberg, M. S. (1980). A theory of indebtedness. In K. J. Gergen, M. S. Greenberg, & R. S. Wills, (Eds.), *Social exchange: Advances in theory and research* (pp. 72-91). New York: Plenum.

Gross, A. E. & McMullen, P. A. (1982). The help-seeking process. In V. J. Derlega J.Grzelak, (Eds.), *Cooperation and helping behavior: Theories and research* (pp. 305-326). New York: Academic.

Gross, A. E. & McMullen, P. A. (1983). Models of the help-seeking process. In B. DePaulo, M. A. Nadler, & J. D. Fisher (Eds.), *New directions in helping: Vol. 2. Help-seeking* (pp. 45-69). New York: Academic.

Gross, A. E., Wallston, B. S., & Piliavin, I. (1979). Reactance, attribution, equity, and the help recipient. *Journal of Applied Social Psychology, 9,* 297-313.

Holmes, T. H., & Rahe, R. H. (1967). The social readjustment rating scale. *Journal of Psychosomatic Research, 11,* 213-218.

Jahoda, M. (1982). *Employment and unemployment.* Cambridge: Cambridge University Press.

Jourard, S. M. (1964). *The transparent self.* Princeton, NJ: Van Nostrand Reinhold.

Kanner, A. D., Coyne, J. C., Schaefer, C., & Lazarus, R. S. (1981). Comparison of two modes of stress measurement: Daily hassles and uplifts versus major life events. *Journal of Behavioral Medicine, 4,* 1-39.

Kieselbach, T. (1985a). Arbeitslosigkeit, Selbsteröffnung und Hilfesuchverhalten. In H. Keupp, D. Kleiber, & B. Scholten (Eds.), *Im Schatten der Wende. Helfer-krisen—Arbeitslosigkeit—Berufliche Rehabilitation* (pp. 122-137). Tübingen: DGVT.

Kieselbach, T. (1985b). The contribution of psychology to the realm of unemploy-ment in the community: Intervention and research concepts. In G. Westcott, P. G. Svensson, & H. F. K. Zöllner (Eds.), *Health policy implications of unemployment* (pp. 367-382). Copenhagen: World Health Organization.

Kieselbach, T. (1986). Zwischen 'blaming the victim' und 'social victim': Forschung und Intervention im Bereich Arbeitslosigkeit. In A. Schorr (Ed.), *Psychologie Mitte der 80er Jahre: Geschichte, Berufsrecht, Weiterbildung, Neue Tätigkeitsfelder, Integration in der Psychotherapie: Vol. 3* (pp. 211-228). Proceedings of the 13th Congress for Applied Psychology of the Association of German Psychologists (BDP), Bonn., Sept. 1985. Bonn: Deutscher Psychologen.

Kieselbach, T. (1987a). Gesellschaftliche und individuelle Bewältigung von Arbeitslosigkeit. In H. Moser (Ed.), *Bedrohung und Beschwichtigung. Die politische und die seelische Gestalt technischer, wirtschaftlicher und gesundheitlicher Gefährdungen* (Fortschritte der Politischen Psychologie, Sonderband 1) (pp.28-55). Weinheim, Basel, Switzerland: Deutscher Studien.

Kieselbach, T. (1987b). Self-disclosure and help-seeking as determinants of vulnerability. Case studies of unemployed from social-psychiatric services and demands for health and social policy. In D. Schwefel, P. G. Svensson, & H. F. K. Zöllner (Eds.), *Unemployment, social vulnerability and health in Europe* (pp. 281-303). Berlin: Springer.

Kieselbach, T. (1988). Youth unemployment and health effects. *International Journal of Social Psychiatry, 34,* 83-96.

Kieselbach, T. (1989). A regional approach for the improvement of the psychosocial situation of the unemployed - the Regional Working Group 'Unemployment and Health' Bremen (FRG). In P.-G. Svensson, B. Starrin, & H. Wintersberger (Eds.), *Unemployment, poverty and quality of working life: Some European experiences* (pp. 295-334). Berlin: Sigma.

Kieselbach, T. (in press-a). *Selbsteröffnung und Hilfesuchen von Arbeitslosen im Sozialpsychiatrischen Dienst.* Weinheim, Basel, Switzerland: Deutscher Studien.

Kieselbach, T. (in press-b). Unemployment. In R. Lerner, J. Brooks-Gunn, & A. C. Petersen (Eds.), *Encyclopedia of adolescence.* Philadelphia: Garland.

Kieselbach, T., & Svensson, P. G. (1988). Health and social policy responses to unemployment in Europe. *Journal of Social Issues, 44,* 173-191.

Kieselbach, T., & Wacker, A. (Eds.) (1985). *Individuelle und gesellschaftliche Kosten der Massenarbeitslosigkeit—Psychologische Theorie und Praxis* (2nd ed.). Weinheim, Basel, Switzerland: Deutscher Studien. (Original work published 1985)

Klink, F., & Scherner, E. (1986). Arbeitslos—am Ende steht der Sozialpsychiatrische Dienst? *Bremer Beiträge zur Psychologie, 58* (whole number).

Liem, R. (1983). *Reconsidering the concept of social victim: The case of unemployment.* Unpublished paper presented at the Annual Meeting of the American Psychological Association, Anaheim, CA.

Mechanic, D. (Ed.). (1982). *Symptoms, illness behavior, and help-seeking.* New York: Prodist.

Nadler, A., Fisher, J. D., & DePaulo, B. M. (Eds.) (1983). *New directions in helping: Vol. 3. Applied perspectives on help-seeking and -receiving.* New York: Academic.

Nadler, A., Fisher, J. D., & Streufert, S. (1976). When helping hurts: The effects of donor-recipient similarity and recipient self-esteem on reactions to aid. *Journal of Personality, 44,* 392-409.

Nelson-LeGall, S., Gumerman, R. A., & Scott-Jones, D. (1983). Instrumental help-seeking and everyday problem-solving: A developmental perspective. In B. M. DePaulo, A. Nadler, & J. D. Fisher (Eds.), *New directions in helping: Vol. 2. Help-seeking* (pp. 265-283). New York: Academic.

Rappaport, J. (1981). In praise of paradox: A social policy of empowerment over prevention. *American Journal of Community Psychology, 9*, 1-25.

Rappaport, J. (1987). Terms of empowerment/exemplars of prevention: Toward a theory of community psychology. *American Journal of Community Psychology, 15*, 121-128.

Rosen, S. (1983). Perceived inadequacy and help-seeking. In B. M. DePaulo, M. A. Nadler & J. D. Fisher (Eds.), *New directions in helping: Vol. 2. Help-seeking* (pp. 73-100). New York: Academic.

Rostila, I. (1985). Arbeitslosigkeit als Lebenslage im Lebensverlauf. In T. Kieselbach & A. Wacker (Eds.), *Individuelle und gesellschaftliche Kosten der Massenarbeitslosigkeit—Psychologische Theorie und Praxis* (pp. 84-90). Weinheim, Basel, Switzerland: Beltz.

Schwefel, D. (1986). Unemployment, health and health services in German-speaking countries. *Social Science and Medicine, 22*, 409-430.

Schwefel, D., Svensson, P.-G., & Zöllner, H. F. K. (Eds.). (1987). *Unemployment, social vulnerability and health in Europe*. Berlin: Springer.

Shapiro, E. G. (1983). Embarrassment and help-seeking. In B. M. DePaulo, M. A. Nadler, & J. D. Fisher (Eds.), *New directions in helping: Vol. 2. Help-seeking* (pp. 143-161). New York: Academic.

Spruit, I. (1983). To be employed, to be unemployed and health in families in Leiden. In I. Spruit (Ed.), *Unemployment, employment, and health* (pp. 137-177). Leiden, the Netherlands: Instituut voor Sociale Geneeskunde.

Tessler, C., & Schwartz, S. H. (1972). Help-seeking, self-esteem, and achievement motivation: An attributional analysis. *Journal of Personality and Psychology, 21*, 318-326.

Warr, P. B., Banks, M. H. & Ullah, P. (1985). The experience of unemployment among black and white urban teenagers. *British Journal of Psychology, 76*, 75-87.

Wills, T. A. (Ed.). (1982). *Basic processes in helping relationships*. New York: Academic.

Wills, T. A. (1983). Social comparison in coping and help-seeking. In B. M. DePaulo, M. A. Nadler, & J. D. Fisher (Eds.), *New directions in helping: Vol. 2. Help-seeking* (pp. 109-139). New York: Academic.

Witzel, A. (1982). *Verfahren der qualitativen Sozialforschung*. Frankfurt: Campus.

Zola, J. (1964). Illness behavior of the working class. In A. Shostak & W. Gomberg (Eds.), *Blue-collar world: Studies of the American worker* (pp. 351-361). Englewood Cliffs, NJ: Prentice-Hall.

11

New Challenges for Career Development: Methodological Implications

William A. Borgen and Norman E. Amundson

In recent years it has become increasingly evident that Western societies are going through a profound economic and social transition as we seek to come to terms with what Freeman and Perez (1988) have called the new "techno-economic paradigm." The microelectronic revolution has signaled major changes in production and information capability (Feather, 1987). The consequences of this technological revolution reverberate through the social and educational structure as well as through the economy.

In terms of work life, the rules for career development have certainly changed (Cohen & Shannon, 1984; Herr & Cramer, 1984). With the shift from traditional manufacturing to the service sector there has been a restructuring of the nature and availability of work. An uninterrupted work life can no longer be taken for granted. Periods of unemployment and career change are to be expected in the normal course of events (Parun & Ploughman, 1988). In terms of employment, while some high-paying jobs have emerged, the greatest thrust in many countries has been in the creation of relatively low-paying jobs that are not secure and that do not utilize a wide range of employee skills (Howard, 1985).

The workers hardest hit by this restructuring have been the young, the handicapped, women, minority groups, and those who are approaching retirement (Mason, 1985). These workers find themselves facing what Bluestone and Harrison (1988) have termed the "Great American U-Turn." Many of the economic gains, in terms of wages, benefits, and security, that have been obtained since the 1940s, have been eroded.

The economic and social scenario just described suggests that the societal context for career development has changed. In view of this change, and the implication that the process of career development may have changed as a result, there is a need for a different foundation for career guidance. The basic assumptions of personal power over job selection underlying traditional career development theories (Ginzburg, 1972; Holland, 1973; Super, 1972) need to be reexamined and perhaps reframed to take account of the current economic and social situations.

GUIDELINES FOR BUILDING A NEW FOUNDATION FOR CAREER DEVELOPMENT

The process of building a new understanding of career development must use as its starting point an exploration of people's experiences (Amundson & Cochran, 1984). In gathering the information required it is also important to cast a wide net. One way of ensuring that a sufficiently comprehensive exploration and analysis has been accomplished is to use as a guideline the heuristic approach proposed by Young, Becker, and Pike (1970) in their textbook on rhetoric. In this book they describe how experiences can be examined from a wide variety of perspectives to: (a) recall a wide range of information, (b) show different relationships between the various segments of information, and (c) facilitate discovery. While their initial intent was to develop a system for use in the exploration of rhetorical composition, their approach can be used as a basis for exploring and analyzing career development experiences.

Young and colleagues suggest that experiences can be considered in terms of their static (particle), dynamic (wave), and network (field) qualities. Using a particle perspective one captures a snapshot of an experience but pays little attention to contextual elements. Viewing experiences as a wave shifts the focus from static qualities to the changes that occur with the passage of time. In terms of a field perspective, the emphasis is on the relationship of the experience to other parts of a system. As an illustration, suppose that one were to consider the emotional experiences associated with unemployment. The static perspective would highlight the particular positive and negative experiences associated with being without paid work. Using the wave metaphor, the experiences would be viewed in terms of how they changed over time. From a field perspective, the experiences would be viewed in terms of how they related to contextual variables like job prospects, support from family, and so on. By using all three perspectives, one obtains a better understanding of the various dimensions of experience.

The particle-wave-field perspective on experience provides one set of dimensions, but Young et al. (1970) suggest that experiences must also be viewed in terms of their particular details. Using the same illustration as above, the emotional experiences of unemployment would need to be understood in terms of the following factors: (a) contrasting features, (b) range of variation, and (c) distribution. In terms of contrast, the emotional experiences would need to be viewed in terms of their similarity and differences with emotional reactions while working. The range of variation emphasizes the fact that people do not feel the same way all the time. A person may feel unhappy, but the degree of unhappiness will undoubtedly vacillate depending on environmental conditions and personal cognitions. As for distribution, the focus would be on the context and how particular people, thoughts, or situations might trigger certain emotional reactions.

As the example illustrates, a comprehensive understanding of an experience stands a better chance of being achieved when one utilizes both particle-wave-field perspectives and characteristics such as contrast, variation and distribution. In the following sections of the chapter we will attempt to further illustrate ways in which a broader perspective can assist in developing contextually relevant approaches to the study of career.

CHOOSING RESEARCH METHODS

The preceding discussion has helped to map the range of research questions that need to be addressed to begin the process of building a new foundation for a contemporary understanding of career development. In approaching the topic in this way we are affirming the importance of reported and observed life experience as a valid starting point from which research methods can evolve. The selection of this starting point is not as straightforward as it may appear. Three desirable features of research are realism, generality, and precision/control. According to Runkel and McGrath (1972), although all these conditions are desirable—indeed mandatory—"the investigator cannot maximize all of them in any one study. And a shift in strategy to increase any one will automatically decrease one or both of the others" (p. 115). Thus, by highlighting realism and life experience, we are making a choice that has implications for research methodology.

The rationale for emphasizing realism can be found in a statement by Goldman (1976):

> Published research in counseling has, on the whole, been of little value as a base or guide for professional practice. Tied to largely inappropriate models derived from the physical sciences, much of the research has been trivial, atomistic, and obsessed with statistics and technical matters of research design. Counseling researchers have often futilely pursued the goals of precision and control, despite the fact that the major objects of study—counselees and the counseling process—do not lend themselves to precise measurement, certainly not at this stage in the development of the behavioral sciences. Major changes in the methods and contents of research are needed. (p. 543)

In our opinion, many of the observations of Goldman in 1976 hold true today, although there are growing signs that new paradigms are also emerging (Howard, 1984). In order to develop a foundation of career development that can have application in the world of the practitioner it is essential to begin with real-life experience and work toward precision and generality (Weinberg, 1959). The importance of this beginning point is further highlighted by Blumer (1969) when he states "the actor acts towards the world on the basis of how he sees it and not on the basis of how the world appears to the outside observer" (p. 17).

Approaching research questions with an emphasis on obtaining descriptions of processes as perceived or observed has implications for the choice of research methodologies used in the study of career development. Goldman (1976) suggests the following:

> Promising trends in the design and conduct of studies include (a) macroscopic rather than microscopic levels of study, (b) field rather than laboratory studies, (c) focusing on the total individual as the unit of study, (d) developing a contractual relationship between researcher and subject, (e) giving due attention to applied evaluation methods, (f) viewing the researcher as the basic research instrument, and (g) anticipating the use of the research findings. (p. 543)

These methods are all indicative of systematic inquiry. The important issue is to choose methods that make sense for the questions that are being asked. In the sections that follow we will outline some of the research efforts that we have undertaken in our ongoing quest for a new understanding of career development and methodological efficacy.

RESEARCH CONCERNING THE EXPERIENCE OF UNEMPLOYMENT

Our studies began with a theoretical depiction of the experience of unemployment as an emotional roller coaster, characterized by loss, grief, and job-search burnout reactions (Amundson & Borgen, 1982). This idea was based on the assumption that involuntary unemployment would represent a loss of a significant life activity and that prolonged, unsuccessful job search would be highly discouraging.

Several studies over the years have contained various descriptions of the effects of unemployment as it is related to people's well being (Bratfisch, 1984; Brenner & Bartell, 1983; Finley & Lee, 1981; Sinfield, 1981; Tiggemann & Winefield, 1984; Warr, Jackson, & Banks, 1982). The negative reactions associated with the experience of unemployment include a sense of inadequacy, depression, lowered self-esteem, increased stress, social isolation, an increased tendency toward minor psychiatric illness, erratic mood shifts, and a progressive loss of optimism about finding employment (Brenner, 1973; Cohn, 1978; Feather & Barber, 1983; Gurney, 1980a, 1980b; Hartley, 1980; Jahoda, 1982; Kasl, Gore, & Cobb, 1975; Liem & Rayman, 1982; Perfetti & Bingham, 1983; Shaw, 1976; Shelton, 1985; Sinfield, 1981; Stokes & Cochrane, 1984; Warr, 1983).

In addition to these studies which were, in the main, cross-sectional, quantitatively based particle investigations, there are some descriptions of the process of unemployment—to use the terminology proposed in this chapter, wave studies. As early as 1935, Zawadski and Lazersfeld described the typical course of the moods of the unemployed as a general feeling of injury, fear, distress, fury, numbness, hopelessness-fear, acquiescence, and apathy. Also, in a more recent article, Heppner and Downing (1982) described the job search and interview process for recent psychology graduates as an emotional roller coaster, with feelings ranging from excitement and elation to anger and depression.

If one surveys recent literature, it seems that the vast majority of studies of unemployment, like the studies of career access and progression, are cross-sectional particle studies in which certain variables judged to be relevant and subject to variation during unemployment were measured with various samples. In examining these studies, it seemed to us that there was insufficient information about the overall process of which these variables were a part. Important questions include: Is there a process that can describe an experience of unemployment? Does this process differ according to demographic, personality, or social factors? Warr (1983) suggested that there was evidence to suggest that the unemployment experience was not the same for everyone, but there did not seem to exist a systematic description of the process of being unemployed over time.

In an effort to investigate the unemployment experience process(es), we conducted several exploratory, descriptive, wave-related interview studies. These studies included samples of men, women, immigrants, youths with high school and university educations, and people with physical disabilities (Amundson & Borgen, 1987a, 1987b; Borgen & Amundson, 1984, 1987; Borgen, Amundson, & Biela, 1987; Borgen, Hatch, & Amundson, 1988).

Methodology

We decided on an open-ended interviewing approach that would facilitate participants telling their stories (Bailey, 1980; Fischer, 1979; Giorgi, 1970) and a critical incident approach developed by Flanagan (1954, 1978). These methods facilitate wave oriented information collection in the realms of contrast, variation, and distribution.

Research assistants were trained to conduct interviews in which participants told of their experience of unemployment with a minimum of interruption or direction. The interview procedure was designed to give participants the opportunity to talk freely about their experiences of unemployment and to focus on some of the high and low points. Near the end of the interview, participants were asked to depict their experience graphically on a time line that charted their remembered experiences and emotions. The stories, critical incidents, and the time line were then discussed with each participant to ensure that there was a correspondence between the information provided in the interview and the summary graph. These discussions increased the likelihood that (a) the participants presented a valid representation of their remembered experiences and emotions, and (b) the interviewer accurately understood the information that had been provided by the participants.

The first step in the data analysis involved transcribing the interviews. We then had research assistants summarize the data and divide the information into "meaning units" (Colaizzi, 1978). Regular reliability checks were made to ensure that the same meaning units were being identified. Using the summaries, the research assistants were then asked to transpose information onto rating sheets. These sheets focused on several components: (a) stated shifts in emotion, (b) time sequence involved with the occurrence of particular emotions, (c) events or behaviors identified as accompanying specific emotional shifts, (d) coping strategies employed, (e) job-search strategies employed, and (f) future expectations. Reliability checks were again conducted to ensure a high degree of consistency.

Once the data had been coded, the rating sheets and life line depiction of each participant's experience of unemployment were used as a graphic representation. More specifically, each time a participant stated a shift in emotion, the shift was noted and named, and an upward or downward pointing arrow was drawn to indicate the direction of the shift. For each shift, the relative spot on the figure was determined by the words used by the participant. For example, the shift "feeling somewhat hopeless" to "feeling cautiously optimistic" would appear lower in the figure than would "feeling hopeful" to "extremely enthusiastic". This process provided two dimensions: the horizontal, denoting time, and the vertical, denoting optimism or pessimism. The accuracy of each figure was checked by comparing it with the figure drawn by each participant at the end of his or her interview. In each case, the figure drawn by the research assistant was an accurate representation of what had been drawn by the participant. Finally, across all studies approximately one-third of the participants were contacted to check the accuracy of the representation.

Next, descriptions were examined for similarities, and people who had described similar patterns of response to unemployment were placed together. Research assistants independently sorted participants' descriptions according to similarity of experience. As a result of this process, a series of patterns was identified.

Results

Results revealed that there was a predominant pattern for about 40 percent of the entire sample across all studies, which totaled over 300 people. This predominant pattern was similar to the original loss and burnout roller coaster model developed in 1982. Subjects who described this pattern of experience included men, women, immigrants, and people with physical disabilities. It is also important to note, however, that other subjects from each of these sample groups also described patterns somewhat different from the most frequently occurring one. These results are consistent with those of Ullah, Banks, & Warr (1985) who state that the "experiences during unemployment are affected by a wide range of features and processes; no single predictor is likely to have a major impact on its own" (p. 293). The results also illustrate the point made by Payne and Hartley (1987) that little is known about the way in which biographical and personality factors vary systematically with each other because there is considerable variation in the experience and circumstances of unemployed people; consequently they cannot be considered to be homogenized by their experience.

Another aspect of the analysis focused on the factors that were identified as being particularly helpful or hindering in relation to the experience of unemployment. An analysis of the categorized responses derived a series of factors that varied in importance somewhat across different subgroups, but that were more striking for the regularity of their occurrence. Like Merriam (1987), we found that most of the frequently occurring positive factors were associated with support from family and friends, opportunities for work, and meaningful activity. Negative factors were related to unsuccessful job-search activities, financial pressures, unproductive contacts with government agencies, negative outlook, and family problems (Amundson & Borgen, 1987b).

The people in the studies exhibited or reported a series of reactions to an interruption in career path progression or a block to job attainment rooted in expectations of relatively easy access to desired occupations. Many of the traditional theories of vocational development do not seem to focus to any great extent on the examination of this assumption, and may be preparing people inadequately to face the reality of current labor market opportunities.

EVALUATING THE METHOD OF RESEARCH

In considering the utility of the approach used in these studies it is important to examine it from several perspectives. From the point of view of reliability of the coding, categorization, and grouping of patterns, a high level of agreement among independent raters was realized. This level of consistency suggests that the data can be reliably summarized and represented according to patterns of experience and positive and negative incidents.

Consideration of threats to validity of the data were treated in several ways. First, during the course of interviewing, the interviewers verbally summarized information provided by participants to check for accuracy. Second, participants were asked to depict their experiences on a time line as a means of comparison. Third, a subset of the participants (about one-third) were contacted to check the accuracy of the summaries and time line. Finally, the issue of a validity claim for the information as it may apply to others has been addressed by replication of studies. Essentially identical experiences and critical incidents were described by participants in three independent studies (Amundson & Borgen, 1987b; Borgen & Amundson, 1987; Borgen, Amundson, & Biela, 1987; Borgen, Hatch, & Amundson, 1988).

The series of studies just described as well as others that focused on unemployed youth and social supports (Marak, 1987), underemployment (Borgen, Amundson, & Harder, 1988), job insecurity (Earnshaw, Amundson, & Borgen, in press), and career reestablishment (Williams, 1988) that we have conducted or supervised suggest that the method of data collection and analysis can provide a rich base of information regarding career path progression through job loss, job search, and career entry or reentry.

These exploratory descriptive studies also provided a map that suggested relevant variables for cross-sectional and longitudinal studies. One such study by Feesey (1987) used several of the critical incident factors as a basis for developing questionnaires. He found that white-collar workers split into high- and low-functioning groups according to several mental health measures, bracketing the blue-collar group. We are currently involved in two longitudinal studies of career establishment using such quantitative measures as causality, work involvement, job satisfaction, and activity and money problems. In these studies two groups of youth are being studied, one for an 18-month and the other for a 2-year period. Quantitative measures and open-ended interviews are being used with participants three times during each study. These studies represent a logical extension of the initial wave studies and have both particle and wave dimensions. That is, the quantitative measures can be viewed within the context of recalled experiences of participants.

As was mentioned earlier, the initial wave studies that we conducted clearly reflect reactions of people prepared for a set of contextual or field conditions that did not exist for them. The results also suggest that more foundational wave studies are needed in order to derive the range of forces that may help or hinder personal effectiveness in career access and progression.

REFERENCES

Amundson, N. E. & Borgen, W. A. (1982). The dynamics of unemployment: Job loss and job search. *Personnel and Guidance Journal, 60,* 562-564.

Amundson, N. E., & Borgen, W. A. (1987a). *At the controls.* Toronto: Nelson Canada.

Amundson, N. E., & Borgen, W. A. (1987b). Coping with unemployment: What helps and what hinders. *Journal of Employment Counseling, 24,* 96-106.

Amundson, N. E. & Cochran, L. (1984). Analyzing experiences using an adaptation of a heuristic approach. *Canadian Counsellor, 18,* 183-186.

Bailey, K. D. (1980). *Methods in social research* (2nd ed.). New York: Free Press.

Bluestone, B. & Harrison, B. (1988). *The great u-turn: An inquiry into recent U.S. employment trends in employment, earnings and family income.* Proceedings of the Conference on Structural Change and Labour Market Policy. Stockholm, Sweden: The Swedish Centre for Working Life (ALC).

Blumer, H. (1969). *Symbolic interactionism.* Englewood Cliffs, NJ: Prentice Hall.

Borgen, W. A. & Amundson, N. E. (1984). *The experience of unemployment.* Toronto: Nelson Canada.

Borgen, W. A. & Amundson, N. E. (1987). The dynamics of unemployment. *Journal of Counseling and Development, 66,* 180-184.

Borgen, W. A., Amundson, N. E. & Biela, P. M. (1987). The experience of unemployment for persons who are physically disabled. *Journal of Applied Rehabilitation Counseling, 18,* 25-32.

Borgen, W. A., Amundson, N. E. & Harder, H. (1988). The experience of underemployment. *Journal of Employment Counseling, 25,* 149-159.

Borgen, W. A., Hatch, W. & Amundson, N. E. (1988). *The experience of unemployment for university graduates: An exploratory study.* Unpublished paper, University of British Columbia, Vancouver.

Bratfisch, D. (1984). *Counselling the unemployed: Employment service strategies in connection with the closure of a large company of great importance to the local labour market—The Swedish experiment.* Paper presented to the Tenth National Consultation on Vocational Counselling, Canada Employment and Immigration Commission, Ottawa.

Brenner, M. H. (Ed.). (1973). *Mental illness and the economy.* Cambridge, MA: Harvard University Press.

Brenner, S. O. & Bartell, R. (1983). The psychological impact of unemployment: A structural analysis of cross-sectional data. *Journal of Occupational Psychology, 56,* 129-136.

Colaizzi, P. F. (1978). Psychological research as the phenomenologist views it. In R. S. Valle & M. King (Eds.), *Existential-phenomenological alternatives for psychology* (pp. 48-71). New York: Oxford University Press.

Cohen, D. & Shannon, K. (1984). *The next Canadian economy.* Montreal: Eden.

Cohn, R. M. (1978). The effect of employment status change on self-attitudes. *Social Psychology, 41,* 81-93.

Earnshaw, A. R., Amundson, N. E. & Borgen, W. A., (in press). The experience of job insecurity for professional women. *Journal of Employment Counseling.*

Feather, F. (1987). *Tomorrow's best Canadian careers.* Toronto: Global Management Bureau.

Feather, N. T. & Barber, J. G. (1983). Depressive reactions and unemployment. *Journal of Abnormal Psychology, 92,* 185-195.

Feesey, T. (1987). *White collar unemployment.* Unpublished Master's thesis, University of British Columbia, Vancouver.

Finley, M. H. & Lee, A. T. (1981). The terminated executive: It's like dying. *Personnel and Guidance Journal, 59,* 382-384.

Fischer, C. T. (1979). Individualized assessment and phenomenological psychology. *Journal of Personality Assessment, 43,* 115-122.

Flanagan, J. (1954). The critical incident technique. *Psychological Bulletin, 51,* 327-356.

Flanagan, J. (1978). A research approach to improving our quality of life. *American Psychologist, 33,* 138-147.

Freeman, C.,& Perez, C. (1988). *Long waves and changes in employment patterns.* Proceedings of the Conference on Structural Change and Labour Market Market Policy. Stockholm, Sweden: The Swedish Centre for Working Life (ALC).

Ginzburg, E. (1972). Toward a theory of occupational choice: A restatement. *Vocational Guidance Quarterly, 20,* 169-176.

Giorgi, A. (1970). *Psychology as a human science: A phenomenologically based approach.* New York: Harper & Row.

Goldman, L. (1976). A revolution in counseling research. *Journal of Counseling Psychology, 23,* 543-552.

Gurney, R. M. (1980a) Does unemployment affect the self esteem of school leavers? *Australian Journal of Psychology, 32,* 175-182.

Gurney, R. M. (1980b). The effects of unemployment on the psychosocial development of school-leavers. *Journal of Occupational Psychology, 53,* 205-213.

Hartley, J. (1980). Psychological approaches to unemployment. *Bulletin of the British Psychological Society, 32,* 309-315.

Heppner, P. P. & Downing, N. E. (1982). Job interviewing for new psychologists: Riding the emotional rollercoaster. *Professional Psychology, 13,* 334-341.

Herr, E. L. & Cramer, S. H. (1984). *Career guidance and counseling through the life span* (2nd ed.). Toronto: Little, Brown & Co.

Holland, J. L. (1973). *Making vocational choices: A theory of careers.* Englewood Cliffs, NJ: Prentice Hall.

Howard, G. S. (1984). A modest proposal for a revision of strategies in counseling research. *Journal of Counseling Psychology, 31,* 430-442.

Howard, R. (1985). *Brave new workplace.* New York: Penguin.

Jahoda, M. (1982). *Employment and unemployment.* Cambridge: Cambridge University Press.

Kasl, S., Gore, S., & Cobb, S. (1975). The experience of losing a job: Reported changes in health, symptoms and illness behavior. *Psychosomatic Medicine, 37,* 106-122.

Liem, R., & Rayman, P. (1982). Health and social costs of unemployment. *American Psychologist, 37,* 1116-1123.

Marak, B. (1987). *Unemployed youth and social supports.* Unpublished Master's thesis. University of British Columbia, Vancouver.

Mason. C. (1985). *Transition to work.* Winnipeg, Man.: Institute for Social and Economic Research.

Merriam, S. B. (1987). The experience of job loss as perceived by young and middle-aged adults and those near retirement. *Journal of Employment Counseling, 24,* 107-114.

Parun, E., & Ploughman, P. (1988). *Structural change and politics in the U.S.A. in the 80's.* Proceedings of the Conference on Structural Change and Labour Market Policy. Stockholm, Sweden: The Swedish Centre for Working Life (ALC).

Payne, R. & Hartley, J. (1987). A test of a model for explaining the affective experience of unemployed men. *Journal of Occupational Psychology, 60,* 31-47.

Perfetti, C. J. & Bingham, W. C. (1983). Unemployment and self-esteem in metal refinery workers. *Vocational Guidance Quarterly, 31,* 195-202.

Runkel, P. J. & McGrath, J. E. (1972). *Research on human behavior: A systematic guide to method.* New York: Holt, Rinehart & Winston.

Shaw, D. (1976). Unemployment hurts more than just the pocketbook. *Today's Health, 54*, 23-26.

Shelton, B. K. (1985). The social and psychological impact of unemployment. *Journal of Employment Counseling, 22*, 18-22.

Sinfield, A. (1981). *What unemployment means.* Oxford, England: Martin Robinson.

Stokes, G., & Cochrane, R. (1984). A study of the psychological effects of redundancy and unemployment. *Journal of Occupational Psychology, 57*, 309-322.

Super, D. E. (1972). A life span, life space approach to career development. *Journal of Vocational Behavior, 16*, 282-298.

Tiggemann, M,. & Winefield, M. (1984). The effects of unemployment on the mood, self-esteem, locus of control, and depressive effect of school leavers. *Journal of Occupational Psychology, 57*, 33-42.

Ullah, P., Banks, M., & Warr, P. (1985). Social support, social pressures and psychological distress during unemployment. *Psychological Medicine, 15*, 283-295.

Warr, P. B. (1983). Job loss, unemployment and psychological well-being. In V. L. Allen & E. Van de Vliert (Eds.), *Role transitions.* London: Plenum.

Warr, P. B., Jackson, P. R., & Banks, M. H. (1982). Duration of unemployment and psychological well being in young men and women. *Current Psychological Research, 2*, 207-214.

Weinberg, H. L. (1959). *Levels of knowing and existence.* New York: Harper & Row.

Williams, L. (1988). *The experience of re-employment.* Unpublished Master's thesis. University of British Columbia.

Young, R. E., Becker, A. L., & Pike, K. L. (1970). *Rhetoric: Discovery and change.* New York: Harcourt, Brace and World.

Zawadski, B., & Lazarsfeld, P. (1935). The psychological consequences of unemployment. *Journal of Social Psychology, 6*, 244-251.

12

Mid-life Career Change Research

Audrey Collin

The topic of career change provides a useful focus when examining the nature of career and ways of studying it. First, it raises the thorny issues of conceptualization and definition, of objectivity and subjectivity. Second, it poses the challenge of identifying meaningful patterns within a web of interrelationships and of studying complex lifelong phenomena. Third, because career change is often a difficult experience for the individual, it demands effort and integrity from the researcher, whose work may eventually form the basis of a counselor's work with a client. This chapter shows how I came to recognize these issues as I set out on my doctoral study of mid-career change, how I attempted to address them, and with what result (Collin, 1984).

BACKGROUND TO THE STUDY

My initial examination of the literature on middle age and on career uncovered a wide range of definitions and meanings apparently ascribed to these various terms (Collin, 1985). Analysis of these suggested that they resulted from the different perspectives on career perceived by the writers—that is, the observer's or actor's view of career—and from the different functions that they used the term to serve, whether to describe or to interpret phenomena. Figure 12.1 identifies four conceptualizations of career arranged on these two axes. The individual's job history recorded by another person forms the substantive career; when others place their interpretation on this history—"local boy makes good," "a brilliant career in the Civil Services"—this is the socially symbolic career. The individual's completion of the "your career to date" section of a job application form would be an example of the phenomenal career, while the working and reworking of one's personal history for and to oneself is the transcendental career. Although it was possible to infer the principles underlying these different conceptualizations in the literature, in general they were not made explicit, nor were their implications discussed.

It was not until the 1970s (Ginzberg, 1972; Super, 1977) that it became accepted that to change careers was not "floundering" (Super, 1957) or some other aberration postulated by the career theorists of the 1950s. The recognition of the

Figure 12.1. Framework for analyzing the meaning of "career."

	the observer's construct of 'career'	the actor's construct of 'career'

'career' as description ↑	**the Substantive 'career'**
	
	• the 'career path' through
	— an occupation
	— an organization
	
	• the individual's progress
	— along such 'paths' in
	  – an occupation
	  – an organization
	— through occupational life in general
	— through life in general
	
	• the individual's subjective experience of such progress
		the Phenomenal 'career'
		
		• the progress of self:
		
		• along a 'career path' in
		— an occupation
		— an organization
		
		• through occupation life in general
		
		• through life in general

↓ 'career' as interpretation	**the Socially Symbolic 'career'**
	
	• the social symbolism of
	— 'career paths' in
	  – an occupation
	  – an organization
	• the individual's progress
	— along such 'paths' in
	  – an occupation
	  – an organization
	— through occupational life in general
	— through life in general
		the Transcendental 'career'
		
		• the significance to self of progress:
		
		— along a 'career path' in
		  – an occupation
		  – an organization
		— through occupational life in general
		— through life in general

need for further occupational exploration in mid-life, whether created by necessity, such as obsolescence and redundancy, or by some personal change, led to several North American studies of career change, for example, Clopton (1972), Gottfredson (1977), Hiestand (1971), LaBuda (1974), Neapolitan (1980), Robbins (1977), Vaitenas and Wiener (1977). These and other studies of the same period focused on the discontinuity of career change rather than the continuity of career, and sought to understand the kind of people who made career changes. They, therefore, examined the characteristics of the changers, such as their self-concept, and the match between person and job; further, they were concerned with classifying the degree of change. In general, their approach was to take a snapshot of a static event, which they then attempted to describe or explain (Collin, 1984).

In many respects, much of the literature and research encountered during this study (up to 1982) lacked rigor. Discussions of the basic concepts of the field were rare. Concepts such as those of development and terms such as "mid-life crisis" and "vocational maturity" were taken as the starting assumptions of research and left unquestioned. Operational definitions of "career change" led to a focus on middle-class subjects, such as individuals in graduate school.

Moreover, both research and literature up to 1982 focused on intra-individual factors in both career and career change and generally paid little attention to the societal and economic context in which this took place. This approach had significant implications. It allowed the assumption of sequential, developmental, and normative patterns of career, even across cultures, and yielded concepts of maturity and deviance. It did not encourage the conceptualization of the interactions between individual and context. The management of these, it could be argued, is significant for the effectiveness of the autonomous person. At the same time, the literature and research mostly addressed the substantive career described in Figure 12.1. Commentators noted the subjective dimension of career, but the research methods generally employed in the various studies did not give access to this dimension.

The conclusion of my literature review was that this field of study was at that time largely immature, with many basic questions of epistemology, methodology, and conceptualization still unaddressed. Not only was much of it flawed in terms of the rigor expected of scientific method, but, as I began to perceive, much of it did not address the relevant issues.

THE STUDY OF MID-CAREER CHANGE

Aims

This appraisal of the literature and research suggested that it would be appropriate to undertake an exploratory study of career change within the overall process of career. Its aim would be to examine the individual's experience and negotiation of change, recognizing both the context of the career and the actor's subjective experience of it. It, therefore, sought to gain access to the phenomenal career described in Figure 12.1. Because of these aims, it was a small-scale, in-depth study, but included examples of career changes in people from working-class occupations. Because career change for women raises issues that are often peculiar to them— such as the childrearing break—the study focused solely on men, for whom career change at mid-life may have been more unusual.

Research Design

The intention to study the phenomenon of career change within the process of career posed particular difficulties. Not the least of these was the lack of time to have two interviews with each person to be studied separated by an interval of time. Because of time constraints, the issues were addressed solely through retrospective accounts. There was no opportunity to adopt the "new paradigm" practice of taking the interpretations back to the respondents (Reason & Rowan, 1981).

It was judged important not to structure the experiences of those to be studied, and hence the terms "career" and "career change" were avoided. Nevertheless, there was a need—if not for an operational definition of "career change," as was done from the positivist standpoint of earlier research—then for some other means of identifying those experiencing significant occupational change. It was, therefore, decided to identify populations who were objectively experiencing occupational change, that is, who were in a discrete and finite transitional state between two occupations. Whether this was for them a career change was a matter for their definition; and because the interview would take place during the transition, I would not know what occupation they eventually went into.

It proved possible to negotiate access to 32 men undergoing the following transitional experiences:

1. The resettlement phase of army service, that is, the men knew that they were within two years of leaving the army and entering a civilian occupation;
2. A full-time university professional magistral degree course, advertised as being for those in mid-career; most men had left their previous employment whether voluntarily or involuntarily;
3. A full-time assessment and training course at an Employment Rehabilitation Centre for those unable to continue their previous employment because of illness or accident; importantly, this population yielded working-class re-spondents; and
4. A residential full-time reorientation course for redundant executives.

Research Interviews

In order to meet the study's aims, it was appropriate to use in-depth, tape-recorded interviews. They were largely unstructured, but followed the individual's life history. Although some topics and questions occurred in all interviews, the topics and issues of relevance and significance to the particular man were pursued in each, thus making each interview unique. This meant that a method of analysis other categorizing and aggregrating had to be found.

The interview sought to elicit the men's occupational history and, in order to examine their present experience of change within the process of career as a whole, related their present to their past and expected future experiences. Much of the interview, therefore, drew on their recollected experiences and feelings, clearly mediated by their present experiences. This further established the subjectivity of the material collected and again had implications for analysis.

Analysis

The mode of analysis was influenced by earlier experiences of literary criticism; indeed, the transcripts of the interviews provided a text. It started by looking for themes, emphases and imagery within individual interviews, and by noting color and intensity of language and voice. Having identified several themes in an interview (although not necessarily having identified all the possible themes therein) I looked for them, or for other forms of them, in all the other interviews, and then turned to the literature for further elaboration and elucidation. Some of the themes that emerged can be seen in the Appendix, which presents part of the edited transcript of the interview with Mr. Dickens and the commentary on it.

Figure 12.2 outlines the iterative process of the analysis, starting with the individual interview, sweeping through all the interviews, and then examining the emerging issues and themes in the light of the combined interviews and the literature. The revised interpretation was then taken back to the individual interview and examined afresh. It was possible to conceptualize some of the constructs that thus emerged about the process of career change in the forms of models already existing in the literature, such as the grief cycle (Adams, Hayes, & Hopson, 1976). For others, new models, some of which are noted below, were constructed.

Presentation of the Material

Consistent with the philosophy and methodology of this study, it is necessary to give the reader access to the raw material collected and indicate the reasons for the interpretations made of it. The Appendix illustrates how this was done. It is clear that this mode of research requires considerable effort on the part of the user of the research, who cannot merely rely on established notions and indicators of validity

Figure 12.2. Analysis, synthesis, and presentation of research material.

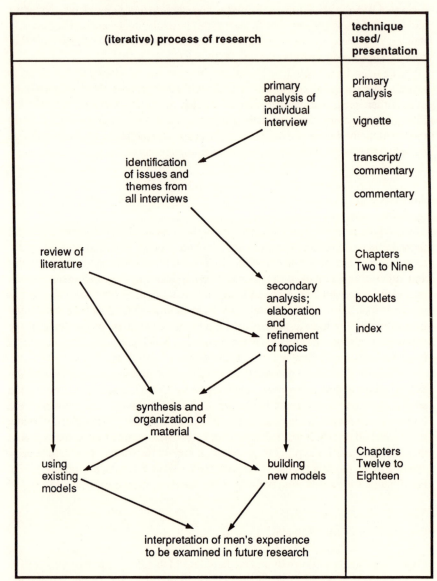

and reliability, but rather must be able to follow the researcher's trail of reasoning and interpretation through the material itself.

MAJOR OUTCOMES OF THE STUDY

Phases in the Process of Career

Not only were those interviewed at various stages in the transition experience, but it also became clear that the beginning of the objective transition was for them not the beginning of their present experience of change (the possible career change). For many, the start of the present experience of change appeared to have been a significant subjective experience that began a process in which they modified the way they conceived of themselves and their world. This modification of their self-concept greatly influenced how they viewed their present situations. (Note how the very act of interpreting, or translating another's experiences into a shared language— "modification of the self-concept"—begins the perhaps inevitable process in research of reducing the transcendental to the phenomenal career and the phenomenal to the substantive.) For example, for Mr. Dickens this was the realization that because illness meant that he could no longer rely on brawn for his livelihood, he would have to cultivate his brain (see the Appendix). This awareness released new opportunities and threats for him. Moreover, even for the soldiers, whose leave-taking of the army was virtually scheduled from their enlistment (and for some this was determined by their family of origin and its circumstances) the significant experiences were again subjective. Mr. Jordan suddenly recognized that the man whose promotion surprised him was not young, but that he himself was old, Mr. Baldwin suddenly acknowledged that he did not equal the excellent annual reports he had been accustomed to receive, so that he would receive no further promotions and would hence leave the army at the age of 38.

Many career theorists have sought to identify the various stages of the typical career; Ginzberg (1972) and Super (1977) proposed modifications to such stage models. Following the chosen methodology, it was not possible to use such stages, derived from outside the experiences of the people studied, to structure their occupational histories. This analysis, however, offered some insight into the process of the phenomenal career, whose phases are not defined by reference to the apparent norms of developmental experiences but by significant subjective experiences.

Career Change as a "Broken Truce"

The recognition of the significance of the subjective career (Collin, 1986a) led to the metaphor of the "broken truce." The individual manages and brings into an acceptable equilibrium the various inputs into and influences upon the career, both intra- and extra-individual. With a change in these, whether voluntary or enforced, internal or external, favorable or threatening, the existing "truce" is broken, and the individual has to take steps to negotiate another truce appropriate to the new circumstances.

The Subjective Career: Implications for Research

The upheavals these men experienced in their subjective world, and which greatly influenced their handling of their present situations, were accessible to the researcher through this mode of research. Had I followed the approach used by other career change researchers and viewed career change as an event, I would have focused on the events before and after the supposed career change, but this would have been an arbitrary point in time, not necessarily related to the processes being experienced by the individual. This raises again the question of the definition of career change.

The Orientation to the Environment

As stated earlier, I was particularly interested in the way in which these men handled the changes they experienced. I also set out on the interviews with an interest in the way they looked toward their future. However, it was not their responses to such questions that indicated to me the next insight into career change I wish to note. I came to my construction of the orientation to the environment through the repetition (19 times) of the phrase "to take advantage of" in Mr. Stephens's interview. Close examination of the other things he was saying suggested that he perceived his world to be largely unrewarding, but that every so often luck would open an unexpected window of opportunity for him. Thus, he had to be constantly prepared and vigilant "to take advantage of" opportunity when it presented itself.

Having had my attention drawn to his perception of the environment, I then examined all the other transcripts to see whether similar views were visible. My interpretation was that many of those interviewed perceived their environment very differently: they saw ample opportunity for themselves and were busily availing themselves of it. From this I inferred a continuum from *perception of the environment as open* to *perception of the environment as closed*. I then went on to examine other facets of the men's responses to their environment and clearly perceived two others: their activity and passivity in response to the environment, and their present or future time perspective. Because of the nature of the interviews and the fact that I had not systematically sought this information, I could not trace clear indications of their position along these three dimensions for all the men, though it was very clear in some cases.

In those cases where the material was available, the men's positions along the three dimensions can be plotted. Of these, the majority construed their environment as open, were active in response to it, and looked to the future. A few saw their environment as relatively closed, were relatively passive in their response, and had a present time perspective. When expressed in this way, one can detect the interdependence of these dimensional constructs.

In the three cases where there appeared to be incompatibility in the men's positions along the three dimensions (Figure 12.3) there was other evidence for the interpretation that the present phase of change was very uncomfortable and being handled badly. For example, Mr. Baldwin construed his world as unyielding and un-rewarding, yet he clearly looked to the future and was very active in response to the environment. Mr. Bolton evidently perceived his world as open and full of opportunity and was active in his response to it, but nonetheless said that "a year seems a remote period to me." He could not project himself forward into the future, and this may have been the explanation for the several ill-judged decisions that had blighted his occupational success. Mr. Townley had no difficulty in envisaging the future and saw his world as presenting many opportunities, but sat back waiting for them to happen to him: "Once it starts it'll come and I don't have terribly much influence on it.". My construct of the orientation to the environment would appear to offer new insights into the individual's negotiation of change and to be more appropriate to the understanding of the phenomenal career than Rotter's locus of control (1966).

Figure 12.3.   Orientation to the environment.

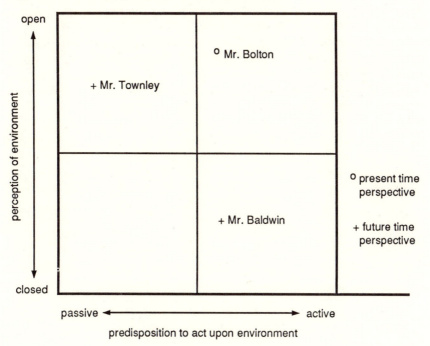

A Systems View of Career

Another outcome I wish to note here developed after the completion of this lengthy process of analysis, and derived from outside the interview material. When introduced to systems thinking, I recognized in it a most appropriate metaphor for the individuals' career, one that conceptualizes both the context of the individual's career and, importantly, changes in it, as well as the adaptations the individual has to make in response to it. It allowed the pulling together into a coherent whole of the scattered influences and events that interact to produce the individual's career, without attributing causal relationships to them. The systems models in Figure 12.4, using Bronfenbrenner's (1977) terms, shows how social class, education, occupational opportunities, and many more factors, can be construed as inputs that are transformed by the self-concept into outputs of career activities, which in turn change the environment and hence generate new inputs (Collin, 1986b). This effectively models the broken truce interpretation, finds a conceptual location for the orientation to the environment as the adaptive subsystems, and identifies as outputs of the system the responses to the opportunity structure described in Collin (1983, 1986b). The maintenance subsystem is identified in the individual's use of career comparisons, models, and members (Collin, 1986a).

CONCLUSION

In conclusion, having identified that the subjective experience of change, the nature of the environment, and the individual's response to it are significant to an understanding of career, this exploratory study was grasping for forms of conceptualization and modes of inquiry that were novel in career research. In other words, this study was moving toward the new directions for the study of career, the ecological and hermeneutical approaches, which have been discussed elsewhere (Collin & Young, 1986).

Figure 12.4. A systems model of "career."

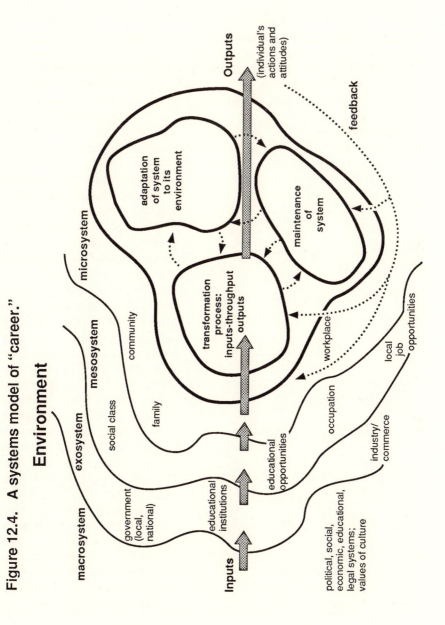

Environment

macrosystem

exosystem

mesosystem

microsystem

government (local, national)

social class

community

family

educational institutions

educational opportunities

occupation

industry/commerce

local job opportunities

political, social, economic, educational, legal systems; values of culture

Inputs

transformation process: inputs-throughput outputs

adaptation of system to its environment

maintenance of system

workplace

Outputs

(individual's actions and attitudes)

feedback

APPENDIX

Sample Interview Text and Commentary

The transcribed text is provided in the left column (a), the commentary in the right (b). The line numbering made it easy to refer to the transcript (a) or the commentary (b) in the text of the research, the symbol (...) denotes an edited cut.

a. *Mr. Dickens*

b. *Mr. Dickens*

58 'enjoyed': see 52b.

59 'crock at the end of the rainbow': he colors the meaning of more money' (61a) with a hint of unattainable dreams and fantasies in this reference to the legendary 'crock.' Money was needed for the fulfillment of some of his early dreams (the desire to travel: 81a, 108a, 116a), but money was in short supply in early adulthood (11b): 'then marriage comes along, and children (...) you put the dreams to the background...'(112-3a). Now, however, although money is still important (121a, 164a ff.), it is no longer a driving force: 'there is a change coming' (128-9a). Like Mr. Jordan (119b, 120a ff.) he can foresee the lessening of financial pressures 130a) and his wife has now been trained for better-paid work 129a, 313-4a). The present driving force is his struggle to regain confidence (see 96b). (This is relevant to the opportunity structure/occupational choice debate: Chapter 8:1 (b ii).) His dream of foreign travel lingers (115a) and could well be fulfilled in the future. He does not have unrealistic 'ambitions' (to become 'Governor of the Bank of England,' 303a), but rather goals that are attainable with effort; those already

60 ended up with them for ten years.
(...) enjoyed it, but I went and left
that because I went for more money
again, which has always been the
crock at the end of the rainbow, (...)
(...) But, er, then I left it to follow
more money and

65 that fell through. The economic situation started to get a bit rough and
this firm I was working with was on
a Government contract. The Government started to cut public spending, and it was one of them that
came under the axe so we had to
become redundant.

*(...) so you've had several jobs from
which you've been made redundant.*

70 Yeah, I've had two that I've been
made redundant, and my last one
I've had to leave because of my (...)
condition, you know, it's forced us
out of the job.
(...) About five years ago I started to
get (...) terrific pain (...). And, er,
the job I was doing was heavy work,
you know, and with the heavy lifting and that, every night it was
hurting my (...). I was

75 having a lot of time off through it,
you know. (...)
(...) I realized that I couldn't keep
on that job, you know, (...) a matter
of time before they got fed up with
me having time off, and I went to
see the Resettlement Officer at (...)
and he put me on the list, you know,
for the, well, if the inevitable did

80 happen—I had to leave—(...) And,
er, they sent me here.

(...) In those early days did you have

achieved have brought great satisfaction (201a, 302a). The goals
would become even more attractive
the nearer he comes to their attainment (see Chapter 9). In these respects he is like Mr. Drive ('ambitions,' 145a) and the Jackamans
('we see a free house....,' 186a); and
unlike Mr. Baldwin (215a) and Mr.
Bolton 267a) who have fantasies,
or Mr. Jordan, who no longer has
dreams (75b).

62 The events mentioned here took
place during the early 1970s. See
43b.

67 Mr. Bolton has also been made
redundant twice.

68 'my (...) condition': he developed a
physical condition (70a ff.) which
eventually caused him to give up
his job (78a).

75 give up his job (78a).
Mr. Bedford, whose employer dismissed him after 76 over two years'
absence after an accident at work. 'I
went to see...': this was about one
year before the interview and seems
to have occurred after the period
when he was 'in real pain, miserable and depressed' (261-8a).

78 'here': the Employment Rehabilitation Centre.

79 The question refers to the time when
he left school: see 9B, 25b.

81 'traveling': see 49b on the work he
enjoys; 59b on his dreams and ambitions.

84 'encouraged': see 22b, 86b, 871.

85 'working-class mentality': see 9b,
27b. He seems to be saying that the
working-class boy accepted without great resistance the constraints
the society imposed upon him (that
is, the opportunity structure).

any dreams for the future, did you ever see yourself doing anything else?

(...) I was very keen on traveling, I'd have liked to have traveled the world at the time, you know. I was keen on reading and, you know, politics, things like that, but, er, as I say, you were never encouraged in any of these things. So, I suppose it's typical

85 working-class mentality at that time and you were on there to do a job of work (...). Like not now, I mean my own lad, he'd doing A levels and everything and he's getting pushed all along the road. We never got that pushing. No matter (...).

(...) I'm a great believer in education, you know.

90 I'd have loved to have done it. I mean I have been sat here trying to do it myself but I've got myself an 'O' level in English, you know, that's a small start but it's a start. (...) with my (...) going I thought I'd better start doing something with my brain because I'd let it

95 go to seed for the last few years, you know, and er, that's why I thought I'd just make a start, and I took it and I got my 'O' level, so I'll keep plugging away till I get some... .

(...)But I believe in education, I mean, as I say I'd sacrifice anything to make sure my lad's got one, you know. (...)

86 'like not now': he recognizes that life has changed (see 146b on changes) and that there are now more opportunities. Moreover, he has himself changed, and learned (229a) of the need to 'encourage' children (22b, 287a ff.).

89/1 See 22b, 98a, 213a. The strong affective tones ('sacrifice anything', 98-9a), his concern for his sons' education (see 22b) and his struggle to improve his own (90a ff.) suggest that this belief is long-held and deep-felt and is not just an idealization of what he himself could not have. This further suggests that his initial job choice (see 9b, 22b) must have badly bruised his early self-concept, so that he now talks of having to 'rebuild my own ego' (153a); see also 152b. Contrast this with Mr. Bolton (5b, 9b), who clung to his early self-concept

89/2 'I'd have loved'. Also cf. Mr. Townley's use of the conditional tense (34b). Mr. Dickens, however, has acted to achieve his aspirations (90a ff.).

92 'start': his several references to this (93a, 95a, 130a, 165a, 266a) do not seem to mean the initiation of action but rather the beginning of a new (and improved) life. They may also have some sense of a new and revised self-concept.

94 'brain': see 25b. After his illness he seems to have taken stock of his assets, for he realized that he had to make a new kind of life for himself. He had not hitherto exploited his intellectual assets.

96 'plugging away': effort, perseverance, striving from another reframe: 'striving' (131a); 'got to bet this'

100 *But looking back at the time (...) had*
things been different, had you have
been perhaps in your son's situ-
ation today you would have liked to
have traveled?
Oh yes, yes. I'd have gone on to
something like writing or anything
like that, you know. I would

105 have liked to have done that really,
(...) but you never get the idea that
you're good enough to do these sort
of things. (...)
(...) So, that was as (...) a dream
more than an ambition, you know,
to write, maybe travel, (...)
(...) *Did you as you got older, did*
you develop other

110 *sort of plans or ambitions? (...) Did*
you develop any new dreams?
No, I didn't, I thought of the same
dream, I still wanted to travel, and
then marriage comes along, and children, and tied down on that. So you
put the dreams to the background,
carry on with reality.
Are they still there then?

115 Yes, I think they are. Yes, I'd love
to...
(..) going and living in other countries and meeting other people and
other cultures and, you know, just
to know these people. (...) I've only
seen them through being in a uni-
form (RAF). (...)
(...) so we weren't getting to meet
them in a proper, civilized way.

(140a); 'got to get in to it' (152a);
'keep fighting through' (156a);
'struggle' 178a); 'pull myself back
up' (254a); 'can't just sit back or
you're defeated' (275a). Such a
response demands the expenditure
of enormous psychic energy, which
can presumably only be generated
for a task essential to the individual:
in this case the strengthening and
mobilization of an emerging self-
concept?

98 See 233a. Education offers self-ful-
fillment (289a, 295a), erodes the
opportunity structure, allows a
working-class boy to see new opportunities (25b). It would be worth
his 'sacrifice' if his sons achieve
this. . Mr. Driver, 273b; Mr.
Southswell, 27B, 37b. Contrast Mr.
Baldwin (187b).

103 See 9b, 25b.

105 'good enough': see 22b. He had no
'encouragement' nor role models
when he was young to help him
evaluate himself, develop a realis-
tic self-concept, and implement it
in his job. He must, therefore, have
abandoned, modified, or shelved
his tentative self-concept of that
time: see 136b.

107 'dream (...) ambition': see 59b.

113 'carry on with reality': a poignant
indication that he did not then have
'a good well-rounded life,' did not
feel himself a 'real human being'
(289a). This seems to be what Mr.
Jordan ('too late for dreams' 75a, b)
is feeling now.

116 Mr. Baldwin (60a, b); Mr. Southwell, 33b value a similar breadth of
experience. Mr. Dickens has an
interest in people (119a) and would
like 'to help' them (247a). He seems

120 (...) Still, I don't think about it much, but it's still an ambition. If ever I got on my feet again I would—and had some money I should soon make use of it.

(...) from what you're saying just then, do you consider that you're not on your feet at the moment?

125 No, no. Far from it.

How do you see yourself?

Er, in limbo, that's the only answer I can give you in short. I don't see what anything happen at the moment. But maybe there is a change coming, my wife's got that (TOPS) course going and in a year or two

130 my youngest—(...) maybe we'll start to pick ourselves up again, (...) But we're always striving to that, you know, no saying I'm giving up, you know. But as the conditions are at the moment it's hard to realize these things, these ambitions, you know. And being . . . as you say being forty (laugh) that's against you as well. (...) I've not been using my brain. I've only been using it to do the silly things like worrying and keeping a job (...) You lack confidence as well when you haven't used your brain for a awhile, you know. I've found that to my cost. (...) You could probably say I'm illiterate in that field, in the field of Maths—or I *feel* that way. (...) I've

to adopt a holistic view of them ('a proper, civilized way' (119a); 'humanity' (247a); 'unhuman' (251a); 'real human beings' (289a)), which contrasts with the 'pigeon-holing' of others (169a), which has been his experience.

120 'ambition': see 59b, 113b. He still hopes to realize them.

127 'in limbo': its discomfort seems to lie in the uncertainty: 'up in the air' (163a); 'no concrete plans' (159a). There is also a sense of disturbance: 'when I get settled down again' (238a). To some extent his future depends upon the center's assessment of him and the occupation and training recommended for him: He is anxious that he will be 'pigeon-holed' as 'stupid' because of his difficulties with Maths (169-70a). Until he knows this assessment he cannot make any plans (162-3a) nor, apart from the continuing struggle with Maths, act to implement his redefined and slowly emerging self-concept. It is difficult to see even the immediate future, though it is clear (238b) that he does look to the future. However, this 'limbo' is not a state of gloom: He expresses great pleasure in recent achievements (202a) and hopes for a brighter future (130a). See Mr. Driver (213b) on other descriptions of the present phase.

128 'Maybe there is a change coming': Like Mr. Jordan (119a, b) he recognizes that there will be fewer family pressures in the future.

133 'ambitions': see 120b.

134 'being forty': see 178b, 317a and Mr. Jordan (22b).

136 'brain': see 25b, 137a.

140 got to beat this, because it's put my confidence back. At 40 you should be fully confident, not lacking it. (...) I always thought that when you got to 40 you could fall back on the experience you've gone through to save you worrying about things, what you've picked up. It doesn't work that way. ... You think you've

145 picked up a lot of experience, but really the experience you've picked up is out of date when this thing comes along, it's sort of changing and you're left. (...) By not keeping on learning through the years you're at a disadvantage when you come to that age, aren't you? Because everything's changed

136/1 'worrying and keeping a job': see 286, 309-10a. Like Mr. Jordan (21b, 76b), he seems to be referring to worry about immediate rather than future concerns (like looking 'across over the horizon', 25b, 219a). He regards such 'worry' as 'silly' 135a, 309a): 'logical thought' (285a) is more effective in dealing with problems. Is this an indication that he is changing from a present to a future orientation (see 238b)?

136/2 'confidence': another refrain: 140a, 141a, 174a, 249a, 251a, 283a. He seems to be speaking of a positive evaluation of himself, a positive self-concept. He has long had a negative self-concept ('you never get the idea that you're *good* enough,' 105a), but he now seems to feel it strengthening, perhaps in response to his learning from life (229a) and to the tentative but assertive steps he has already taken (the 'O' level, 91a). Both self-concept and social learning theories offer explanations. See also Mr. Driver (315a,b) on confidence.

139 Maths: see 4a,b; 169a ff.. 'I feel': an acknowledgement of subjective experience.

140 'at 40': confidence and maturity, further aspects of the stereotypes of 'middle age' (see Mr. Baldwin, 185b). Mr. Flint says that he expects to be at his best, physically and mentally, at the age of 43.

145 'out-of-date': is he speaking here of knowledge? Cf. 229a,b. See 148b.

146 'changing': he is aware of change at several levels: e.g., personal (230a: cf. Mr. Bolton, 362b); family circumstances (128a, 317a); societal (26a, 86b, 150a, 197b).

148 'learning': another refrain: see 229b. Here he seems to mean keeping up with new ideas, being flexible (see 145b).

150 absolutely dramatically in the last 10, 20 years and I haven't been going along with it, really not keeping up with it. I've got to get in to it. Just for my own satisfaction, if nothing else, to re-build my own ego (laugh), because it's got a bit *shattered* over the

153 'rebuild my own ego': he seems to be expressing his awareness of the present strengthening of his self-concept (see 96b) which, he has indicated (22b, 105b), has hitherto been far from positive. This 're-building' is a conscious and a demanding (96b) process started, it seems, after his illness (see 93a ff. and 154b). It is of significance to the opportunity structure/occupational choice debate, for it shows how the individual, having redefined the self, may then redefine the opportunity structure, see the possibility of eroding it or perceive the total self-in-situation in a new light and so transcend the structure.

154 'shattered (...) despondent': cf. 76b, 261b. When he first became ill, 'everything started to crumble': his known world, his expectations of it, and of himself. This jolt to his perceptions (see 259b) led to a reappraisal of himself and his world (see 153b) and to a determination to so modify himself that he could cope with his changed circumstances. (Cf. Mr. Baldwin [10b] who also received a jolt to his perception of the world.) After the initial shock he fight back and is not 'despondent': see 'worrying' (136b) and Mr. Jordan (21b).

155 last few years. But I'm not *despondent* or anything, `down and out about it; it's just part of life—you've just got to keep fighting through, that's what I intend to do.
You said you thought that at present you were in limbo. Would you say that you'd got any plans for the future now?
No, none. No concrete plans that I could say to you in all honesty that I want to do this and do that.

158 See 237-8a.

160 I'm still between the Devil and the deep blue sea. Once I can get myself—if things—if I can settle myself . . . I can start planning. But I can't plan at the moment. Everything's up in the air. (...) And if I'm working at the same time (as his wife),

165 of course, that will be even to the better. We can maybe even start planning things then. Of course, she wants a lot of things in the house (...) that we're not been able to afford yes, we've got those plans, that's what we're thinking about doing. (...)

(...) Because, as I say, I don't want them to

170 pigeon-hole me because of that, Maths. Because I'm not *stupid*--it makes you feel stupid. It's just something I've neglected and I'm finding it hard to get a grip on.

(...) As soon as they come in front of me I tighten up. If I could just get myself some confidence back,

175 even the simplest Maths would do just to get the hand, to do them properly.(...) I can do the ordinary subtractions, multiplication, division but when it starts getting to the technical Maths—I blow! (laugh). I struggle with my fractions, (...) I don't feel as though I'm 40 and over the hill, I still feel

159 'concrete plans': see 127b. Contrast this with the Jackamans 182b). Mr. Dickens, however, is not only changing his occupation: He is also in process of changing himself and therefore cannot project very far forward.

161 'deep blue sea': see 127b. There is no suggestion elsewhere of a dilemma.

168 Plans at the material, practical level.

169 'pigeon-hole me': this is what he experienced when he left school (9b) and he is now having, with great effort, to break out of the mold others made for him. (Driver 50b, Bolton 365b). He is anxious lest he be 'pigeon-holed' again. It is thus very important for him that he masters Maths, which symbolizes another arena in which he fights the battle between social stereotyping and individual autonomy. He had previously 'neglected' significant parts of himself, like his intellect, and had almost accepted others definitions of himself. He is now trying to throw off that incomplete identity and allow his strengthened self concept to emerge.

173 'I tighten up': because he is not engaging in merely cognitive problems: it is a fight for his identity.

178 The discrepancy between chronological age and the subjective experience of it (cf. Mr. Southwell, 107b). Although he knows he is 42, he feels 'a young man' (182-3a). The discrepancy is heightened by the negative stereotypes of 'middle age' (183a) which have no meaning in his experience. He recognizes that the stereotypes are out-of-date (190-1a, 195a) and says that he will

180 young enough. (...) I still feel as
though I'm 30, 30, yes 30—I could
go as far back as 20-odd. I haven't
got that 40 in my mind. Uncon-
sciously I know I'm 42, but I don't
feel—I'm not going into an old cap
and a pipe. I feel a young man.
Do you think that middle age is
different now from what
185 *it used to be?*

Yes—because you're still, I think
you're *still* a young man, whereas
years ago by middle age was the
one start of the decline in feeling—
bad psychological thing at one time
when you reached 40. (...) Folks
reaching 40 were looking down the
hill and that was it, that's all
190 they had to go. I think it's not like
that now— I think even men of 50
can look forward to something,
today anyway.
Why do you think that is?
Because there are more opportunities for them, I think. Even old
men—I was reading in the paper
how some
195 old man went and passed (...) his
'A' level Maths—78. I thought if
he can do it, I feel I can at least try
and do it. That gave me a gee (?) I
feel there's opportunities for every-
body. They weren't there all the
time: At one time 40 was the end of
the road. I don't know—unless
you're really ill I think you're

200 still fit enough - at 40 you're still a
young man.
When you got your 'O' level, what
did you feel then?

not be put off by his age (281-2a).
See Mr. Southwell (89b) on age
stereotypes.

187 'years ago': see 146b for his sense
of change at various levels. he sees
that some of the stereotypes of
'middle age' (178b) are no longer
relevant. However, some of the other
men (see Mr. Baldwin, 185b) are
still influenced by these stereotypes.

191 Mr. Jackaman (154b) sees 50 as a
greater stumbling block than 40.

193 'opportunities': he uses this concept several times (e.g., 208) and
seems to perceive his environment
as open and offering opportunity.

195 'if he can do it': see Mr. Hampden
(63b) on comparisons with others.
Mr. Dickens probably had no relevant model upon whom to base
himself when he left school (9b,
22b). This 'old man' offers him a
model of the kind of achievement
he values, a contrast to the 'old cap
and pipe' image of 'middle age'
183a).

199 'really ill': he does not now con-
strue himself in these terms (cf.
261a ff.) and can thus look forward
to the kinds of opportunities he
mentions; 'fit enough': fitness
seems important to him: 261a ff.

Oh, magic, magic. The biggest ego-booster I'd had in years! (laugh) O yes, great!

(...) I'll never forget that experience. I'm only

205 too sorry I didn't get stuck in when I was younger. I could have — when I was at X—I could have gone to night school for my Maths and things, though I never went. I regret that—that's one thing I *do* regret, not *taking* my chances: I've had the chance but I've not taken them so if you suffer at the end of it it's your own fault really.

202/1 'magic, magic': a current popular expression of delight. Compare this with Mr. Bolton's relief (385b) on achieving his professional status. Perhaps the difference in their responses could be accounted for by the fact that for Mr. Bolton the achievement was the end of his long, hard struggle to vindicate his self-concept, whereas for Mr. Dickens it opened his eyes to his many possibilities; it positively reinforced his new evaluation of himself.

202/2 'ego-booster': see 136b, 153b. It was a confirmation of his newly emerging and fragile self-concept, a reward for his struggle and public achievement, as well as an important event in the family. Social learning and self-concept theories both offer explanations.

205 'I could have': cf. 'It *could* have been my own fault' (292a ff.). He seems to be saying that there may have been opportunities for him when he left school and later ('I've had the chance', 208a), but he did not take them because he was not aware of them (25b, 218b). This was largely because he was not 'encouraged' to do so, nor to become the kind of person who could do so (9b, 22b), He thus apparently believes that there are means (particularly education) to overcome the opportunity structure but that not all children are made aware of them nor of their potential to use them. Cf. 'could have' with Mr. Bolton (194b); Mr. Jordan (2a, 13b, 113b); Mr. Townley (34b). Mr. Dickens is akin to Mr. Driver (238a), Mr. Jackaman (77b).

207 'I regret': his own behavior: Mr. Jordan (11a) 'regrets' his wife's.

208 'chance': opportunity (see 193b). He does not use the word 'luck' in the interview.

209 'your own fault': he accepts responsibility for his own life, even though he had no 'encouragement' when young (218b). Contrast Mr. Jordan (39b).

210 *What other chances do you think you've had in life which you've not taken?*
(Pause) I think—I would say that had been the main one—my education.
Would you say that, going back to the time you left

213 'my education': see 89b. The possessive pronoun suggests that he sees education as essential to personal development.

215 *school, that you regret the kind of decision you made then to take up the apprenticeship?*
Yes, yes I think I do.

REFERENCES

Adams, J., Hayes, J., & Hopson, B. (1976). *Transition: Understanding and managing personal change*. London: Martin Robertson.

Bronfenbrenner, U. (1977). Toward an experimental ecology of human development. *American Psychologist, 32*, 513-531.

Clopton, W. (1972). *An exploratory study of career change in middle life*. Unpublished doctoral dissertation, University of Cincinnati.

Collin, A. (1983). A mid-career perspective on the opportunity-structure/occupational choice debate. *British Journal of Guidance and Counselling, 11*, 52-67.

Collin, A. (1984). *'Mid-career change': An exploratory study of the process of career' and of the experience of change in 'mid-life'*. Unpublished doctoral dissertation, Loughborough University of Technology, Loughborough, England.

Collin, A. (1985). The learning circle of a research project on 'mid-career change': Through stages to systems. *Journal of Applied Systems Analysis, 12*, 33-53.

Collin, A. (1986a). Career development: The significance of the subjective career. *Personnel Review, 15*, 22-28.

Collin, A. (1986b, March). *A systems and ecological approach to career: Towards a new conceptualisation of life course*. Paper presented at the annual conference of the British Sociological Association on the Sociology of the Life Cycle, Loughborough, England.

Collin, A., & Young, R.A. (1986). New directions for theories of career. *Human Relations, 39*, 837-853.

Ginzberg, E. (1972). Toward a theory of occupational choice: A re-statement. *Vocational Guidance Quarterly, 20*, 169-176.

Gottfredson, G. D. (1977). Career stability and redirection in adulthood. *Journal of Applied Psychology, 62*, 436-445.

Hiestand, D. L. (1971). *Changing careers after thirty-five: New horizons through professional and graduate study*. New York: Columbia University·Press.

LaBuda, H. R. (1974). *Motivations affecting the earlier occupational decisions and current occupational changes of a group of middle-aged men: An exploratory study*. Unpublished doctoral dissertation, Wayne State University, Detroit, MI.

Neapolitan, J. (1980). Occupational change in mid-career: An exploratory investigation. *Journal of Vocational Behavior, 16*, 212-225.

Reason, P., & Rowan, J. (Eds.). (1981). *Human inquiry: A sourcebook of new paradigm research*. Chichester, England: Wiley.

Robbins, P. A. I. (1977). *Career change in males in middle adulthood and its implications for higher education*, Unpublished doctoral dissertation, University of Connecticut, Storrs, CT.

Rotter, J. B. (1966). Generalized expectancies for internal versus external control of reinforcement. *Psychological Monographs, 80*, 1-28.

Super, D. E. (1957). *The psychology of careers*. New York: Harper and Row.

Super, D. E. (1977). Vocational maturity in mid-career. *Vocational Guidance Quarterly, 25*, 294-302.

Vaitenas, R., & Wiener, Y. (1977). Developmental, emotional and interest factors in voluntary mid-career change. *Journal of Vocational Behavior, 11*, 291-304.

13

The Politics of Methodological Decisions: How Social Policy and Feminism Affect the Study of Careers

Jane Gaskell

The study of careers can be carried out in a large variety of ways, as the chapters in this book illustrate. In this chapter, I will argue that different methods are appropriate for different purposes, and that therefore the discussion of our purposes as researchers must be part of our discussion of method. The discussion of purposes involves us all in an examination of our political agendas and social contexts.

The purposes research is expected to serve vary over time, and they will vary according to the social location, disciplinary training, and political preferences of the researcher. The variation is appropriate, indeed inevitable, but it does not mean that "anything goes." As ethical researchers, we must be able to argue for the appropriateness of our goals. The connections between why we do research and how we do it are complex and rarely self-evident. Linking purposes and methods as consciously and clearly as possible allows us to reflect more critically on appropriate methodological decisions.

I will illustrate this argument by reflecting on the methodological decisions I have taken, as a sociologist, in my own research on the career decisions of young women over the course of nearly 20 years. These methods have changed as I became more aware of and suspicious of the political and theoretical underpinnings of the methodological techniques I adopted in my early work. After starting with status attainment models, I came to adopt a model that emphasizes the social context in which careers are developed, and that therefore takes a single occupation (clerical work), adopts an explicitly feminist stance, and uses comparative case studies. I will try to explain the reasons for my choices and point to the purposes I think they serve. In the process, I notice the way my goals have been shaped by the social environment in which I have moved as a researcher, and the resulting impact of changing economic and political conditions on how sociological research on careers has been carried out, not just by me, but by many researchers who in one way or another share my social location and political ideals.

The chapter is organized into two major sections, illustrating two political purposes that I have clarified in relation to my own work. First, my purpose is primarily to inform educational and social policymakers who must make decisions about how to organize workplaces and schools, rather than to inform individuals who must act within these structures. This choice involves me in trying to understand social structures, rather than individuals, but also puts the problem of how structure and individual action come together at the forefront of my concern. Second, my purpose is to increase opportunities for women at work, rather than to fit people into the existing structure of the workplace. I try to place my work within feminist debates about the meaning of equality and the nature of power. My purpose then is to inform change in the structures around work, particularly in relation to equality for women, and I examine my research design to determine whether it is well tailored to serve these ends.

THE STRUCTURE OF INEQUALITY: INDIVIDUAL AND STRUCTURAL VARIABLES

The prevailing sociological paradigm when I started to do research on young women and their career plans in the 1970s was status attainment research, for example, Blau and Duncan (1967), Jencks (1972), Sewell and Shah (1967). This appeared to be a straightforward technique for determining what factors had an effect on aspirations and ultimately on attainment at school and in the labor market. The researcher would take various indices of individual characteristics—socioeconomic status, educational achievement, IQ, attitude measures, self-concept measures, and the like—and see how well they would predict occupational attainment. Attributes had to be ranged numerically on scales that went from high to low, and then had to be entered into multiple regression equations that would estimate the amount of variance explained by each.

This was exactly what I did in my thesis, distributing a questionnaire to high school girls, asking them about their families, their attitudes, their grades and their plans, and then using a path analysis to explore which variables were related to aspirations (Gaskell, 1973). I found what I had expected to find, which was lucky, because I would not have known what to do with anything else, and my supervisors would have assumed that there was something wrong with the study. Higher grades and higher social class backgrounds were related to aspiring to more education and a higher status job. I also found that attitudes towards "sex roles" helped to explain some of the variance in aspirations. The less traditional girls were more likely to want more education and better jobs.

What is striking about this research is that it focuses solely on the girls themselves. It asks about their characteristics, and it assumes these characteristics are what will matter as students move on into jobs. The unit of analysis is the individual. The focus is on individual differences. The question is how these individual traits are related to success, as measured in a variety of ways.

The research tradition is based in the assumptions of structural functionalism, and has an implicit set of policy implications (Horan, 1978). The research is grounded in Parsons's (1951) pattern variables, in the assumed move of industrial societies from ascription to achievement, from gesellschaft to gemeinschaft. The implicit belief is that in democratic and industrialized societies, it is efficient and equitable to relate aspirations and occupational achievement to IQ or school achievement, and not to ascriptive variables like social class, ethnicity, sex, or race (Halsey, 1977).. When relationships are found with ascriptive characteristics, the results are deplored, and it is argued that schools or the workplace must change. However, exactly how they might be changed cannot be explored, since the characteristics of the institutions have not been the subject of the research.

There is a second kind of policy implication of this kind of research. Whatever other variables are linked to success—attitudes, self-concept, grades, or whatever—become the characteristics that we should encourage, in order to allow more people to be successful. The clearest example of this was the consistent finding that school success was related to getting a better-paid job (Boyd et al, 1985; Economic Council of Canada, 1964). The policy implication was that young people should stay in school in order to get a good job, and that the society should emphasize schooling in order to solve problems of unemployment and poverty. Similarly, if confidence is related to success, programs should be set up to make young people more confident. If good math grades matter, we need to reemphasize mathematics.

There is a large psychological literature that also looks at what individual characteristics are related to course choice, to educational plans, to work aspirations. It is perhaps more understandable that psychologists should be interested in individual-level variables, and should draw policy conclusions from them. For example, Meece, Eccles, Kackala, Goff, and Futterman (1982) set out an entire model of course choice that takes into account individual predilections. There is a lot of work on self-concept, efficacy, feelings of control, confidence, and so on (Brookover, Thomas, & Patterson, 1962; Porter, Porter, & Blishen, 1982). The implications of the research are that if we can isolate the characteristics of successful young people, we will be able to help more young people be successful.

These models take the structure of the labor market and the school system for granted, and inquire only about what individuals need to get through it successfully. They implicitly adopt a benign and unvarying version of social structure. They are interested in differences among individuals, not differences among structures.

Status attainment models assume an open, fully competitive labor market in which individual characteristics are identified and the rewards people get depend on their own characteristics. Particular contexts disappear from view. Status attainment models assume an average worker in an average workplace, and then see the effects of changes in this worker's characteristics on his or her success. They assume that the important difference among jobs is in the level of rewards they provide, but that there are no significant differences in the way they attract and treat labor since all employers will attempt to maximize profit within the constraints of a competitive economy. There is no attention to the structure of the labor market, to the levels of unemployment, or to the organization of the firm, the industry, or the occupation.

These models adopt the same implicit version of school. One's fate depends on one's own characteristics. We can generalize across different settings—to schools in different cities, in different countries. There is no attention to the structure of course offerings, to the way academic streaming is organized, to the role of the principal and the teacher, to the effect of counseling and so on.

As soon as this is pointed out, it is clear that there is an alternative research strategy. This is to look at social structure instead of looking at individuals, and to see what social structures are related to higher aspirations and to more people getting better jobs. For example, one could compare local labor markets to see what kinds of labor markets lead to more young people being employed or working at higher-paying jobs. One could look at the effects of different job training programs, to see which ones were more successful in placing their students. One could look at which kinds of schools sent more students to university, which program innovations had an effect on retention rates, or, as Rutter et al.'s (1979) well-known study did, look at school atmosphere and its effect on students' futures in the labor market.

There is, of course, a lot of sociology that does this, that examines social structure and its impact on individuals. The 1963 study by Cicourel and Kitsuse on guidance counselors and how they classify and sort students into academic and non-academic streams is an educational example. There are studies of the internal labor markets of firms, and how they identify 'talent' and structure opportunities for promotion (Berg, 1981; Osterman, 1984). There are studies of the way in which labor markets are segmented, and how different labor markets work (Edwards, Reich, & Gordon, 1975).

There is also a social psychological literature that points in the same direction, to the impact of the social environment on individual characteristics, and begins to specify the environments that encourage high aspirations and the settings that reinforce confidence. Effective schools research and the literature on human resource management both look at how the environment can change people.

The distinction between looking at individual characteristics and looking at social structures is a useful one for highlighting different approaches to understanding career development. What is important is to understand that each approach is partial, each is a set of concerns that will sometimes be useful, depending on the researchers' questions. For policy, the approach of looking at structures is more useful, for politicians, administrators, and community groups address the organization of institutions (schools, workplaces, social security programs, etc.) that affect large numbers of people. For individual counseling, the approach of understanding individual differences will often be more useful, for here the attempt is to change people rather than the institutions in which they work.

However, both approaches have problems, conceptually and empirically, as an adequate explanation. The approach of emphasizing individual characteristics too often makes incorrect assumptions about social structure, overgeneralizes from one setting to another, and pretends individuals can act in the world as autonomous agents. The approach of emphasizing social structure assumes an "oversocialized conception of man," in Wrong's (1961) useful but sexist phrase, misrepresents individual consciousness as an internalized version of the social structure and sees structures reproducing themselves without an adequate account of human agency. It is theoretically and politically inadequate.

Even though researchers with finite budgets, energy, and time must make choices about whether to emphasize social structures or individual characteristics, in all real situations both are important. It is clear that looking at individual characteristics must be only part of the story. Researchers need to look not only at individual characteristics but at the structures within which individuals move in order to explain anything. How to put structures and individual characteristics together is at the heart of the problem and at the heart of one of the major conundrums of sociological theory, addressed by major theorists from Marx to Weber to Durkheim (Alexander, 1982). Sometimes a researcher will want to concentrate on only one and sometimes on another, but understanding their interaction will be preferable in most circumstances.

Giddens's (1979) notion of structuration begins to provide a theoretical answer that I find useful. Giddens sees social structure as being constantly created and recreated through a type of individual action that takes place in determinant social conditions. To understand individual action then remains central. However, that individual action is always clearly located in a social context, and the context informs and constrains the action. The reproduction of social structures is central to the inquiry, but the importance of individuals in the reproduction is emphasized.

As a research strategy this leads me to comparative case studies of educational institutions where students develop their orientations to work. Instead of focusing simply on students and their aspirations and responses to school and work, I have come to explore these as they are developed in particular settings, and as they are responses to these settings. I am interested in the ways statements about work reflect not just individual characteristics, but the nature of the labor market and of the workplace. I have become interested in the ways different educational institutions can produce different versions of the workplace, and can affect the way students understand their own futures.

To take an example, the high school and the college I studied portrayed the demands of clerical jobs in different ways. In the high school, the clerical courses were for the "failures," those students who could not make it in the academic stream. Teachers constructed a curriculum that assumed minimal effort and intelligence on the part of students, as they also responded to the structure of the high school in their teaching. Students chose clerical courses if they wanted an easy curriculum. The system had a particular structure to which both students and teachers responded by recreating the conditions in which clerical work was seen as a very low status option.

In the college setting, the system was different. The office education department streamed their courses from the low-level ones (introductory typing and bookkeeping) to the more advanced and desirable programs like legal secretary and word processing. In many of the courses, office work was portrayed as a difficult, demanding job that required high levels of literacy. Both students and teachers responded to and recreated this version of the job. Attitudes towards "careers" were being shaped by the structure of the training, as this was incorporated, challenged and occasionally reframed by individuals.

This is important to me because as an educator, I see my research as involved in helping to define the characteristics of educational settings that provide opportunities and learning experiences for students. If this is the point, exploring the characteristics of institutions and they ways they affect students makes more sense than focusing on the students themselves. To know how to change educational experiences, we have to study those experiences, and see how they are organized and how they might be reorganized. By and large, this means studying institutions as the unit of analysis, not individuals. It means asking questions about the characteristics of instruction, instead of about the characteristics of individual students.

The same general point applies to the workplace. Studies need to explore how the organization of the workplace affects job satisfaction, opportunities for advancement, and equality of access to good jobs (Baron & Bielby, 1980). The structure of job interviews, internal labor markets, and mentoring relationships at work can be studied. The structure of hierarchy in the workplace need not be taken for granted so that we can see how individuals are distributed through it. Rather, the way in which the structure of unequal opportunities is put together must be queried. Comparative studies of workplaces focus on questions of structure, and allow the researcher to address the question of how institutional structure, rather than individual psyche, affects individuals and their careers.[1]

FEMINISM: THE POLITICS OF GENDER AND RESEARCH

Status attainment models were designed to explore inequality at work, but it was primarily class inequality that was of interest. I have argued that they were not well designed to explore class inequality because they ignored structural issues. They were even less able to account for issues of inequality in relation to women.

In my work, I put the experience of women front and center, because it has been so often ignored. I would describe my work as feminist in that it is interested in equality for women, both practically at work and school, and theoretically in the models we use to understand work and school. I try to see how the scholarship that has been done on men and overgeneralized to "people" has misrepresented the notion of career to fit men's experiences. I am interested in developing analyses that will help women who are struggling for equality at work, and in changing scholarship so that our models can encompass the experience of both females and males.

The status attainment model was developed and elaborated on male populations. Blau and Duncan (1967), for example, in their extremely influential book on occupational attainment in the United States dealt only with men, stating that:

> men's careers occupy a dominant place in their lives today . . . a knowledge of the occupational structure and of the conditions that govern men's chances of achieving economic success by moving up in the occupational hierarchy is . . . essential for understanding modern society. (pp. 7-8)[2]

Women were considered only as wives who might influence their husbands' careers, as another variable in the male equation. Clearly women's lives were just not that important. Moreover, as some researchers would point out in footnotes, it was difficult technically to incorporate women into the model. How does one treat the status and pay of a housewife? How should we deal with time outside the labor force? Why does women's educational attainment not provide the same occupational rewards for them as it does for men? Separate equations had to be done for men and women, because the variables seemed to work in different ways for each sex.

How to enter women into the research has been a subject much discussed in the feminist literature (Sokoloff, 1980). When women's careers are addressed, issues arise that had not been addressed in the research on men. How can we deal with sexual discrimination and segmented labor markets for women in status attainment equations? How should researchers enter the world of the family, of children and child-care arrangements, into a discussion of the labor market? Addressing the issues that are important in understanding women's experience at work means rethinking the models we start with.

Incorporating women's experience has been the challenge that women have posed to most areas of scholarship in the 1970s and 1980s. As I have argued elsewhere, while this process starts by simply adjusting a few variables and adding women to existing research paradigms, ultimately it involves questioning the taken-for-granted assumptions built into their very base. This is true for research on careers.

The impetus to look at women's career lives came from the women's movement in the 1970s. What had been taken for granted, that women's work lives were neither very interesting nor very important, was challenged as more women entered the labor force, and as more women entered the academic labor force and did the research.

The question that quickly became paramount was why did women earn so much less than men? Now in the late 1980s women earn about 60 cents for every dollar earned by a man, and these numbers have changed very little over the past 20 years. Status attainment models lead researchers to search for the causal factors in the characteristics of women themselves. How are they different from men? What factors are related to women earning more?

What is immediately striking is that the differences in women's work force experience cannot be accounted for in this way. Education is the best predictor of labor force status, however, women in the labor force are better educated than men, even though their earnings are so much lower. Attitude variables do not help much. Socialization differences have been overplayed in an attempt to get the old models to fit (Gaskell, 1983).

Incorporating a new set of variables related to family life does help to some extent. Women's lives in the paid labor force are influenced by their lives in the family. In both places, women "work." Both sites of work need to be considered to make sense of women's careers. Here, incorporating women's experience requires reconsidering our terminology—what counts as work, what is a career (Biklen, 1985)—and adding a whole new area of inquiry. It means recognizing that in studying men, we have made assumptions about domestic life that have not been examined, and that the research is therefore both limited and historically specific in its application.

What is necessary is to begin to look more closely at the structures within which men and women play out their schooling and their work lives. People work in families as well as for pay, and the nature of that work affects their careers. People work in schools and jobs where gender is a socially important fact, where discrimination exists, and where segmentation is a dominant feature. The gendered organization of these institutions cannot be ignored.

Segmentation of the labor market is particularly important for understanding women's experience in the labor force, as women by and large do different jobs from those done by men. Women are concentrated in a few occupations that employ mostly women—clerical, sales, service, and a few semiprofessional jobs such as teaching and nursing. They are more likely than men to be employed in secondary jobs—that is, in small marginal firms. This occupational segregation by sex is very resilient, cannot be explained by individual characteristics, and shows few signs of declining. The characteristics of women's jobs can explain much about women's behavior in the labor market.

There are two characteristics of the jobs women do that help explain the low economic returns women experience to their schooling. First, as Oppenheimer (1970) has pointed out, women's jobs systematically underpay for the years of education they demand. The roots of this can be traced historically. That women could be paid less than men was an established tradition before industrialization, and it was carried over with the support of employers and male workers into the new jobs women came to do in the industrializing world (Hartman, 1976).

Moreover, the jobs that women do provide few opportunities for on-the-job training, requiring instead extensive training before employment (Wolf & Rosenfeld, 1978). Clerical work and the semiprofessions all have this character. The organization of training can reinforce low pay by providing a plentiful supply of qualified workers at no cost to the employer. Training for women's work has been eminently accessible, lodged in the public schools more often than training for men's work.

The characteristics of this training and of these jobs have become the focus of my research on women's careers. As the particular organization of a particular occupation is important if one adopts the notion of segmentation, I chose to examine clerical work, a job shaped historically by its transformation from a predominantly male to a predominantly female occupation at the turn of the century. More women are employed as clerical workers than in any other single job category. About a third of all Canadian women are clerical workers. The nature of this job and the way one must prepare for it have shaped the education of women in Canada, their work experiences, and their "careers." There is little research that has addressed this fact, and there needs to be more.

Focusing on the structure of the occupation strikes me as politically preferable, because it does not "blame the victim", in other words, it does not blame women themselves for the deficits they experience in the workplace. Focusing on what it is about women that will explain why they earn less tends to suggest that women must change if they want to be equal. Focusing on the organization of work and training suggests that must be the locus of change if women are to experience equality.

Moreover, a vision of the egalitarian society is implicit in different research models. Most research on equality for women has examined how to get more women out of female job ghettos and into job categories that are better paying and populated by men. For example, there has been a good deal of stress on getting women into science and technology, on getting them into blue collar jobs, and on getting them into law school and medical school.

This vision of equality has much to recommend it. Women have been excluded in a variety of ways, and women want entrance. Women have had few options and they need more. However, this vision of equality is a partial one. It suggests that to get paid like men, women must move into jobs that men have had. It accepts the devaluation of women's traditional work, as secretaries and housewives, and nurses, in arguing that women must leave these fields for higher rewards elsewhere.

It tends to accept the kinds of hierarchies that exist in the world, while it makes the case that women should participate on an equal basis with men. It takes the structure of inequality for granted, while it demands women not be relegated to the bottom rungs. It accepts the idea of meritocracy as a way of allocating positions, while it attempts to have standards applied to men and women equally. One consequence is that as women move into higher positions, men have to take their share of positions at the bottom. Furthermore, while some women win opportunities to move up, the great majority of women are left with little. Women and men are left scrambling for the right to be unequal.

The emphasis on access to nontraditional employment too often confirms the low status of women's traditional areas of employment. Women who remain in traditional spheres are "just" secretaries, nurses, and housewives. They are seen to deserve their low pay and status because they have ignored the call to go for "bigger and better things" in the world of nontraditional employment.

The feminist vision has been a somewhat different one. It demands respect for the work women do, it calls for "equal pay for work of equal value." It challenges the process of valuation that puts women's work at the bottom. The process of revaluing women's work must be combined with the process of opening up opportunities in nontraditional areas.

Again, this objective points beyond status attainment models to a research process that illuminates the way both employees and employers come to value and understand the workplace. This involves historical inquiry. It involves ethnographies of particular settings where definitions of value are contested, where the "structuration" of the workplace is achieved.

CONCLUSIONS

Methodological questions involve questions of purpose, of what one wants to know and why. No methodology can take a photograph of the social process we want to understand. All methods are lenses that influence what we find, as well as what we ask. The researcher must take a stand as a political actor; he or she must decide from what vantage point the question should be asked, and how best to serve these inevitably partisan purposes.

This entails a broadening of methodological questions beyond the usual issues of appropriate technique to political and theoretical issues that are often ignored in discussions that purport to be about method. Donmeyer (1985) usefully summarizes three levels at which a piece of research may be evaluated, and in so doing sets out three levels at which methodological decisions must be made by the researcher. He writes:

> First order mistakes occur when the evidence cannot support propositions that have been framed by using a particular language. Second order mistakes occur when the language used to frame propositions is not adequate for particular purposes. Third order mistakes relate to the inadequacy of the purposes themselves. (p. 19)

First-order mistakes involve careful gathering and weighing of evidence. Here are the technical questions of reliability, and of validity, of sampling error and interviewer bias in interviews. Good research must sift and weigh evidence carefully. As Lather (1986) has argued, we must develop and refine techniques that ensure the credibility of our data, and minimize the distorting effects of personal bias on the logic of evidence. Although I have not dealt with these questions here, I take them to be critical, and the usual focus of methodological discussion.

Second-order mistakes involve the usefulness of a conceptual framework for the purposes they are being asked to advance. Here researchers must ask methodological and theoretical questions in light of their overall purposes. For example, will interviews or questionnaires answer the questions better? How should questions be asked? Should the unit of analysis be individuals or institutions? Should students or teachers be questioned? The researcher must clarify how questions of individual agency and structure are being handled, and what the methodology is going to illuminate and conceal. These decisions involve knowledge of competing frameworks and conceptual languages, and an appreciation of their different implications. The question of what the research is trying to understand, what the political purposes are, should underlie these kinds of decisions.

These considerations have lead me to adopt interviews, observations, and the collection of institutional documents as appropriate methods. To examine the process of structuration, one needs to understand how participants see the settings in which they act, and to understand how the institution takes the form it does.

Third-order mistakes involve an analysis of the political purposes themselves. The relativist view that one person's purpose is as good as another's, and that differences among research frameworks are simply a matter of personal political preference, trivialize the most important questions about our commitments as researchers and educators. To justify one's research choices is to engage in discourse about political questions, about the nature of good education in a good society. This dialogue is a critical one. It brings political discussion to the heart of the academic process.

Political self-consciousness means not just personal confessionals at the beginning of research reports, but rather a serious conceptual analysis of the frameworks that are being used, and an argument for their utility. Politically situating the research in this way can help the research have an impact, while at the same time it improves the conceptual logic and academic value of the study. In arguing for a feminist method that concentrates on structuration, these questions are placed on the research agenda, to be taken up by any of you who wishes.

NOTES

1. See Don Fisher's chapter in this volume for some discussion of case studies that do this.
2. Blau and Duncan were not the only ones. Both of Jencks's books involved surveys of only male populations.

REFERENCES

Alexander, J. (1982). *Theoretical logic in society: Positivism, presuppositions and current controversies*. Berkeley, CA: University of California Press.

Baron, J. N., & Bielby, W. T. (1980). Bringing the firm back in. *American Sociological Review, 45*, 737-765.

Berg, I. (1981). *Sociological perspectives on labor markets*. New York: Academic.

Biklen, S. (1985). Can elementary school teaching be a career? *Issues in Education, 3*, 215-231.

Blau, P. M. & Duncan, O. D. (1967). *The American occupational structure*. New York: Wiley.

Boyd, M., Goyder, J., Jones, F., McRoberts, H., Pineo, P., & Porter, J. (1985). *Ascription and achievement: Studies in mobility and status attainment in Canada*. Ottawa: Carleton University Press.

Brookover, W. B., Thomas, S., & Paterson, A. (1962). Self-concept of ability and school achievement. *Sociology of Education, 37*, 271-278.

Cicourel, A. V., & Kitsuse, J. I. (1963). *The educational decision makers*. New York: Bobbs Merrill.

Donmeyer, R. (1985). The rescue from relativism: Two failed attempts and an alternative strategy. *Educational Researcher, 14,* 13-20.

Economic Council of Canada (1964). *Toward a sustained and balanced education and economic growth* (Second Annual Review). Ottawa.

Edwards, R., Reich, M., & Gorden, D. (Eds.) (1975). *Labor market segmentation.* Lexington, MA: D.C. Heath.

Gaskell, J. (1973). *The influences of the feminine role of the educational and occupational aspirations of high school girls.* Ed.D. thesis, Harvard University.

Gaskell, J. (1983). Education and women's work: Some new research directions. *Alberta Journal of Educational Research, 29,* 224-241.

Giddens, A. (1979). *Central problems in social theory: Action, structure, and contradiction in social analysis.* Berkeley: University of California Press.

Halsey, A. H. (1977). Towards meritocracy? The case of Britain. In J. Karabel & A. Halsey (Eds), *Power and ideology in education* (pp. 173-185). New York: Oxford University Press.

Hartman, H. (1976). Capitalism, patriarchy, and job segregation by sex. In M. Blaxdall & B. Reagan (Ed.), *Women and the workplace* (pp. 137-169). Chicago: University of Chicago.

Horan, P. (1978). Is status attainment research atheoretical? *American Sociological Review, 43,* 534-540.

Jencks, C. (1972). *Inequality.* New York: Basic Books.

Jencks, C. (1979). *Who gets ahead: The determinants of economic success in America.* New York: Basic Books.

Lather, P. (1986). Openly ideological research. *Interchange, 17,* 63-84.

Meece, J. L., Eccles, J., Kackala, C. M., Goff, S. B., & Futterman, R. (1982). Sex differences in math achievement: Towards a model of academic choice. *Psychological Bulletin, 91,* 324-348.

Oppenheimer, V. (1970). *The female labor force in the United States.* Berkeley, CA: Institute of International Studies.

Osterman, P. (1984). *Internal labor markets.* Cambridge, MA: MIT Press.

Parsons, T. (1951). *The social system.* New York: Free Press.

Porter, J., Porter, M., & Blishen, B. (1982). *Stations and callings.* Toronto: Methuen.

Rutter, M., Maughan, B., Mortimore, P., Ouston, J., & Smith, A. (1979). *Fifteen thousand hours: Secondary schools and their effects on children.* Cambridge, MA: Harvard University Press.

Sewell, W., & Shah, V. (1967). Socio-economic status, intelligence and the attainment of higher education. *Sociology of Education, 40,* 1-23.

Sokoloff, N. (1980). *Between money and love: The dialectics of women's home and market work.* New York: Praeger.

Wolf, W. C., & Rosenfeld, R. (1978). Sex structure of occupations and job mobility. *Social Forces, 56,* 823-844.

Wrong, D. H. (1961). The oversocialized conception of man in modern sociology. *American Sociological Review, 26,* 183-193.

A Structural Model Approach to Occupational Stress Theory and Women's Careers

Bonita C. Long and Sharon E. Kahn

One of the most exciting developments in vocational psychology in recent years is the emergence of complex theoretical models of women's career development that identify gender-role beliefs and structural constraints on women's work as potential influences on career progress (Astin, 1984; Betz & Fitzgerald, 1987; Farmer, 1985; Gottfredson, 1981). The complexity of these models suits their subject, given many women's conflicts between family and job responsibilities—conflicts that may both delay a woman's entry into the work force and interrupt her pursuit of career objectives—as well as the overt and covert discrimination most women confront at work. Fassinger's (1985) use of structural equation modeling is an example of a multivariate approach appropriate to the integrative nature of women's career choice. When she operationalized the Betz and Fitzgerald (1987) model of career choice, Fassinger found that a combination of ability, achievement orientation, and feminist orientation determined women's orientation toward family and career, and that this orientation, in turn, determined women's career choices.

Because a woman's feelings about herself and her abilities to cope with the demands of family and work affect her interpersonal relationships, her career advancement, and, subsequently, her self-perception, researchers and practitioners involved in developing counseling interventions must take into account both environmental factors (home and workplace structures) and individual factors. Understanding the processes for coping with these demands is central to under-standing women's career adjustment because stress and coping strategies relate to job satisfaction, work performance, and subsequent job tenure, as well as overall psychological well-being.

Women employed in male-dominated careers experience particular problems stemming from gender-role stereotypes and occupational sex discrimination (Brief, Schuler, & Van Sell, 1981; Falkenberg, 1985; Greenglass, 1982; Nelson & Quick, 1985). These women, as Falkenberg (1985) suggests, are exposed to greater levels of work stress than their male counterparts because women form a minority group subject to male-dominated policy-making. Moreover, there is evidence that such stereotypes and discrimination restrict women's work opportunities, and encourage women to select occupations from a more limited set of options than are available to men (Hesse-Biber, 1985). Those few women who do manage to gain a footing in a male-dominated field tend to be concentrated at lower levels (Gottfredson, 1978). Thus, despite the increase of women in the workplace, women in nontraditional jobs where the majority of their peers are male remain underrepresented and underutilized.

Even when women in male-dominated jobs are successful and do receive promotion to managerial positions, they are in a distinct minority—less than 10 percent (Cahoon & Rowney, 1984)—and there is evidence that these women report higher overall levels of stress and psychosomatic symptoms than do men in similar positions (Cooper & Davidson, 1982; Cooper & Melhuish, 1984; Davidson & Cooper, 1984). A number of researchers list stressors encountered by the female manager: covert and overt prejudice and discrimination; isolation; lack of mentors, role models, and supports; limited promotions; and conflicting demands between career and family life (Beehr & Newman, 1978; Cahoon & Rowney, 1984; Falkenberg, 1985; Nelson & Quick, 1985; Terborg, 1985). The similarity of these stressors to those encountered by women who have not entered managerial positions in male-dominated careers remains unaddressed by vocational psychology theory.

Despite their professional success many dilemmas confront women in management positions: How are these successful women managing their marginality in the world of work? In particular, how do the stressful events in women's lives differ among women in different family roles and at various levels of career progress? For example, women who work in masculine-typed jobs with high levels of responsibility and job-related stress may have relatively easier family lives because many such women are single, childless, or, if married, have sufficient income to pay for household services (Terborg, 1985).

In addition to the structural factors inherent in the interaction between family/work roles, and work/nonwork stress, personality factors are important variables in research on women's career adjustment (Betz & Fitzgerald, 1987; Parkes, 1986). For example, gender-role beliefs, particularly liberal attitudes toward women's roles and the construct of instrumentality (Spence & Helmreich, 1978) have been found in women to relate to strong career motivation and high career aspirations (Fassinger, 1985). The stronger and more consistent career commitment and involvement of women who pursue success in male-dominated fields may add to or buffer their experience of stress (Betz & Fitzgerald, 1987). In other words, does the success of women in management positions and/or their unique personality characteristics enable these women to cope more effectively than women in other jobs?

Empirical studies of the relationships between stress and coping describe the individual's appraisal of stress and coping resources as the primary determinants of coping responses (Lazarus, DeLongis, Folkman, & Gruen, 1985; Osipow & Davis, 1988). There exists little examination of how gender stereotypes may modify the meaning of coping style or response in particular social contexts. Women in masculine-typed managerial positions have broken some of the structural constraints in the work force, but no doubt they continue to confront other barriers to their career progress. These women also may have gender-role beliefs that facilitate or interfere with the ways they cope with work-related stress. Research that combines issues of gender, work, stress, and coping, may be able to develop theoretical models that can direct organizational and individual interventions to create work environments that are healthy for women.

A STRUCTURAL MODELING APPROACH

Despite the large quantity of research on factors related to occupational stress, the lack of unifying theory to describe relationships among variables makes it difficult to determine the relative strength of variables regarding their influence on women's career adjustment. Thus, the development of testable models of stress and coping processes of women becomes a necessary next step.

The sophisticated multivariate technique of structural equation modeling is a methodology that allows the examination of causal and interactional relations among variables in an integrated, testable form (Bentler, 1980). Although this methodology can be applied to virtually any analysis (that is, correlational, nonexperimental, and experimental data), it is typically used on survey data based on large samples. As a method of theory testing, causal modeling can help determine whether a hypothesized population model sufficiently represents actual data. This statistical technique employs the simultaneous specification of two models: a measurement model and a structural model. The measurement model describes relationships between the measured, observed variables and the hypothetical, unobserved constructs. The measurement model can be tested by confirmatory factor analysis because relationships between the observed or measured (that is, manifest) variables and unobserved variables or constructs (that is, latent variables) are specified by an a priori theory, and not by the actual correlations and covariances observed in the data. The structural model component accounts for relationships among the theoretical constructs. As such it is similar to a path analysis model, except that it hypothesizes causal relationships among the unobserved constructs rather than among the observed variables. Therefore, in contrast to multiple regression and path analysis, there is no assumption that observed variables must be measured perfectly.

The best known of the structural equation modeling approaches is LISREL (Joreskog & Sorbom, 1979, 1981). According to Cliff (1983), LISREL represents "perhaps the most important and influential statistical revolution to have occurred in the social sciences...since the adoption of analysis of variance by experimental psychology in the 1940's" (p. 115). To summarize, a structural equation model is considered methodologically superior to other causal modeling techniques (e.g., path analysis) for at least three important reasons. First, no assumption of error free measurement is made with respect to the measures used (that is, manifest variables). Second, measurement errors are allowed to correlate over time. Third, causal relations between the hypothetical constructs (that is, latent variables) rather than between observed variables can be tested.

As an illustration of the use of causal modeling, our study of women's experiences of work-related stress and coping applies the method of structural equation modeling to test directly the modified Lazarus and Folkman (1984) model of stress and coping. We have developed measured variables to tap each of the latent constructs postulated in the model. Eventually we will generate matrices and equations required to test the model using the LISREL computer program (Joreskog & Sorbom, 1986).

Subjects are 255 women in nontraditional occupations (less than 35 percent of this population are females, 1981 Canada Census data) at the managerial, supervisory, or administrative levels. Interviewers contacted the women monthly for six months and then after one year. For initial analysis, data will be used from the first three of the six assessments, each assessment being one month apart. Subsequent analysis for cross-validation purposes will be conducted using the three remaining assessments. Personality trait measures, gender-role attitudes, and demographic information were assessed (time 1) one month prior to assessments of a work-related stress, stress appraisals, work environment, and coping strategies (time 2). One month later (time 3) potential consequences of coping were assessed (that is, satisfaction and health). Similar data were collected at times 4, 5, and 6 and were collected in this longitudinal fashion because the passage of time helps to eliminate possible competing explanations of phenomena.

Figure 14.1 is a schematic representation of the causal model with boxes representing the measurements, referred to as manifest variables. The circles represent the constructs, referred to as latent variables, which underlie the measurements. The straight arrows from the constructs to their respective manifest variables indicate that the constructs precipitate the observed performance on these measures.

The model specifies hypothesized relationships among eight theoretical constructs (latent variables—symbolized by circles): $F_1, F_2, F_3,$ and f_1, f_2, f_3, f_4, f_5. As the arrows indicate, $F_1, F_2,$ and F_3 (exogenous constructs) are considered to affect f_1 and f_2 (endogenous constructs); f_1 and f_2 are considered to affect f_3; and f_3 to affect f_4 and f_5. Thus the model in Figure 14.1 postulates that personality traits (F_1), gender role attitudes (F_2), and demographics (F_3) may be linked to stress appraisals (f_1) and perceptions of the environment (f_2). Coping strategies (f_3) are determined by appraisals and the environment, and stress-related consequences (f_4 and f_5) may depend on the coping strategies brought to bear on the situation. For example, the greater the gender stereotypical beliefs (F_1), the more threatening workplace demands may appear (f_2), and the more likely passive coping strategies (f_3) will be utilized. Finally, the consequences may include diminished health (f_5) as well as job and life dissatisfaction (f_4). Support for these hypothesized relationships is evidenced in the work of Folkman and Lazarus and their colleagues (Folkman & Lazarus, 1986; Folkman, Lazarus, Dunkel-Schetter, DeLongis, & Gruen, 1986; Folkman, Lazarus, Gruen, & DeLongis, 1986) and Long (in press).

In the illustrative model presented here, there are two or more indicators for each latent variable. The variables are labeled X or Y depending on whether they measure exogenous or endogenous variables: Personality is measured by X_1 and X_2

Figure 14.1. Structural Equation Model of Occupational Stress in Women

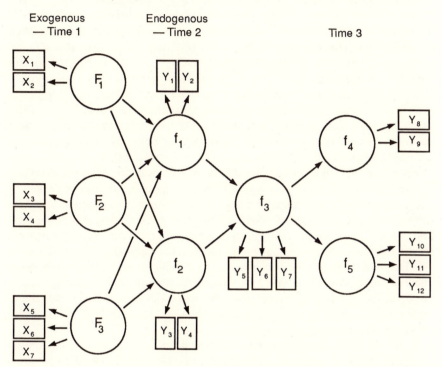

F₁ = Personality Traits   F₂ = Gender Role Attitudes   F₃ = Demographics

f₁ = Appraisals   f₂ = Environment   f₃ = Coping
f₄ = Satisfaction   f₅ = Health

X₁ = Self-efficacy   X₂ = Instrumentality   X₃ = Attitudes
X₄ = Femininity   X₅ = Marital Status   Toward Women
X₆ = Age   X₇ = Years in Position

Y₁ = Uncertainty   Y₂ = Control   Y₃ = Work Demands
Y₄ = Work Supports   Y₅ = Avoidance Coping   Y₆ = Active Problem-
                                                              Solving Coping
Y₇ = Reappraisal Coping   Y₈ = Life Satisfaction   Y₉ = Job Satisfaction
Y₁₀ = Anxiety   Y₁₁ = Depression   Y₁₂ = Somatic
                                                               Symptoms

(self-efficacy, instrumentality); gender-role attitude is measured by X_3 and X_4 (attitudes toward women, femininity); demographics are measured by X_5, X_6, and X_7 (marital status, age, years in position); appraisal is measured by Y_1 and Y_2 (uncertainty, control); environment is measured by Y_3 and Y_4 (work demands, work supports); coping is measured by Y_5, Y_6, Y_7 (avoidance, active problem-solving, reappraisal); satisfaction is measured by Y_8 and Y_9 (life and job satisfaction); and health is measured by Y_{10}, Y_{11}, and Y_{12} (anxiety, depression, somatic symptoms). Each indicator has a directional arrow leading to it from its latent variable.

The aim of LISREL analysis is the achievement of a reasonable fit for a model such that the structural and measurement relationships postulated by the model conform reasonably well to the data. The parameter estimates for such a model provide evidence for the relative importance of different explanatory variables (the *Fs* in Figure 14.1) in accounting for the variance of the endogenous variables (the *fs* in Figure 14.1). Direct and indirect effects and total effects also are computed by the program. Because the measurement component of the model can be tested for psychometric inadequacy independent of the testing of the theory under investigation (that is, the structural component of the model), both construct development and theoretical weaknesses can be evaluated in the early stages of confirmatory studies. With regard specifically to theory development, LISREL provides a heuristic method for identifying hypothesized relationships that are not significant, and significant relationships that were not hypothesized. Thus, the overall aim of using LISREL causal modeling techniques in this research is to aid in theory development and subsequent testing.

In this study, cross-validation of the model will occur by utilizing several methods. Split-sample analysis has been recommended as a method to cross-validate the model testing results (Cliff, 1983). One hundred of the 255 women will be used for the split-sample method in order to determine the invariance of the model with another sample. In addition to the split-sample analysis, replications of data are available from assessments at time 4, 5, and 6 (for example, initial testing— time 1,2,3; cross-validation replication—time 1,4,5). Furthermore, an examination of the long-term stability of the relationships can be assessed by a cross-validation of data from time 6 to 1-year (time 1,6,7). This will aid us in determining the stability of the model across time.

In order to examine the causal predominance within causal model testing, several conditions must exist. For example, to determine the causal predominance of coping over health or vice versa, three criteria must be met. First, a statistical relationship between coping and health must be established. Second, a time precedence must be established (e.g., coping and health measures taken at two points in time). Third, a model of causal predominance must be specified. In this study the model used was developed in large part by Lazarus and Folkman (1984) and is consistent with other models (Brenner, Sorbom, & Wallius, 1985; Osipow & Davis, 1988). Although valid testing of a causal model is appropriate when these assumptions are met, Cliff (1983) asserts, "Causal relations can only be established through patient, painstaking attention of all the relevant variables, and should involve active manipulation as a final confirmation" (p. 125).

Future research will be needed to manipulate the components of the model systematically so as to discover the structure and processes underlying the appraisal and coping processes and subsequent effects on work and health outcomes. A complete test of the invariance of the core model would require at least three strategies. (a) Assessing the fit of the model to new samples, using the same scales as in earlier studies; that is, testing the invariance over the subject context (for example, cross-validation). For example, the model could be tested on female managers in traditional occupations such as nursing. (b) Evaluating the relationships over time by using repeated measures; that is, establishing the invariance over the time context. The present data will allow us to test this invariance for short- and long-term stability. (c) Studying the effect of adding variables that theoretically should be related to the core stress chain, that is, moderating or buffering variables. For example, social support variables, not included in the present model, are hypothesized to effect coping responses both directly and through the variable of appraisal (Lazarus & Folkman, 1984).

CONCLUSION

Structural equation modeling is a powerful approach with great potential for advancing career research and theory. The use of structural equation modeling can facilitate more precise statements of theory, allow more exact theory testing, and provide more explanatory, rather than simply descriptive, understanding. To this end, our current research investigates the unique workplace demands on women in male-dominated positions, the role of gender-role attitudes in assessing stress and coping resources, and the psychological manifestations of workplace stress. Thus, the structural model approach is a useful tool to assist concept and theory development and can be employed to help understand the process linking work-related stress and coping and career adjustment.

NOTE

Completion of this chapter was supported in part by a Social Science and Humanities Research Council Grant No. 482-87-006.

REFERENCES

Astin, H. S. (1984). The meaning of work in women's lives: A sociopsychological model of career choice and work behavior. *Counseling Psychologist, 12,* 117-126.

Beehr, T. A., & Newman, J. E. (1978). Job stress, employee health, and organizational effectiveness: A facet analysis, model, and literature review. *Personnel Psychology, 31,* 665-699.

Bentler, P. M. (1980). Multivariate analysis with latent variables: Causal modeling. *Annual Review of Psychology, 31,* 419-456.

Betz, N. E., & Fitzgerald, L. F. (1987). *The career psychology of women.* Orlando, FL: Academic.

Brenner, S., Sorbom, D., & Wallius, E. (1985). The stress chain: A longitudinal confirmatory study of teacher stress, coping, and social support. *Journal of Occupational Psychology, 58,* 1-13.

Brief, A., Schuler, R., & Van Sell, M. (1981). *Managing job stress.* Boston: Little Brown.

Cahoon, A., & Rowney, J. (1984). A comparative study of organizational stress. In R. J. Burke (Ed.), *Current issues in occupational stress: Research and intervention* (pp. 79-113). Downsview, ONT: York University.

Cliff, N. (1983). Some cautions concerning the application of causal modeling methods. *Multivariate Behavioral Research, 19,* 115-126.

Cooper, C. L., & Davidson, M. (1982). The high cost of stress on women managers. *Organizational Dynamics, 10,* 44-53.

Cooper, C. L., & Melhuish, A. (1984). Executive stress and health: Differences between men and women. *Journal of Occupational Medicine, 26,* 99-104.

Davidson, M., & Cooper, C. L. (1984). Occupational stress in female managers: A comparative study. *Journal of Management Studies, 21,* 185-205.

Falkenberg, L. (1985). *Women in minority positions and organizational stress.* Working papers series #85-021. Concordia University, Montreal.

Farmer, H. (1985). Model of career and achievement motivation for women and men. *Journal of Counseling Psychology, 32,* 363-390.

Fassinger, R. (1985). A causal model of college women's career choice. *Journal of Vocational Behavior, 27,* 123-153.

Folkman, S., & Lazarus, R. S. (1986). Stress processes and depressive symptomatology. *Journal of Abnormal Psychology, 95,* 107-113.

Folkman, S., Lazarus, R. S., Dunkel-Schetter, C., DeLongis, A., & Gruen, R. J. (1986). Dynamics of a stressful encounter: Cognitive appraisal, coping and encounter outcomes. *Journal of Personality and Social Psychology, 50,* 992-1003.

Folkman, S., Lazarus, R. S., Gruen, R. J., & DeLongis, A. (1986). Appraisal, coping, health status, and psychological symptoms. *Journal of Personality and Social Psychology, 50,* 571-579.

Gottfredson, L. S. (1978). An analytical description of employment according to race, sex, prestige, and Holland type of work. *Journal of Vocational Behavior, 13,* 210-221.

Gottfredson, L. S. (1981). Circumscription and compromise: A developmental theory of occupational aspirations. *Journal of Counseling Psychology, 28,* 545-579.

Greenglass, E. R. (1982). *A world of difference: Gender roles in perspective.* Toronto: Wiley.

Hesse-Biber, S. (1985). Male and female students' perceptions of their academic environment and future career plans: Implications for higher education. *Human Relations, 38,* 91-105.

Joreskog, G., & Sorbom, D. G. (1979). *Advances in factor analysis and structural equation models.* Cambridge, MA: Abt Books.

Joreskog, G., & Sorbom, D. (1981). *Lisrel V user's guide.* Chicago: International Educational Enterprises.

Joreskog, G., & Sorbom, D. (1986). *LISREL VI.* Mooresville, IN: Scientific Software.

Lazarus, R. S., DeLongis, A., Folkman, S., & Gruen, R. (1985). Stress and adaptive outcomes: The problem of confounded measures. *American Psychologist, 40,* 770-779.

Lazarus, R. S., & Folkman, S. (1984). *Stress, appraisal, and coping.* New York: Springer.

Long, B. (in press). Sex role orientation, coping strategies, and self-efficacy of women in traditional and nontraditional occupations. *Psychology of Women Quarterly.*

Nelson, D. L., & Quick, J. C. (1985). Professional women: Are distress and disease inevitable? *Academy of Management Review, 10,* 206-218.

Osipow, S. H., & Davis, A. S. (1988). The relationship of coping resources to occupational stress and strain. *Journal of Vocational Behavior, 32,* 1-15.

Parkes, K. R. (1986). Coping in stressful episodes: The role of individual differences, environmental factors, and situational characteristics. *Journal of Personality and Social Psychology, 51,* 1277-1292.

Spence, J., & Helmreich, R. (1978). *Masculinity and femininity: Their psychological dimensions, correlates and antecedents.* Austin, TX: University of Texas Press.

Terborg, J. R. (1985). Working women and stress. In T. A. Beehr & R. S. Bhagat (Eds.). *Human stress and cognition in organizations* (pp. 245-286). Toronto: Wiley.

Selected Bibliography

Alexander, J. (1982). *Theoretical logic in society: Positivism, presuppositions and current controversies*. Berkeley, CA: University of California Press.

Amundson, N. E., & Borgen, W. A. (1982). The dynamics of unemployment: Job loss and job search. *Personnel and Guidance Journal, 60*, 562-564.

Amundson, N. E., & Borgen, W. A. (1987). Coping with unemployment: What helps and what hinders. *Journal of Employment Counseling, 24*, 96-106.

Baltes, P. B., Reese, H. W., & Nesselroade, J. R. (1977). *Life span developmental psychology: Introduction to research methods*. Monterey, CA: Brooks/Cole.

Becker, H. S. (1952). The career of the Chicago public school teacher. *American Journal of Sociology, 57*, 336-343.

Becker, H. S. (1956). The development of identification with an occupation. *American Journal of Sociology, 61*, 289-298.

Becker, H. S., Hughes, E. C., Geer, B., & Strauss, A. (1961). *Boys in white: Student culture in medical school*. Chicago: University of Chicago Press.

Becker, H. S., & Strauss, A. (1956). Careers, personality and adult socialization. *American Journal of Sociology, 62*, 253-263.

Bentler, P. M. (1980). Multivariate analysis with latent variables: Causal modeling. *Annual Review of Psychology, 31*, 419-456.

Betz, N. E., & Fitzgerald, L. F. (1987). *The career psychology of women*. Orlando, FL: Academic.

Blumer, H. S. (1969). *Symbolic interactionism: Perspectives and method*. Englewood Cliffs, NJ: Prentice-Hall.

Bogdan, R. C., & Biklin, S. K. (1982). *Qualitative research for education: An introduction to theory and methods*. Boston: Allyn and Bacon.

Bogdan, R. C., & Taylor, S. J. (1975). *Introduction to qualitative research methods: A phenomenological approach to the social sciences*. New York: Wiley.

Borgen, F. H. (1986). New approaches to the assessment of interests. In W. B. Walsh & S. H. Osipow (Eds.), *Advances in vocational psychology: Vol 1. The assessment of interests* (pp. 83-125). Hillsdale, NJ: Erlbaum.

Borgen, W. A., & Amundson, N. E. (1984). *The experience of unemployment*. Scarborough, ONT: Nelson Canada.

Borgen, W. A., & Amundson, N. E. (1987). The dynamics of unemployment. *Journal of Counseling and Development, 66,* 180-184.

Borgen, W. A., Amundson, N. E., & Biela, P. M. (1987). The experience of unemployment for persons who are physically disabled. *Journal of Applied Rehabilitation Counseling, 18,* 25-32.

Bronfenbrenner, U. (1979). *The ecology of human development: Experiments by nature and design.* Cambridge, MA: Harvard University Press.

Bruner, J. (1986). *Actual minds, possible worlds.* Cambridge: Cambridge University Press.

Burgess, R. G. (1984). *In the field: An introduction to field research.* London: George Allan and Unwin.

Burgess, R. G. (1985). *Field methods in the study of education.* London: Falmer.

Carr, D. (1986).*Time, narrative, and history.* Indianapolis: Indiana University Press.

Chapman, M. (Ed.). (1984). Intentional action as a paradigm for developmental psychology: A symposium. *Human Development, 27,* 113-144.

Chusid, H., & Cochran, L. (in press). The meaning of career change from the perspective of family roles and dramas. *Journal of Counseling Psychology.*

Cicourel, A. V., & Kitsuse, J. I. (1963). *The educational decision makers.* New York: Bobbs Merrill.

Colaizzi, P. F. (1978). Psychological research as the phenomenologist views it. In R. S. Valle & M. King (Eds.), *Existential-phenomenological alternatives for psychology* (pp. 48-71). New York: Oxford University Press.

Collin, A. (1985). The learning circle of a research project on 'mid-career change': Through stages to systems. *Journal of Applied Systems Analysis, 12,* 33-53.

Collin, A. (1986). Career development: The significance of the subjective career. *Personnel Review, 15*(2), 22-28.

Collin, A., & Young, R. A. (1986). New directions for theories of career. *Human Relations, 19,* 837-853.

Collin, A., & Young, R.A. (1988). Career development and hermeneutical inquiry: Part II - Undertaking hermeneutical research. *Canadian Journal of Counselling, 22,* 191-201.

Cochran, L. (1985). *Position and the nature of personhood.* Westport, CT: Greenwood.

Cochran, L. (1986). *Portrait and story.* Westport, CT: Greenwood.

Cochran, L. (in press). *The sense of vocation: A study of life and career development.* Albany: State University of New York Press.

Cook, T. D., & Campbell, D. T. (1979). *Quasi-experimentation: Design and analysis issues for field settings.* Chicago: Rand-McNally.

Cranach, M. von, Kalbermatten, U., Indermuhle, K., & Gugler, B. (1982). *Goal-directed action.* New York: Academic.

Cranach, M. von, Mächler, E., & Steiner, V. (1985). The organization of goal directed action. In G. P. Ginsburg, M. Brenner, & M. von Cranach (Eds.), *Discovery strategies in the psychology of action* (pp. 19-61). Orlando, FL: Academic.

Cranach, M. von, & Valach, L. (1984). The social dimension of goal directed action. In H. Tajfel (Ed.), *The social dimension of social psychology* (pp. 285-299). Cambridge: Cambridge University Press.

Crites, J. O. (1983). Research methods in vocational psychology. In W. B. Walsh & S. H. Osipow (Eds.), *Handbook of vocational psychology*. (Vol. 1, pp. 305-353). Hillsdale, NJ: Erlbaum.

Ericsson, K. A., & Simon, H. A. (1984). *Protocol analysis: Verbal reports as data.* Cambridge, MA: MIT Press.

Fassinger, R. (1985). A causal model of college women's career choice. *Journal of Vocational Behavior, 27,* 123-153.

Freeman, M. (1984). History, narrative, and life span developmental knowledge. *Human Development, 27,* 1-19.

Gaskell, J. (1983). Education and women's work: Some new research directions. *Alberta Journal of Educational Research, 29,* 224-241.

Giddens, A. (1979). *Central problems in social theory: Action, structure, and contradiction in social analysis.* Berkeley: University of California Press.

Gibbs, J. C. (1979). The meaning of ecologically oriented inquiry in contemporary psychology. *American Psychologist, 34,* 127-140.

Giorgi, A. (1970). *Psychology as a human science: A phenomenological approach.* New York: Harper & Row.

Giorgi, A. (1985). *Phenomenology and psychological research.* Pittsburgh: Duquesne University Press.

Glaser, B. S., & Strauss, A. (1967). *The discovery of grounded theory: Strategies for qualitative research.* Chicago: Aldine.

Hammersley, M., & Atkinson, P. (1983). *Ethnography: Principles and practice.* London: Tavistock.

Harré, R., & Secord, P. F. (1972). *The explanation of social behavior.* Oxford: Blackwell.

Holland, J. L. (1985). *Making vocational choices: A theory of careers* (2nd ed.). Englewood Cliffs, NJ: Prentice Hall.

Jepsen, D. A. (1984). The developmental perspective on vocational behavior: A review of theory and research. In S. D. Brown & R. W. Lent (Eds.), *Handbook of counseling psychology* (pp. 178-215). New York: Wiley.

Joreskog, G., & Sorbom, D. G. (1979). *Advances in factor analysis and structural equation models.* Cambridge, MA: Abt.

Kalbermatten, U., & Valach, L. (1985). Methods of an integrative approach for the study of social interaction. *Communication and Cognition, 18,* 281-315.

Kieselbach, T. (1985). The contribution of psychology to the realm of unemployment in the community: Intervention and research concepts. In G. Westcott, P. G. Svensson, & H. F. K. Zöllner (Eds.), *Health policy implications of unemployment* (pp. 367-382). Copenhagen: World Health Organization.

Kieselbach, T. (1987). Self-disclosure and help-seeking as determinants of vulnerability. Case studies of unemployed from social-psychiatric services and demands for health and social policy. In D. Schwefel, P. G. Svensson, & H. F. K.
Zöllner (Eds.), *Unemployment, social vulnerability and health in Europe* (pp.
281-303). Berlin: Springer.

Kieselbach, T. (1988). Youth unemployment and health effects. *International
Journal of Social Psychiatry, 34,* 83-96.

Kvale, S. (1983). The qualitative interview: A phenomenological and hermeneutical mode of understanding. *Journal of Phenomenological Psychology, 14,* 171-
196.

Lerner, R. M., & Busch-Rossnagel, N. A. (Eds.). (1981). *Individuals as producers
of their development: A life-span perspective.* New York: Academic.

MacGregor, A., & Cochran, L. (1988). Work as enactment of family drama. *Career
Development Quarterly, 37,* 138-148.

Mandler, J. (1984). *Scripts, stories, and scenes: Aspects of schema theory.* Hillsdale,
NJ: Erlbaum.

Manicas, P. T., & Secord, P. F. (1983). Implications for psychology of the new
philosophy of science. *American Psychologist, 38,* 399-413.

McAdams, D. P. (Ed.). (1988). Biography, narrative, and lives [Special Issue].
Journal of Personality, 56(1).

Morgan, G. (Ed.) (1983). *Beyond method: Strategies for social research.* Beverly
Hills, CA: Sage.

Myers, R. M. (1986). Research on educational and vocational counseling. In A. E.
Bergin and S. L. Garfield (Eds.), *Handbook of psychotherapy and behavior
change* (3rd ed.) (pp. 715-738). New York: Wiley.

Nesselroade, J. R., & Ford, D. H. (1987). Methodological considerations in
modeling living systems. In M. E. Ford & D. H. Ford (Eds.), *Humans as self
constructing living systems: Putting the framework to work* (pp. 47-79).
Hillsdale, NJ: Erlbaum.

Ochberg, R. L. (1986). *Middle-aged sons and the meaning of work.* Ann Arbor:
UMI Research Press.

Ochberg, R. L. (1988). Life stories and the psychosocial construction of careers.
Journal of Personality, 56, 173-204.

Oliver, L. W., & Spokane, A. R. (1983). Research integration: Approaches,
problems, and recommendations for research reporting. *Journal of Counseling
Psychology, 30,* 252-257.

Oliver, L. W., & Spokane, A. R. (1988). Career intervention outcome: What
contributes to client gain. *Journal of Counseling Psychology, 35,* 447-463.

Outwaite, W. (1986). *Understanding social life: The method called verstehen* (2nd
ed). Lewes, East Sussex, England: Beacon.

Packer, M. J. (1985). Hermeneutic inquiry in the study of human conduct. *American
Psychologist, 40,* 1081-1093.

Polkinghorne, D. (1983). *Methodology for the human sciences: Systems of inquiry.*
Albany: State University of New York Press.

Polkinghorne, D. (1988). *Narrative knowing and the human sciences.* Albany: State University of New York Press.

Reason, P., & Rowan, J. (Eds.). (1981). *Human inquiry: A sourcebook of new paradigm research.* Chichester, England: Wiley.

Ricoeur, P. (1984). *Time and narrative: Vol. 1.* (K. McLaughlin and D. Pellauer, Trans.). Chicago: University of Chicage Press. (Original work published 1983)

Ricoeur, P. (1985a). *Time and narrative: Vol. 2.* (K. McLaughlin and D. Pellauer, Trans.). Chicago: University of Chicage Press. (Original work published 1984)

Ricoeur, P. (1985b). *Temps et recit: Vol. 3.* Paris: Seuil.

Rosenwald, G. C., & Wiersma, J. (1983). Woman, career changes, and the new self. *Psychiatry, 46,* 213-229.

Sarbin, T. (1986). *Narrative psychology.* New York: Praeger.

Schulenberg, J. E., Vondracek, F. W., & Nesselroade, J. R. (1988). Patterns of short-term changes in individuals' work values: P-technique factor analyses of intraindividual variability. *Multivariate Behavioral Research, 23,* 377-395.

Sloan, T. S. (1986). *Deciding: Self-deceptions in life choices.* New York: Methuen.

Spokane, A. R. (1985). A review of research on person-environment congruence in Holland's theory of careers [Monograph]. *Journal of Vocational Behavior, 26,* 306-343.

Spokane, A. R. (1987). Conceptual and methodological issues in person-environment fit. *Journal of Vocational Behavior, 31,* 217-221.

Spokane, A. R., & Oliver, L. W. (1983). The outcomes of vocational interventions. In W. B. Walsh & S. H. Osipow (Eds.), *Handbook of vocational psychology Vol. 2* (pp. 99-136). Hillsdale, NJ: Erlbaum.

Stewart, A. J., Franz, C., & Layton, L. (1988). The changing self: Using personal documents to study lives. *Journal of Personality, 56,* 41-74.

Sullivan, E. V. (1984). *A critical psychology: Interpretation of the personal world.* New York: Plenum.

Thompson, J. B. (1981). *Critical hermeneutics.* Cambridge: Cambridge University Press.

Valach, L., Cranach, M. von, & Kalbermatten, U. (1988). Social meaning in the observation of goal directed action. *Semiotica, 71*(3/4), 243-259.

Vondracek, F. W., Lerner, R. M., & Schulenberg, J. E. (1983). The concept of development in vocational theory and intervention. *Journal of Vocational Behavior, 23,* 179-202.

Vondracek, F. E., Lerner R. M., & Schulenberg, J. E. (1986). *Career development: A life-span developmental approach.* Hillsdale, NJ: Erlbaum.

Wampold, B. E. (Ed.). (1987). Special issue: Quantitative foundations of counseling psychology research. *Journal of Counseling Psychology, 34,* 363-489.

Westwood, S. (1984). *All day and every day: Factory and amity in the making of women's lives.* London: Pluto.

Willis, P. (1981). *Learning to labor: How working class kids get working class jobs.* New York: Columbia University Press.

Young, R. A. (1988). Ordinary explanations and career theories. *Journal of Counseling and Development, 66,* 336-339.

Young, R.A., & Collin, A. (1988). Career development and hermeneutical inquiry: Part I - The framework of an hermeneutical approach. *Canadian Journal of Counselling, 22,* 153-161.

Young, R. A., Friesen, J. D., & Pearson, H. M. (1988). Activities and interpersonal relations as dimensions of parental behavior in the career development of adolescents. *Youth and Society, 20,* 29-45.

Young, R. E., Becker, A. L., & Pike, K. L. (1970). *Rhetoric: Discovery and change.* New York: Harcourt, Brace and World.

Name Index

Subject Index

About the Editors and Contributors

Richard A. Young is Associate Professor of Counselling Psychology at the University of British Columbia. His research interests include the study of career theory, and he is currently conducting research with John Friesen on the influence of parents on the career development of adolescents. In recent years, he has published articles on the ecology of career development, career theory, and hermeneutical approches to the study of career.

William A. Borgen is Associate Professor and Head of the Department of Counselling Psychology at the University of British Columbia. His work in recent years has centered on the study of career education/counseling, particularly the psychological impact of unemployment, group employment counseling, and the experience of post-high school transition. He is the author of several articles and books in the career field.

Norman E. Amundson is Associate Professor in the Department of Counselling Psychology at the University of British Columbia. His research interests include the dynamics of unemployment, group employment counseling, and the post-high school transition experience. He is the co-author, with William Borgen, of *Employment Groups: The Counselling Connection.*

Charles Bujold is Professor in the Department of Counseling and Guidance at Université Laval in Quebec City. His major research interests include the study of personal and vocational identity, career education, career decision making, and the psychology of work. Among his recent publications is the text on career development theories entitled *Choix Professionnel et Développement de Carrière.*

Larry R. Cochran is Professor in the Department of Counselling Psychology at the University of British Columbia, with a major interest in career and life patterns. His most recent work is *The Sense of Vocation: A Study of Career and Life Development.*

Audrey Collin is Principal Lecturer in the Department of Human Resource Management, Leicester Polytechnic, U.K. Her research interests include the employment of older workers and mid-life and mid-career change. She has published papers on these and other career-related topics in such journals as *Human Relations, Journal of Applied Systems Analysis,* and *Canadian Journal of Counselling.*

Donald Fisher is Associate Professor in the Department of Social and Educational Studies at the University of British Columbia. Among his recent published works are articles in *Minerva, Sociology, Sociological Review,* and *Knowledge.* In recent years, Dr. Fisher has taught a graduate course in field research.

John D. Friesen is Professor in the Department of Counselling Psychology at the University of British Columbia. His research interests include the influence of family dynamics on personal, social, and career development. Among his recent published works is *Structural-Strategic Marriage and Family Therapy* (1985).

Jane Gaskell is Professor and Head of the Department of Social and Educational Studies at the University of British Columbia, where she is an educational sociologist. Her current work is on the organization of clerical education. Among her recent published works is *Woman and Education: Canadian Perspectives,* with Anne McLaren (1987).

Edwin L. Herr is Professor and Head, Division of Counselling and Educational Psychology, The Pennsylvania State University. He is the author of several books in the field of career behavior, including *Career Guidance and Counseling Through the Life Span,* with Stanley Cramer (1988). Dr. Herr has broad interests in the career field, and his many published works address career theory, research, and practice.

Sharon E. Kahn is Associate Professor of Counselling Psychology at the University of British Columbia, where she is also Director of Employment Equity. Dr. Kahn has expertise in gender studies and her research interests include women's career development, work stress, and coping process.

Thomas Kieselbach is Senior Researcher in the Research Unit "Work, Unemployment and Personality Development" of the Department of Psychology, University of Bremen, Federal Republic of Germany. His current research in the area of psychosocial consequences of unemployment, health psychology, and community psychology has resulted in publications in European and North American journals.

Bonita C. Long is Associate Professor of Counselling Psychology at the University of British Columbia. She has published articles in the areas of cognitive and exercise stress-management interventions, employee health promotion programs, and stress and coping processes in the workplace. Her current research interests include conceptual and theoretical aspects of stress and coping processes, particularly for populations in work settings, but also for the chronically ill.

Donald E. Polkinghorne is Professor of Counseling at California State University, Fullerton. He is the author of *Methodology for the Human Sciences* (1983) and *Narrative Knowing for the Human Sciences* (1988). His present research interests are in the use of qualitative research processes in clinical judgment and philosophy of the human sciences.

Arnold R. Spokane is Professor of Education and Director of the Counseling Psychology Training Program at Lehigh University, Bethlehem, Pennsylvania. He was previously associated with the University of Maryland. Dr. Spokane's research interests include the study of person-environment interaction in vocational behavior, and the evaluation of vocational counseling outcomes. He is the author of the forthcoming book *Career Intervention*.

Ladislav Valach, a social psychologist, is employed as a research methodologist in the Department of Psychiatry at the University of Berne, Switzerland. Dr. Valach is actively involved in work on the theory of goal-directed action, and in recent years has authored (with M. von Cranach and U. Kalbermatten) several articles on this topic published in such journals as *The European Journal of Social Psychology, Semiotics, Communication and Cognition, Psychologie,* and *Psychotherapie*.

Fred W. Vondracek is Associate Professor of Human Development at The Pennsylvania State University, where he has served academic and administrative roles. His research interests are in the area of life-span career development, and he is currently conducting research on a longitudinal study of development in adolescence. He is the author (with R. M. Lerner and J. E. Schulenberg) of *Career Development: A Life Span Developmental Approach* (1986).